FRANK SMYTH AND MYLES LUDWIG

THE DETECTIVES

CRIME AND DETECTION IN FACT AND FICTION

J. B. LIPPINCOTT COMPANY

Philadelphia and New York.

A QUARTO BOOK

Published by J.B. Lippincott Company,
Philadelphia and New York.

First Published 1978

© Copyright 1978 Quarto Limited.

This book was designed and produced by Quarto,
666 Fifth Avenue, New York, N.Y. 10019,
and 13 New Burlington Street, London W1.

Devised by Myles Ludwig. Written by Frank Smyth,
with additional material by David Hardy.

Phototypeset in Britain by Filmtype Services Limited,
Scarborough, Yorkshire.
Printed in Hong Kong by Toppan Printing (H.K.) Ltd.

Library of Congress Cataloguing in Publications Data

Smyth, Frank
The Detectives
1. Crime and criminals//case studies
2. Crime investigation//case studies
3. Detectives//case studies
I Ludwig, Myles Eric, joint author
II Hardy, David joint author
III Title
HV6025.S56   364–.92–6   78–1835

ISBN–0–397–01253–5
ISBN–0–397–01252–7 pbk.

CONTENTS

They inspired Poe, Dickens and Balzac

THERE HAVE BEEN LAW-GIVERS and judges since the earliest times, but the systematic pursuit of the criminal is a much more recent phenomenon. In medieval England, the victims of crime were commonly left to trace the wrongdoer, perhaps by raising a 'hue and cry', and to bring him before a magistrate. The first detective was probably Jonathan Wild, who advertised himself as 'Thief-taker General of Great Britain and Ireland', in the early 1700s. Wild was a 'bent cop', since he organized most of the crimes which he subsequently 'solved'. Another criminal, Eugene Vidocq, turned detective in the same century, and it was his memoirs that inspired Edgar Allan Poe to write *Murder in the Rue Morgue*. The story is recognized as being the first of the genre of detective fiction, and it marked the beginning of the long association between the fiction and the fact of crime investigation. Poe's hero, C. August Dupin, is partly

Humphrey Bogart and Martha Vickers in the classic production of Raymond Chandler's 'The Big Sleep'.

based on Vidocq, and Dupin is the prototype from whom many other fictional characters were evolved. Another Dupin adventure, and three more detective stories by Poe, all appeared in *Tales* in 1845.

Eugene Vidocq formed the French *Brigade de Sûreté*, but the rest of the world was slow to follow his lead. It was not until 1829, two year after Vidocq's retirement, that Sir Robert Peel brought about the foundation of the London Metropolitan Police. As British Home Secretary, Peel had brought about many penal reforms. His blue-coated 'Bobbies', or 'Peelers' as they became derisively known, were not popular. Londoners took several years to accept them, and when, in 1842, plain clothes 'Bobbies' were introduced, there was widespread public alarm. Surely these new lawmen would be no better than spies or *agents provocateurs*? Slowly, the agitation died down, and soon newspaper editors discovered that their readers actually relished the police news. Charles Dickens was one of these editors, and his magazine *Household Words* did a great deal to

popularize the detective as a lonely, dedicated worker. In fact, Dickens became almost too enthusiastic at times. In an article on how detectives worked, the magazine said, 'Sometimes, they are called upon to investigate robberies, so executed, no human ingenuity appears to ordinary observers capable of finding the thief. He leaves no trail or trace. Every clue seems cut off; but the experience of a detective guides him into tracks quite invisible to other eyes.'

Like his friend Poe, Dickens decided that the detective might make a popular fictional character. As early as 1838, in *Oliver Twist*, he had explored this possibility in the character of Mr Brownlow, who investigated Oliver's mysterious background and then revealed his conclusions in the final chapter. This set a style for numerous other fictional detectives. In *Bleak House*, Inspector Bucket is a central figure, and the book, published in 1835, went further in establishing the detective in the eyes of the public.

It was another friend of Dickens,

Wilkie Collins, who set about vindicating the stained character of a Scotland Yard detective. In 1860, Inspector Jonathan Whicher was despatched to the town of Frome, Somerset to investigate the murder of an infant named Francis Kent. The local police chief, Inspector Foley, was convinced that the child had been killed by gypsies, but Whicher found evidence to indicate that the crime had been committed by the child's 16-year-old sister, Constance. Unfortunately for Whicher, his circumstantial evidence was over-ruled by the magistrate. The Kents were a prominent family in the area and the idea of Constance being a murderer was scandalous.

An enormous public outcry followed the acquittal, and Whicher was forced to resign from Scotland Yard. He was convinced, however, that he had been right in arresting the girl. For four years he hunted for fresh evidence at his own expense and in the teeth of public anger. Finally, bankrupt and broken, he was forced to give up – just one year before Constance confessed. Ironically, she was arrested by Inspector Adolphus 'Dolly' Williamson, who had been Whicher's assistant, as sergeant, on the case. 'Dolly' Williamson went on to become the first Chief Constable of the Criminal Investigation Department, as the Yard's detective department later became. In 1868, three years after Constance Kent's final conviction and sentence to life imprisonment, Wilkie Collins published his novel *The Moonstone*. The book's hero, Sergeant Cuff, was based so closely on Inspector Whicher that he was immediately recognizable to any newspaper reader. So, too, was the character of Superintendent Seegrave, whom Wilkie portrayed as a stupid country hayseed who was, in real life, Inspector Foley.

Organized

American readers liked the books of writers like Poe, who wrote four more detective tales after *Murder in the Rue Morgue* before tiring of the genre and turning to horror. They read Dickens and Collins with fascination, but also with slight puzzlement. For, although uniformed police forces, based on Sir Robert Peel's concept, patrolled the streets of the principal Eastern cities such as New York, Washington and Boston as early as the 1850s, the idea of detectives as such was slow to catch on in the United States. Over 90 per cent of the vast continent was virtually lawless. It was policed sparsely by local, elected sheriffs, and a handful of appointed state marshals.

The first organized crime fighting force west of New England was the one with the least sophisticated image in the public mind, and yet it has always been among the most efficient in North America. In 1832, the Texas cattleman Stephen F. Austin, hired ten, tough-but-honest horsemen to police his pioneer settlements, and to protect the inhabitants against Indians and cattle thieves. These men were so successful that in October 1835 they were officially commissioned as a law enforcement brigade, under the title Texas Rangers. During the next ten years they combined their duties as lawmen with the role of light cavalry in the

A 'ticket' for the hanging of Jonathan Wild, perhaps the first of the detectives.

war for independence from Mexico, and their reputation grew quickly. The Mexicans called them *Los Diablos Tejanos*, 'the Texas Devils', and their impression on the fierce Lipan Apaches was equally strong. An Indian scout named Flacco said of Ranger Captain Jack Hayes, 'Me and Red Wing not afraid to go to hell together. Captain Jack not afraid to go to hell by himself.'

Methodical

Despite the 'rough-riding' image, the Rangers were detectives in the true sense of the word. They tracked their quarry over vast distances, and meticulously gathered evidence. Today, they are still required to maintain a horse, they work as part of the Texas Department of Public Safety, and at their headquarters in Austin they maintain a crime laboratory second only to that of the F.B.I. Their personal cars are equipped as mobile crime laboratories, and the modern rank and file Ranger, unlike his counterpart in any other police force in the world, is required to be an expert on every phase of modern laboratory criminology.

Something of the independent spirit of the Texas Rangers fired Allan Pinkerton. Pinkerton was born in Glasgow, Scotland in 1819, the son of a police sergeant. At first he shunned his father's calling and became a barrel maker, a modest-but-safe livelihood in those days. In 1842, he moved to the United States and settled in Cook County, Chicago. It was while out cutting timber for his barrels that he came across evidence that a gang of counterfeiters were at work in the area, and he methodically amassed enough evidence to warrant their arrest. As one observer said, 'Pinkerton went out to the woods a cooper, and came back a copper.'

As a result of this capture Pinkerton was appointed sheriff of Cook County, but soon found the work lacking in scope. In 1850 he resigned this post and founded the Pinkerton National Detective Agency. The object of the agency was to bring law to the Wild West. It was a giant task, but Pinkerton's operatives, working under the motto 'We Never Sleep', scoured the country for decades, hunting down such desperados as Frank and Jesse James, The Younger Brothers, the Reno Brothers, and Butch Cassidy and the Sundance Kid. In each case the criminals were either captured or run out of business.

Allan Pinkerton's role in the growth of American crime detection continued to expand. In his early days as a settler in Illinois he had known Abraham Lincoln. When the Civil War was over, one of Lincoln's first acts was to authorize Pinkerton to establish on a regular basis the 'secret service' which Pinkerton had operated for the Union Forces. It became the direct forerunner of the Office of Strategic Services, which in turn became the Central Intelligence Agency. The Pinkerton influence did not end there. State and city legislatures asked Pinkerton's advice on setting up their own official detective forces, advice which he gladly and generously gave. As long as 20 years after Pinkerton's death in 1884, one of his operatives, William J. Burns, was asked by the United States Attorney General to set up a coast-to-coast crime fighting force to be called the Bureau of Investigation. In 1924, under the directorship of a bright young lawyer named J. Edgar Hoover, it became the Federal Bureau of Investigation.

Extensive

If Pinkerton's influence on the real world of detection was a great one, his influence on the genre of detective fiction in America was also extensive. In 1874, he published a highly sensationalized account of his work in a book called *The Expressman and the Detective*. It was an immediate best seller and Pinkerton, leaning more and more towards fiction, published four more books during his remaining years. When he died,

Charles Dickens saw the possibilities of detective fiction, and Mr Brownlow of Oliver Twist was an early creation.

his sons William and Robert took over the agency, while his son A. Frank Pinkerton climbed into his father's literary shoes. His novels were published under the overall title of *The Frank Pinkerton Detective Series*.

The Pinkerton influence on the fiction of crime detection was not contained within his family. Samuel Dashiell Hammett, a middle-class, high-school drop out from Maryland, worked for the Pinkerton Detective Agency in Baltimore. He was a good detective, and his career with Pinkerton's was varied. Among his cases were the successful arrest of a man who had stolen a Ferris wheel, the shadowing of mobster Nick Arnstein, and the clearing of film star Fatty Arbuckle in the famous rape case which ruined the career of this fat comedian.

During the First World War, Hammett contracted tuberculosis. This affected his health so badly that he was unable to continue in active detective work after the war was over. Inspired by Allan and Frank Pinkertons' success as writers, he began to write detective stories, based on his own career. The style was dramatically different, however. Gone were the mannered creations of the late nineteenth century; Hammett's characters were hard-bitten, hard-drinking low-lifers, not unlike himself. He and Erle Stanley

Sir Robert Peel, the first police chief.

Gardner were the top writers for the *Black Mask* pulp magazine, which first published most of Hammett's stories. It was Sam Spade, the archetypal 'gumshoe', that made Hammett's reputation as a writer. Spade, with his terse dialogue and whiskey bottle in the desk drawer, was skilfully characterized by Humphrey Bogart who played the role in the film of *The Maltese Falcon*.

Spade was the first of a long line of tough detectives. Raymond Chandler, whose first short story was published in 1929, four years after Spade appeared, recognized that Hammett had produced a new style of American hero. Chandler refined him slightly, gave him a philosophy,

An elementary search for clues by an eagle-eyed Sherlock Holmes on the screen.

and he became the immortal Philip Marlowe. Writing about this new style of hero that he and Hammett had brought to life, Chandler said: 'Down these mean streets a man must go who is not himself mean, who is neither tarnished nor afraid. The detective in this kind of story must be such a man. He is the hero, he is everything. He must be a complete man and a common man and yet an unusual man. He must be, to use a rather weathered phrase, a man of honor . . .' Chandler wrote seven Marlowe novels along the lines he had prescribed, and he was so successful that the poet W. H. Auden described his stories as 'works of art'.

Intuitive

Edgar Allan Poe, although himself an American, drew largely on European sources as inspiration, and it was not until 1931 that a European fiction writer abandoned Poe's 'ratiocination' method of detection. Poe's method of investigation meant that the problems were solved through formal reasoning. With the publication of the first Maigret novel, Georges Simenon showed his preference for a more intuitive approach. Simenon is one of the most prolific writers of the past 100 years. His famous character, Maigret, solved his cases by thoroughly soaking up the atmosphere of the scene, sitting in cafes and thinking himself into the character of the criminal while smoking one of his 15 pipes and sipping pernod or beer. Maigret leaves the background research to one of his subordinates, usually the faithful Sergeant Lucas. Two other top fictional detectives share these characteristics with Maigret. G. K. Chesterton's Father Brown likes to steep himself in the role of the murderer, 'moving' as he says in one book 'the criminal's arms and legs'. The hero of Rex Stout's novels, Nero Wolfe, rarely moves his vast bulk from the old New York brownstone house in which he lives. He leaves the research and the strong-arm stuff to his assistant Archie Goodwin. In fact, few real-life lawmen have ever been able to afford the luxury of this 'armchair' approach to detection. It is here that the popular crime fiction novel departs most from the real world.

Even as Pinkerton was writing, the great days of the lone detective,

The search for 'Son of Sam'

Even today, much detective work is astonishingly time-consuming. It takes hours of work to match a fingerprint taken at the scene of the crime with one from police files. Nor can such problems be solved entirely by the deployment of huge teams of detectives, or the use of advanced scientific techniques. The New York Detective Bureau has access to a machine which will match fingerprints by scanning them with a laser beam; offenders or suspects can even be 'voice-printed'; and another device will 'select' a known criminal's photograph from the file to match an eye-witness description. Despite all of this, crime continues to flourish.

In 1977, the Bureau needed a task force of 300 men to work on the case of the multiple murderer who called himself 'Son of Sam'. This special item, itself bigger than many cities' entire police

departments, was largely occupied in sifting and checking information submitted by the public. At one stage, the telephone company recorded 1,000 'busy' signals on the Bureau's lines in a single hour. Many garrulous callers merely wished to contribute suggestions, often based on the story-lines of television detective series which were running at the time, but others genuinely believed that they had solid information. Of the 7,000 names proposed by the public as suspects, not many more than 1,000 were ever checked out by the overstretched detectives. It was a large police team, with a big switchboard at its disposal, but could there ever have been enough men or enough telephone lines? Certainly there weren't enough detectives, for they never got round to checking a tip-off about an eccentric postal worker called David Berkowitz, who was ulti-

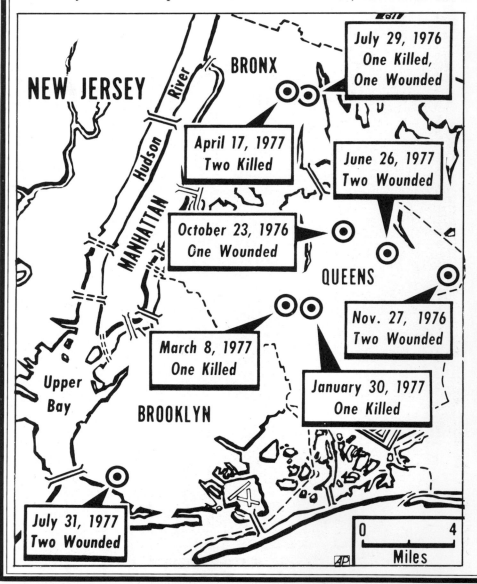

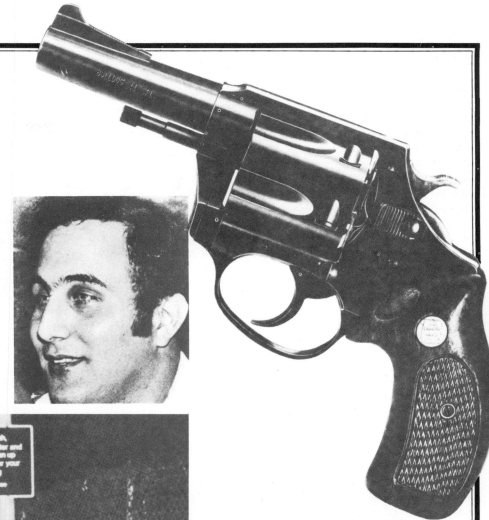

mately to be arrested as 'Son of Sam'. Berkowitz might never have been caught but for the fact that he couldn't find a parking space the night he killed his last victim, Stacy Moskowitz. He parked too near a fire hydrant, and thus attracted the attention of a traffic cop.

Small wonder that it remains standard procedure for a team of detectives always to note down the numbers of all cars parked anywhere near the scene of a crime. Sometimes a criminal who is disturbed while committing a crime may escape by stealing the nearest car – leaving behind as evidence the one in which he came. For the same reason, the files on parking summonses in the area of a crime are always checked. It is axiomatic that the most trivial, and even unbelievable, act of carelessness can trap the criminal.

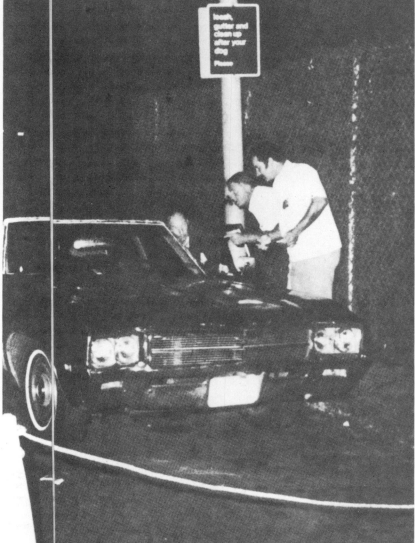

David Berkowitx, the postal worker who was arrested as Son of Sam. He was accused of killing six people and wounding seven others. One survivor was crippled and another blinded. The killer's weapon was always the same – a ·44 caliber Bulldog 5-shot double-action model revolver.

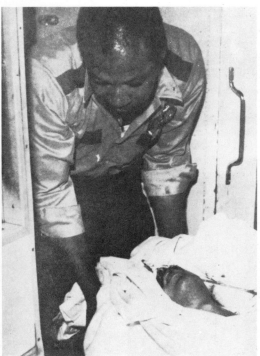

working by observation and deduction, were numbered. In France, the Sûreté remained the world's leading detective force for most of the nineteenth century. One of the Sûreté's most inventive scientists was Alphonse Bertillon. Bertillon was a strange, unhappy man who had realized the importance of harnessing science to crime fighting. It was during the nineteenth century that he was perfecting his Bertillon system of identification, whereby certain unchanging measurements were made of various parts of a criminal's body, and these measurements were placed on record. Dr Alexandre Lacassagne was a forensic expert with the Sûreté before becoming the first Professor of Pathology and Forensic Medicine at the University of Lyons.

Professor Joseph Bell at Edinburgh University impressed one of his students with his knowledge of the advancing science of forensics. His keen, almost uncanny powers of deduction and reasoning at autopsies made a lasting impression on one of his young medical students, Arthur Conan Doyle. By the end of the nineteenth century, Dr Bell was immortalised as the greatest detective in fiction under the name Sherlock Holmes.

Clinical

By 1910, Scotland Yard had accepted fingerprints as foolproof evidence, and began to build up fingerprint records. The rest of the world quickly followed suit. Within the next few years, the science of ballistics, the study of bullets and their markings, advanced rapidly, as did other branches of forensic science. By 1930, the detective was inextricably linked with the scientist.

In 1932, police chiefs in Britain and Continental Europe began to consider pooling some of their resources in the international fight against crime, but it was not until after the end of World War II, in 1946, that their dream became reality. During that year, five top detectives, from Britain, Sweden, Switzerland, Belgium and France met to found the International Criminal Police Commission, which quickly became known as Interpol.

Today, Interpol occupies a rather clinical looking building in St Cloud, near Paris, topped off by the flags of its 94 member nations. It is not a police 'force' in the same way that Scotland Yard and the F.B.I. operate, but its staff of under 100 operatives compare records, pass on messages, correlate efforts in international crime fighting, and link member countries where their needs coincide. Since its inception, Interpol has done a major job of cracking international crime. In its first few years of existence it broke down the white slave trade, and it is currently doing the same to the narcotics market.

Realistic

Interpol emphasises and reflects on a large scale the team work which is now essential to detection even in the smallest country town in Britain or the United States. The day of the individual is over, except in the sphere of the private investigator. Even he, to be more than moderately successful, has to belong to a large agency with wide-spread branches and scientific departments of its own. As a crime writer once remarked, 'the modern whodunnit, in which the private detective solves the mystery while the police plod on behind, is not untrue to life but simply out of date.' Even as such heroes of literature as Hammett's Sam Spade and Chandler's Philip Marlowe were taking their first literary walks along those mean streets, they were out of date. Their famous real-life counterparts, such as private investigator Ray Schindler, were already using what amounted to small scale police forces of their own.

Now the fashion in fiction, as in fact, is for showing the team spirit. Ed McBain's *87th Precinct* novels are perhaps the best of these starkly realistic pieces of fiction. Perhaps in the future they will be known as 'police procedural novels' rather than 'detective novels'. Even such TV series as *Kojak, Police Woman* or *Dan August* stress that the leading character is backed up by a team of patrol men, fellow detectives and backroom boys.

Even Kojak, the TV supercop played by Telly Savalas, needs a back-up team.

A detective for the defense

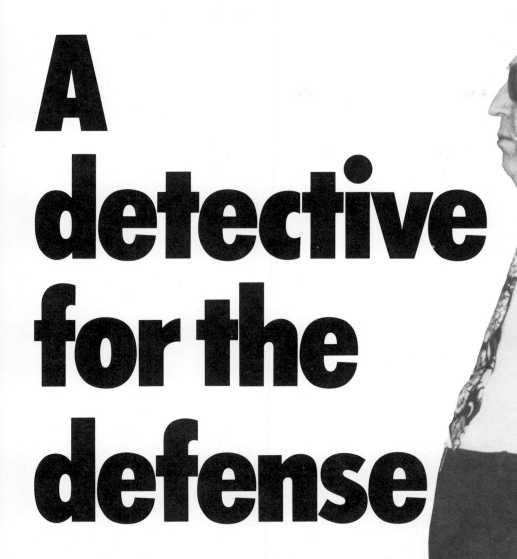

Raymond Campbell Schindler . . . and death in the Bahamas

By DEFINITION, the private investigator has, on the whole, a more difficult task than his official counterpart. In most of the United States, where a private eye is hired to investigate a criminal case, he has access to sometimes vital evidence only at the discretion of the local police chief, and if the police rule against him for any reason, he is immediately working at a disadvantage. In Britain and parts of Continental Europe, few official forces will collaborate with a civilian investigating a crime privately – despite what much popular detective fiction would have readers believe. So the real-life Philip Marlowe very often has only his intelligence, his powers of deduction, and his grasp of logic to go on. On the other hand he does have one advantage over regular lawmen; if he is engaged to prove his client innocent, he merely has to do just that. He is there to show who didn't commit a crime, not who did.

One of the undoubted masters of this concept was Raymond Campbell Schindler, who is still remembered for his investigation of the Sir Harry Oakes murder. Erle Stanley Gardner, creator of 'Perry Mason', described Schindler's success with this case as 'triumphant'. He was a short, tubby man who liked good food and who closely resembled television's 'Cannon'. In a highly paid and highly publicized career spanning over fifty-five years, Ray Schindler helped convict many criminals, but he was never happier than when working for an accused client in whose innocence he completely believed.

Born in Mexico, New York, in 1882, the son of a minister, young Ray was taught the meaning and virtue of total integrity at his father's knee. In April, 1906, when he was 24 years old, Schindler was in California when the great San Francisco earthquake occurred. In the wake of the disaster he took a job as an insurance investigator, sorting out which claims were genuine, and which had been rigged to look like the results of the tragedy. He was a huge success. He caught the attention of William J. Burns, owner of the famous detective agency, and appointed manager of the Burns New York office.

Three years later he left to found his own organization, and Schindler's

The aftermath of the 1906 San Francisco earthquake. It was in this devastation that young Raymond Schindler first made his name as an investigator. His career prospered and he helped to free many clients, putting many crooks behind bars in the process.

County 'Freddy' de Marigny, high-handed and unpopular victim of a conspiracy, whose wife commissioned private detective Ray Schindler. Schindler proved, in the face of fingerprint evidence, that Freddy could not have had the time to commit the murder.

outfit soon rivalled those of both Burns and Pinkerton in its reputation for skill and integrity.

The client who came to see Schindler at his plush Manhattan office in July 1943 was vastly rich, but she was in extreme distress and the avuncular Schindler lent her a handkerchief to dab away her tears as she sobbed out her story. She was 19-year-old Nancy Oakes, daughter of multi-millionaire Sir Harry Oakes who, as Ray Schindler already knew, had been found brutally battered to death in the Bahamas on July 7. The Nassau police were holding Nancy's 33-year-old husband, the rich Count Marie Alfred Fouquereau de Marigny, for the murder; and, ex-plained Nancy tearfully, he didn't seem to have a chance. The whole white community of the island hated him for his high-handed manners. But she knew he was innocent. Could Mr Schindler please help?

Ray Schindler regarded her thoughtfully for some time. Then he told her: 'All right, my dear. I will do my best – but on my usual condition. If my investigation turns up evidence that your husband is guilty, I will hand that evidence over to the prosecution.'

The following day, Nancy and Schindler flew down to Nassau to face the formidable task of rescuing 'Freddy' de Marigny from a hangman's noose – or that of a lynch mob, for already there were suggestions that he should be strung up without trial. The evidence was certainly stacked against him. Almost from the start of their acquaintanceship, he and his father-in-law had quarrelled, sometimes in public. On one occasion Sir Harry had threatened to horsewhip the Count.

De Marigny could not account for his whereabouts at the time of the murder, nor could he produce the shirt he had been wearing that evening. Sir Harry's body had been badly burned after the killing and de Marigny's beard and arm-hairs had been singed. He admitted to having spent the night within a block of Westbourne, the large, 15-room beach house where Sir Harry had been killed. But worst of all, one of his fingerprints had been found on a Chinese screen in the victim's bedroom.

Elopement

To most investigators the situation looked hopeless. But Schindler had given his word to the stricken wife, and he began his investigation.

Schindler first investigated de Marigny himself, his character and his past. He discovered that the accused man, a French citizen from Mauritius, had been married twice before meeting the pretty red-headed Nancy. They had met at a Bahaman yacht club, where de Marigny kept a racing boat, and had eloped to New York and married at the Bronx County Courthouse in May 1942.

At first, Nancy's father had been furious, but appeared to have been pacified when de Marigny had refused to accept a penny from him. The Frenchman had money himself, and told Sir Harry that he was perfectly capable of keeping Nancy in the manner to which she had become accustomed. Nevertheless, Sir Harry had offered his son-in-law a directorship and shares in his profitable mine in Canada. De Marigny turned the offer down – thus annoying his tetchy father-in-law again. As a mutual friend explained to de Marigny: 'Harry can't understand anybody who isn't trying to get money out of him. He's funny that way. If he sees you are, it makes him

Nancy Oakes, with her millionaire father. Oakes did not approve of her marriage but was proud of his friendship with the Duke of Windsor and was furious at the Count's insults.

mad, but when he sees you're not, it makes him madder.'

Schindler then started his check on Sir Harry. He discovered a background which must have appealed to him in view of his own past. Sir Harry was born in Sangerville, Maine, in 1874, the son of a fairly unsuccessful surveyor. When gold was discovered on the Klondike in 1896, he bummed his way up to the gold fields and spent 13 unproductive years in prospecting. Then, wandering penniless around Canada, he was befriended by a Chinese restaurant owner who lent him money to stake a claim on Lake Shore, near Ontario. The mine turned out to be one of the most valuable ever discovered on the North American Continent – it yielded an estimated two hundred million dollars. After that, he literally seemed to have the Midas touch – every venture in which he invested turned to gold. In 1923, tiring of the inroads made into his fortune by the United States Treasury, he settled in the Bahamas and was thus able to become a British subject. Despite his 'rough-diamond' background – he had little social sense and used obscene language even when dining at the grandest tables – he was a snob, and by pouring money into charities he gained a knighthood in 1939.

Schindler discovered that one of Sir Harry's greatest satisfactions was his close friendship with the Duke of Windsor, who had become Governor of the Bahamas after leaving the British throne. The abdication had of course been brought about by his marriage to American divorcee Mrs Wallace Simpson.

Chided

It seemed that Sir Harry's friendship with the Duke might have a bearing on the case, for on at least two occasions de Marigny had insulted Windsor. Once he had told him: 'You are not my favourite ex-King of England.' On another occasion, when Sir Harry and his son, daughter and son-in-law had been invited for cocktails at Government House, 'Freddie' and Nancy had not turned up. Sir Harry and the Duke and Duchess ran into them at another party later in the evening, and chided them for their 'bad manners'.

'To hell with the Duke,' said de Marigny, and turned back to his

Harry Oakes, the rough diamond who struck it rich in the Klondike Gold Rush (left). This left him with a Midas Touch for business and he eventually settled in the Bahamas, where he became a British subject – and was given a knighthood.

drink. None of this had helped his popularity, either with Sir Harry or the other white socialites of the island.

With the background of the two principals established, Schindler turned to the day of the murder.

On the afternoon of July 7, Sir Harry had played a set of tennis at his mansion, Westbourne, with the Honourable Harold Christie, a member of the island's State Legislature.

They had been joined by four other people for dinner, and Christie had arranged to stay the night. Apart from the servants, Christie and Sir Harry were the only people staying in the house that night as Lady Oakes and her son were away. The two men had retired to their bedrooms, separated by a bathroom and a dressing room, at about 11.30, and Christie had quickly fallen into a sound sleep.

Scorched

During the night, however, a storm blew up, and the thunder and lightning woke him. The humidity of the room had attracted mosquitoes, and Christie was prevented from getting much more rest because of them and the noise of the storm. At seven he rose, dressed and went into his host's bedroom. An appalling sight met his eyes. Oakes lay on his back on the bed, naked. His head had been battered, and blood was spattered everywhere – on the walls, floor, bedclothes and surrounding furniture. Most horrifying of all was the fact that his killer had poured gasoline over the body, particularly the eyes and genitals, and set fire to it.

Oddly enough an electric fan which had been going in the room seemed to have extinguished the flames fairly quickly, so that the corpse and the bedclothes were merely scorched. Christie panicked; first he had tried to revive the dead man by pouring water into his mouth; then, after blundering around the room and covering his hands with blood, had finally gone back to his own bedroom and called the police.

De Marigny's story was that he had been at his cottage some five miles from Westbourne, where he and his close friend George de Visdelou were staying. Nancy was away in the United States. When the storm arose, de Marigny had lit

several hurricane lamps, and in doing so had singed the hairs on his arm and his small Vandyke beard. At about 1.00 am he drove two guests to their homes and the route took him past Westbourne which, he said, had been in darkness at the time.

He returned immediately to the cottage, said goodnight to de Visdelou and his girlfriend, and went to bed. Later, de Visdelou had taken his guest home and on returning had parked his car behind de Marigny's and, with his ignition key in his pocket, had gone up to his room.

As Schindler's investigation continued, he became uneasily aware of some kind of conspiracy to nail de Marigny at all costs to protect the killer. By this time the detective was sure that his client was innocent. But everywhere he went, his footsteps were dogged by the police, and

every witness he questioned was later cross-examined by official detectives to see what Schindler had learned from them. He was up against that worst of all barriers faced by the private eye – official hostility.

What was quite clear was that the official investigation had been handled badly from the start. The Duke of Windsor, Sir Harry's friend, had been urged to call in either Scotland Yard or the F.B.I. Instead, he had flown in Captain Edward Melchen of the Miami police, who had once acted as his body guard. Melchen had brought with him Captain James O. Barker, supervisor of the Miami Crime Laboratory. It was he who found the print of de Marigny's right-hand, little finger, on the Chinese screen which stood near Sir Harry's bed.

The allegation was that de Marigny

Nancy Oakes is questioned (left) by reporters, after arriving in New York on her way to hire Ray Schindler. Above: Bahamian real estate operator Harold Christie, against the floor plan of the house in which he found Sir Harry's body. Below: Lawyer Godfrey Higgs discusses the case with Schindler. Right: Judge and jury visit the murder house.

A CU-5 camera, which obtains fingerprints during forensic investigations. Schindler was furious to find that one had not been used in the Oakes case.

had waited until George de Visdelou was asleep, had got up, driven to Westbourne, killed Sir Harry, disposed of his own bloodstained shirt, and then returned to his bed. Captain Melchen had made great play with the fact that de Marigny had been unable to produce the shirt he was wearing that night, and that his suit had been newly pressed. The explanation was simple: 'I don't know where the maids put the dirty laundry,' de Marigny said. 'I never ask them. And my manservant presses my suit every morning as a matter of course.'

Schindler found the theory impossible to believe. To get his car out from in front of de Visdelou's, de Marigny would have to have gone to the other man's room, taken his keys, backed his car out, taken his own car to Westbourne, replaced his car in its original position, driven de Visdelou's car back into its former place, and replaced de Visdelou's keys; all without waking anyone, on a night on which hardly anyone Schindler spoke to had slept, because of the heat and the storm.

Schindler knew that it was just possible for de Marigny to have driven to Westbourne, clubbed his father-in-law to death, and driven back during the time that de Visdelou was out taking his girlfriend home. The investigator even tried the drive himself under several different weather conditions, but he realized that de Marigny did not have time to cause the fire as well.

This he proved by obtaining samples of the bedding, clothing and carpets which had been found scorched in Sir Harry's bedroom. The Nassau authorities did not seem to take his interest in these matters

seriously. He discovered that the quickest time in which the materials would burn to the state in which they were found was 45 minutes. Other evidence showed that Sir Harry had been clubbed while standing in the room, and then carried to the bed after the fire had been started, and the remains of the gasoline poured over him then. Feathers from the torn pillow had been found scattered over the body, and Schindler proved that they could not have been scattered by the electric fan – they must have been sprinkled by hand. All this convinced Schindler that the killer must have stayed in the room for almost an hour after the murder which was impossible for de Marigny in the time available to him.

Carelessness

Schindler was appalled at the carelessness of the Miami detective's investigation as he proceeded with his own. No proper autopsy had been performed, and no X-rays had been taken to determine what weapon had inflicted the four triangular holes in the skull that had caused death. The police had arbitrarily claimed that a wooden picket from a fence on the property had been used, but could not produce it. In any case, Schindler was able to prove that the instrument needed to cause such terrible injuries would have to be much heavier and stronger than a wooden stake. In addition, doctors had found a strange black fluid in Sir Harry's stomach, but no attempt had been made to analyze it.

There had been guards on duty on the estate during the murder night, but the police had not questioned them, and they had vanished into the native population. A strange boat had been seen tying up alongside a jetty near Westbourne, and men from it had gone ashore. Again no enquiries had been made. Furthermore, an experienced Bahamian police officer, Edward Sears, claimed that he had seen Harold Christie driving through Nassau at the very time he was supposed to have been asleep two doors away from where the murder was taking place. Christie denied it vehemently.

The worst carelessness, however, had been in the investigation of the murder room. Dozens of people, from servants to the police themselves, had tramped in and out of

Above: After the case, a delighted Nancy celebrates the acquittal of her husband with defense lawyers Godfrey Higgs and Ernest Callender. Below: Count Freddy stands in the dock at Nassau Supreme Court. Right: A broad smile and a victory sign as the Count is driven away from court a free man after being found not guilty of murdering his father-in-law. The verdict embarrassed the authorities and the real murderer was never discovered. The case was Schindler's toughest – and it was his greatest investigative triumph.

the bedroom, plastering finger prints everywhere, and even the Chinese screen on which de Marigny's finger print had been found had been picked up and carried out into the corridor before being dusted for prints. Captain Barker, the so-called forensic expert, had ruined the bloody prints – some of them whole hand prints – on the walls and furniture by dusting them while they were still wet. And the blood had never been analyzed to see if it was Sir Harry's. When Schindler asked why, he received the amazing reply: 'The fingers were stubby and de Marigny's were not, so we ignored them.' Schindler's answer was blunt: 'I shall never understand how an honest investigator could have permitted this to happen. In my opinion it is criminal negligence.'

From all this chaos had come the one piece of evidence which might have hanged Schindler's client – the fingerprint. Schindler, in view of the activities of the police so far, viewed this with the deepest suspicion. To begin with, the print had been 'lifted'; dusted with finger print powder and then removed from the surface with a strip of clear tape, so that the outline of the print remained intact.

But this process is normally only used if the surface from which it comes is immovable – and the screen was light enough to carry with one hand. So why had Barker departed from established police procedure? Also, when a print is lifted a photograph of it is taken on the original surface. Barker had not taken such a photograph. He told Schindler, rather testily, that he had not brought a print camera with him

Freddy and Nancy are reunited. They went on a fishing trip and planned their future. After the trial, the marriage lasted only another six years.

from Miami because he thought he could use a Nassau police camera, but theirs was broken. Schindler pointed out that the Royal Air Force base in Nassau had its own crime department, equipped with a fingerprint camera. Why, in view of the very serious nature of the matter, had Barker not borrowed it? Barker made no recorded reply.

At this stage, Schindler enlisted the aid of one of America's leading fingerprint experts, Maurice O'Neill of New Orleans. O'Neill was intrigued by the print; it had a background of circles under it, which he could not explain. With Nancy Oakes' assistance they borrowed the Chinese

screen from the police, and went to work on it. For several weeks they examined every single print on its surface, lifted them all, and submitted them to rigorous scrutiny. None of them bore the circular marks which showed on the de Marigny print. In fact nowhere on the screen was anything even resembling them. Most curious of all was the fact, in examining the exact spot in which Barker claimed the original print had appeared, no print, not even a smudged one, existed. The only possible explanation was that Captain Barker had lied, and had rigged the evidence.

On de Marigny's behalf, Schindler

hired an able team of lawyers, an Englishman named Godfrey Higgs and a sharp-witted Bahamian named Ernest Callender.

He briefed them thoroughly on the neglect of the case by the police, and on his own carefully gathered evidence. Most of all he emphasised the evidence of the print, and the suspicious circumstances under which it had been taken.

The case went before the Supreme Court of the Bahamas, presided over by Irish Chief Justice Sir Oscar Daly, on October 18, 1943. During a three day cross-examination, Callender severely undermined the prosecution's case, finally destroying Barker with one of the most thunderous denunciations ever made of a policeman in a court of law. 'Not guilty', was the only possible verdict. Triumphantly vindicated, de Marigny was carried shoulder high from the courtroom, to the cheers of the waiting crowd.

Obscurity

Schindler had done what he set out to do, but he was not satisfied. He was convinced that he could bring the true killer to book if given proper co-operation by the authorities; but that co-operation was not forthcoming. The New York detective had embarrassed the Bahaman authorities enough, and the case was never solved.

Captain Barker's career was in ruins. He was fired from the Miami police and took to drugs for consolation. In 1952 he was shot to death by his own son.

De Marigny's marriage to Nancy lasted another six years, before he disappeared into obscurity in South America.

Raymond Campbell Schindler, arguably the greatest American private investigator, died in his bed at Tarrytown, New York, on July 1, 1959. One of his obituaries was written by Erle Stanley Gardner, creator of *Perry Mason*. Of the Oakes case he said: 'The fact that the fingerprint, unquestionably that of de Marginy's little finger, authenticated by the police testimony as being on that wooden screen, didn't put the noose right around de Marigny's neck is one of the greatest investigation triumphs of modern times. I know of no detective who has ever faced a tougher assignment or discharged it more triumphantly.'

The detective doctor

. . . and a murder down Lambeth way

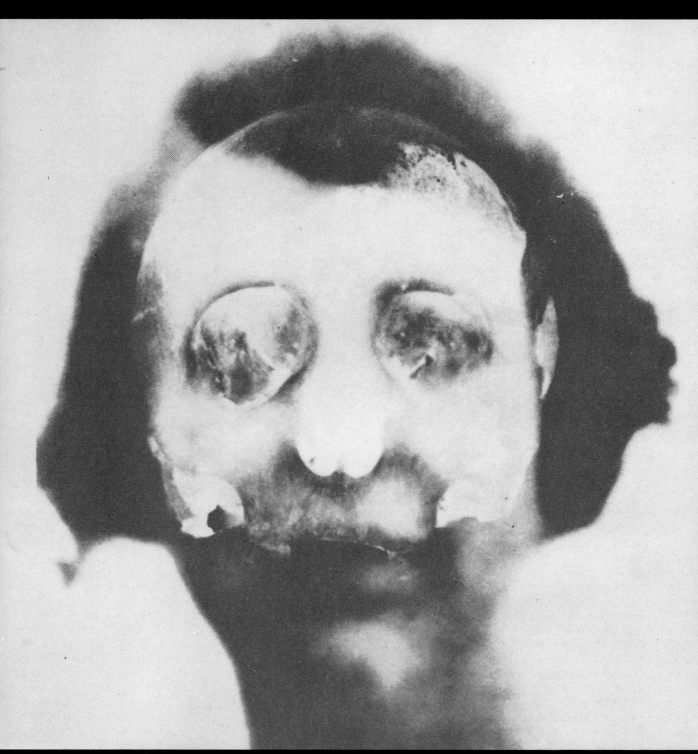

A photograph of Rachael Dobkin's skull, superimposed on a snapshot of the murdered woman.

WITHOUT A *corpus delicti*, it is very difficult to prove that a murder has taken place. Hence, the efficient disposal of the victim's body is of prime importance to the murderer. By the same token, a conviction can often rest wholly on the ability of the pathologist to identify remains.

A top pathologist is not only a skilled surgeon but a master detective in his own right, and a good man can often solve a case in his laboratory, leaving the police with the simple task of making an arrest. Such a man is Professor Keith Simpson, successor to such great names as Sir Bernard Spilsbury and Professor Francis Camps as Britain's top Home Office pathologist.

Dr. Simpson is a neat, almost dapper man who habitually wears a smart black derby hat and a sombre overcoat. Early in his career he proved his ability as detective-doctor during the Dobkin case, which became a minor classic in the annals of crime detection.

Hard-pressed

It began in Lambeth one blazing Friday in July, 1942. Lambeth, like the other London boroughs bordering the River Thames, had been steadily blasted by Hitler's bombs for almost two years. Many of its neat streets were gapped and broken like rows of rotten teeth. Kennington Lane had suffered particularly badly, and a Baptist church at 302 had been totally destroyed. The church had had an old, disused graveyard attached to it, and a gang of demolition workers clearing away the rubble constantly came across ancient portions of coffins and skeletons.

Each of these had to be reported to the South London coroner's office, an already hard-pressed department in the years of the blitz, so when a workman uncovered a skull and a few bones on that Friday morning he merely groaned with the boredom of having to make yet another report, and pushed the relics to one side. Later in the day a police van took them to Southwark morgue to await what should have been a routine autopsy.

The following morning, Dr Simpson arrived in Southwark to begin sifting through the pathetic remains, which were parcelled up in a brown paper bag. The body had been un-coffined, so that, although it had

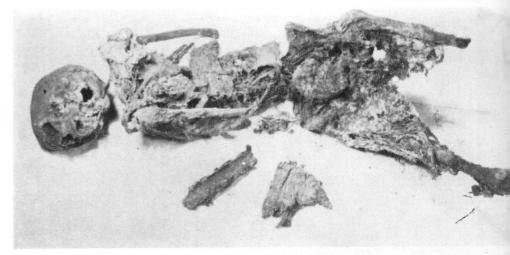

The blitzed cellar of the Baptist Church (above) where the remains of Rachael Dobkin's body were discovered after a London air raid in 1942. Pathologist Dr Keith Simpson (right) was called in. He expected it to be a routine examination, but he was wrong. The body (left) presented a real challenge. His careful investigation of the corpse, with its severed head and limbs, started a manhunt which led a killer to the gallows. It was also a case which helped to establish Dr Simpson in the front rank of the scientific detectives.

29

been found at the edge of the old graveyard, the doctor thought it unlikely to have had an orthodox burial. A cursory glance showed that he was right. Signs of burning on the skull and rib cage showed clearly, and the lower arms and legs had been severed. A bomb victim? He was pretty certain that it was not, but to make sure he had the bones removed to his own laboratory at Guy's Hospital where he could make a thorough examination.

Instrument

On Monday morning he began the delicate task of cleaning grit and soil from the skeleton, and then reassembling the bones into their natural form. The body was that of a woman, he discovered, and death had taken place between one year and eighteen months previously. The dead woman's height was simple to establish. Like other Western pathologists, Dr Simpson used Pearson's Formulae for Reconstructing Living Stature from Dead Long Bones, a standard procedure. Using the remaining intact long bone, the left humerus, he was able to calculate that she had been 5 ft 1 in tall.

Clinging to the skull was a patch of the scalp, with a strand or two of dark brown, greying hair attached. Judging by the skull vault sutures (the fine joins which close finally at certain ages) he calculated that she had probably been between 45 and 60 years of age. At the base of the skull were the marks of a sharp, heavy instrument which presumably had severed the head from the body. The elbow joints and knees showed similar marks. Could bomb fragments have severed the head and the limbs? Dr Simpson thought not. He had already noted that the body had been sprinkled with lime which, contrary to popular belief, tends to preserve rather than destroy human tissue. In this case its presence helped him, for it had preserved the tiny bones of the voice box intact, along with patches of the skin of the throat. The voice box had been crushed, and the skin bore traces of bruising which indicated manual strangulation. Although the lower jaw was missing, the upper jaw still held four teeth, which had had dental work done upon them.

The lime had also fortunately preserved much of the lower abdominal area, and Dr Simpson discovered a

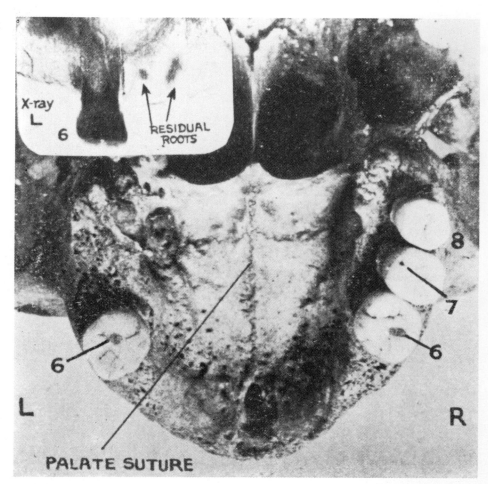

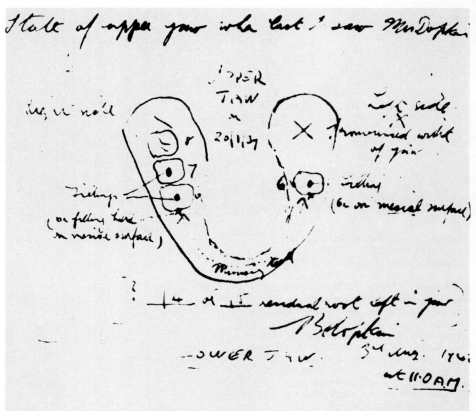

Rachael Dobkin's dental record provided a vital link in the identification of her body. The remains of the jaw (top, with an X-ray, tallied with diagrams (above) supplied by her dentist. This finally convinced Dr Simpson that the body was that of Mrs Dobkin, who had been missing for 18 months.

fibroid tumour in the womb. All this should help identification.

At this point, Dr Simpson contacted Divisional Detective-Inspector Fred Hatton, of the Metropolitan Police 'M' Division, and told him of his findings which he now considered to to be a murder victim, killed by strangulation, and then dismembered. Who was she?

Inspector Hatton, whose heavy gait reflected his methodical manner, ordered a list of all women reported missing during the last two years and began to wade through them. The task took some weeks, but finally he came up with a likely name.

She was Mrs. Rachael Dobkin, and her sister had reported her missing in April, 1941, eighteen months previously. This fitted Dr Simpson's outside estimate of the date of death. Rachael had been exactly 5 ft 1 in in height, and her dark brown hair was beginning to grey.

Just before her disappearance she had complained of abdominal pains, and doctors at the London Hospital had diagnosed a fibroid tumour of the womb, which she had refused to have removed.

Dr Simpson was convinced that the heap of bones which lay in the laboratory and the missing Mrs

Dobkin were one and the same, but he asked Inspector Hatton for the dead woman's dental records as a final check. Luckily, Mrs Dobkins' sister knew the name of the dentist, and when his records arrived they matched exactly the state of the teeth and sockets in the upper jaw of the Lambeth skull. Beyond a shadow of a doubt the bones were those of Rachel Dobkin.

No good pathologist leaves loose ends untied for a courtroom lawyer to tug at and unravel. So, as a double check, Dr Simpson obtained a picture of the dead woman, had it blown up to lifesize, and superimposed it on

the skull. Again the result was a perfect match. The eye shape, the angle of the nose, the set of the mouth, all coincided precisely with the features in the photograph.

Dr Simpson then told Inspector Hatton how the crime had been committed. Eighteen months before, Mrs Dobkin had been strangled by a person with a powerful grip, presumably a man. Judging by traces of clotted blood on the back of the skull, the killer had either banged her head viciously on a hard surface while committing the deed, or had thrown her lifeless body to the ground with great force.

Within a few hours of the killing,

Inspector Fred Britten (above) whose careful work pointed to Mrs Dobkin, pictured below on her wedding day.

again judging by clots and the straight scars on the remaining bones, he had cut off the head, the forearms, and the lower legs. He had then attempted to burn the torso, and had finally buried the remains in lime. To do all this, Dr Simpson maintained, the man would have to be strong, unimaginative, and certainly very desperate, a man pushed to his limits. The dead woman was far from attractive, and she had not been sexually interfered with, as far as could be judged at this distance from her death. So the man who killed her had to be close to her, so close that she had some kind of hold on him. Her husband, perhaps?

According to Mrs Dobkin's sister, Rachel had been deserted by her husband, Harry Dobkin, some years previously, and she had since lived alone. As far as Rachel's sister knew, the couple had not seen each other since, but there had been some trouble over alimony payments.

Inspector Hatton asked for a check on the records of local magistrate's courts, which dealt with alimony, and at the same time put out a trace for the missing man, with the rider that he was not to be alarmed. If Harry Dobkin was guilty, Hatton did not want him taking fright and diving to earth. Fortunately for Dobkin's hunters, no word of the discovery of Mrs Dobkin's body had so far leaked to the press.

The search was not a difficult one. Dobkin proved to be living a few miles away from Lambeth, in south London, and to the satisfaction of both Dr Simpson and Inspector Hatton, investigating officers discovered that he had been 'fire-watching' (on the look-out for fires started by bombs) in Kennington Lane in 1941, at about the time Rachel Dobkin had apparently died.

The police asked Dobkin to call at Southwark police station 'on a minor matter'. He turned up without trouble, and was told that human remains found in Kennington Lane

had proved to be those of his wife. Inspector Hatton watched him with interest. He was a heavily built, dark-featured man with powerfully developed arms and shoulders. Enquiries had shown that he worked in the building trade, and his education was slight. Magistrate's court records had also shown that, some months before, he had fallen behind on his alimony payments to Rachel and had been jailed for the offense. As soon as he came out of prison, she had been there waiting for him, badgering him.

'Strong, unimaginative, and very desperate,' Dr Simpson had said, and this was enough for Inspector Hatton. He arrested Dobkin for the murder of his wife.

Ironic

Dobkin's lack of imagination perhaps helped his imperturbability. He denied having had anything to do with Rachel's death, even when confronted with Lambeth magistrates during the initial hearing. But when indicted for the offense, and sent to the highest criminal court in the land, the famous Old Bailey, for trial by jury, his calm broke. In the witness box, quietly laying down the facts in a firm tone, was Doctor Keith Simpson.

As the details were revealed, Dobkin became restless, gripping steel spikes which surrounded the dock and sweating profusely, his face drained of all color. When Dr Simpson stood down, the jury was satisfied. The twelve members returned after only a short deliberation, and pronounced Dobkin guilty as charged. He collapsed in the dock.

By a stroke of irony, Dr Simpson was to see Dobkin again. By pure accident he was the pathologist on the Home Office rota delegated to perform an autopsy, strictly routine this time, on the body of the murderer at Wandsworth Prison, on the morning he was hanged just before Christmas, 1942. Dr Simpson was outwardly impassive about the task, as any good detective-surgeon would have been. In the Dobkin case, he had carefully assembled a set of unassailable facts, checked them against each other time and again, and had arrived at what he knew to be the truth. As a human being he may have deplored the cause and the effect of the case, but as a scientific detective he was totally satisfied.

The deadly traces

Wherever he went, the killer left his trail

The dapper Mr Deeming, alias Williams, was a little too free with his invitations to death. He killed in the Windsor district of Melbourne, in the English village of Rainhill, and in Johannesburg, South Africa. The contemporary Press called him 'The Criminal of the Century.'

SURVEYS CARRIED out in the United States of America and Europe have shown that the professional criminal tends to be more conservative than almost any other social group, not only in his political outlook but in every aspect of his life. Resistance to any kind of change is a foible of the criminal mind, and it is a characteristic for which the police have cause to be thankful. Once a fraud, a housebreaker or a killer establishes a method of working, he rarely deviates from that method. He might change his appearance, he may even travel half way round the world, but by and large his habits will remain set. It was this rigidity which brought Frederick Bailey Deeming to his death on the gallows in the 1890s.

One summer's day, a Mr Stamford was showing a prospective tenant over a villa he owned in Andrew Street, Melbourne, Australia, when he noticed a sickening smell. The villa was a two-story building, and the smell seemed to be coming from the downstairs bedroom. The potential lessee told Mr Stamford that quite obviously his drains were in appalling condition, and that he had changed his mind about the place. Stamford went angrily to see his agent, a Mr Connors, to demand an explanation.

Enormous

Connors was puzzled. The last tenant, an Englishman named Drewen, had done a great deal of work on the house before leaving two months previously. He had partly relaid the bedroom floor and had built a new fireplace in the room. Surely he would have noticed if anything was wrong. Connors and Stamford went back to the villa to examine it more closely. They saw that a rectangle of concrete had been laid to serve as a hearthstone, but the fierce heat of the Australian summer had dried out the cement too quickly, and the concrete was beginning to crumble. It was from here that the smell seemed to emanate. Stamford stepped forward and kicked at the hearth, and a whole section fell into a shallow cavity beneath. When he peered into the hole, he was horrified to see the decaying body of a young woman staring up at him, her head almost severed from her body.

Detective Sergeant Considine of Melbourne Criminal Investigation Department was on the scene within half an hour, accompanied by a police surgeon. The doctor's report was straightforward. The body was that of a woman in her late 20s or early 30s. She had been beaten about the head and body, and death had resulted from her throat being cut with enormous force. She had been dead for about two months.

Detective Sergeant Considine interviewed the agent Connors about his previous tenant. The man's name, said Connors, had been Drewen, a mild-mannered Englishman. 'He took the place on December 16,' he said, 'and paid three weeks' rent in advance. He seemed all right and I didn't ask for references. In any case, he told me he had just arrived from England and knew nobody in Australia. He said he had his wife with him and wanted a house quickly because he was finding that his hotel expenses were far too high for him.' A neighbor in Andrew Street was able to give the sergeant a description of Drewen. He was about 5 ft 7 ins, with a fair moustache and beard, and was aged about 40. The neighbor also stressed the 'mild-mannered' nature of Drewen, which, he said, made his subsequent behavior even more surprising. 'He was a funny sort of

chap,' he said. 'I saw him a few times and tried to be friendly with him, but he wasn't interested. A few days before his wife moved in – I suppose it was his wife – Drewen had a bag of cement and some tools delivered, and from the noise I heard later I guessed he was very busy in the house. His wife arrived on Christmas Eve with several trunks covered with labels, and it looked as if she had not long disembarked. Shortly afterwards, they began to quarrel, and the row went on until midnight. I never heard her voice again, but early next morning I could hear Drewen hammering and banging. I didn't see him during the next couple of days, not until he went out and returned with a carrier who took away some luggage. As for his wife, I never saw her again.'

Acting on Sergeant Considine's instructions, detectives began circulating a description of Drewen throughout Melbourne, and checking the shipping offices. They also set about locating the firm of carriers which had moved Drewen's luggage.

Sergeant Considine began searching the villa for any scraps of evidence which might have been left behind. Drewen appeared to have cleared up thoroughly, and had burned some papers and magazines in the fireplace. Among the charred remains was the front page of a mining magazine, and a few storm matches like those used on ships. There was also an invitation card. It read, 'Mr Albert Williams requests the pleasure of the company of . . . at dinner at the Commercial Hotel, Rainhill.' The space for the name of the guest was blank. It occurred to the sergeant that 'Mr Albert Williams' could be an alias for Drewen. But where was Rainhill? There was no town of that name with a Commercial Hotel in Australia. Considine looked up a gazetteer of the British Isles, and found a town

Victim Emily Mather (above) . . . she was Deeming's bride. Left: the murder house in Melbourne, and the body in the hearth, as depicted by a Press artist. While newspapers dwelt on the horror of his crimes, Deeming maintained a casual attitude right from the moment of his arrest. 'I was just fixing up the bedroom fireplace,' he told police . . . 'winter is coming on.' He was equally unmoved when the judge sentenced him to be hanged.

with the company of McLean Brothers and Rigg, which would have cost them £2,000 had it succeeded.

Considine checked the description of Dobson and found that he had a fair beard and hair, and was aged about 40. Now the sergeant decided to seek the aid of the Melbourne newspapers. He called a press conference and announced that the man who had defrauded the jewellery company was believed to be the same person who had killed the woman at the villa. He had travelled from England just before Christmas, and Considine asked if any fellow passengers could recall him. The response was encouraging. Five people recognized the description as that of a fellow passenger called Albert Williams. One woman said, 'It was easy to be taken in by him. He was well mannered and affable, but a trickster and very fond of women. Everybody on board knew of his affairs with different women except his wife. When he arrived in Melbourne, he tried to get money out of three fellow passengers by putting up mining schemes which were obviously bogus.'

Workmanship

Another passenger recalled, 'Williams told me he was a mining engineer. Engineering happens to be my profession too, and I would say that he had had some practical experience of mining and knew what he was talking about. He was good with hand tools and had made himself a pair of pliers out of a couple of knitting needles. The workmanship was excellent.'

A third informant shame-facedly admitted to having had a visit from Williams two or three days before Christmas. On that visit he had loaned money to Williams and had not seen either the money or the miner again.

Certainly Williams seemed to be a busy man, who did not believe in letting the grass grow under his feet. His timetable since arriving in

Not only did Deeming (far left) sometimes use the name Williams, he had many other aliases. These false names, and a list of alleged crimes, were extravagantly displayed in a newspaper feature about his felonious career. Even this 'criminological tree' was far from complete, the newspaper hinted heavily. At this stage, he had not stood trial.

called Rainhill in Lancashire, between Liverpool and St Helens. The Sergeant sent off a cable to Scotland Yard, giving Williams/Drewen's description and the details of the invitation card, asking them to check on his credentials.

Meanwhile, detectives checked hardware stores, seeking the shop where Drewen had bought his tools and cement. It turned out that the equipment had been sent to the villa in Andrews Road at the order of a customer giving the name of Dobson. Was this another alias? The name rang a bell with Sergeant Considine. Just before New Year an Englishman with the name of Dobson had swindled Kilpatrick and Company, a Melbourne firm of jewellers, out of some valuable gems. Some days later, the same man had tried a similar ruse

ALBERT WILLIAMS—HIS MARK.

AN EXTRAORDINARY CRIMINAL CAREER.

THE CRIMES AND ADVENTURES OF A DESPERATE RUFFIAN.

A LIFE'S RECORD OF MURDER AND FRAUD.

When the past life of Albert Williams is revealed in all its naked hideousness—and we have been able to trace his devil's handiwork from his first essay in the field of criminal adventure up to his arrest at Southern Cross—it will be found that the Victorian detectives have brought to a close the record of the most desperate and unscrupulous ruffian of modern times. We have tried to arrange in the form of a criminalogical tree the crimes and adventures that, up to the present, have been alleged against him, also the occupations followed by him in different parts of the world, and that have been reported to us by telegraph and otherwise within the past few days. From present appearances it would seem that this table is far from complete, and that the revelations of the next few days may make material additions to it. Some people would place the crimes of "Jack the Ripper" on his shoulders. On the other hand there are one or two items in the appended table which, though alleged in certain quarters, may prove to be groundless.

WILLIAMS, ALBERT.

BORN NEAR LONDON ABOUT 1843.

ALIASES—

GEORGE.

Working as bricklayer at Euroa, 1893.
Steals quantity of jewellery.
Disappears suddenly.

DEEMING.

THE CAPE
Forgery for £2000.
Killed a Zulu with a jack-knife.
Slew 13 lions in a day.
Buried a wife at Johannesberg.
Robbed mail coach of 5000 sovereigns in 1878.
An Adherent of Cetewayo's
Sundry minor frauds.

SYDNEY.
Time payment frauds, 1882.
Fraudulent insolvency, 1887.
Absconded from bail, and had a fire.
Belonged to Y.M.C.A.
Robbed his employer.
Deserted wife and family.
Imprisoned for bogus advertisement.
Sundry frauds on jewellers.
Got engaged to be married.
Worked as gasfitter and an engineer.
Alleged to have made away with wife and two children.

BRISBANE.
Sundry frauds in 1886.

WELLINGTON.
Perpetrates several swindles.

DAWSON.

Had wife and family in Birkenhead, 1889.
Wife and family disappear.
Perpetrates sundry frauds.

DREWN.

Takes a house in Melbourne.

MOLLETT.

Rockhampton in 1882.
Marries widow with two children at Charters Towers.
Robs and deserts his wife.
Married to daughter of German settler, Brisbane, 1883.
Commits sundry frauds.
Disappears.

DOBSON.

A married man, with family in Melbourne, 1884.

LAWSON.

Married Scotch girl at Hull, 1890.
Steals jewellery £285 at Hull.
Passes valueless cheques.
Escapes to Monte Video.
Brought back and gets nine months.
Stole money at Beverley.
Deserts newly wedded wife.
Robs the bride.
Poses as Australian Wool King

WILLIAMS.

Married at Birkenhead.
Murders wife and four children at Rainhill.
Buries them beneath hearthstone.
Marries Miss Mather at Rainhill, 1891.
Murders her in Melbourne, 1892.
Buries her beneath hearthstone.
Advertises for another wife.
Commits sundry frauds.
Said to be concerned in theft of 5000 sovereigns from Iberia.

DUNCAN.

Advertised for a wife at Melbourne, 1892.

SWANSTON.

Engaged to marry Miss Rounsvelle.
Arrested at Southern Cross.

The detectives are disposed to regard it as intentional. It is possible that other packages or trunks may yet be found, and special attention is being devoted to this point.

Emily Mather (the woman who was murdered at Windsor).

She is described as having been rather pretty, with rosy cheeks. She was the pet of the village, her kindly disposition and modest de-

Deeming in the dock: 'I don't think no more of my life than of that bit of paper.'

Melbourne on December 15 had been full. The day after he arrived he had rented Mr Stamford's villa. On December 17, he had ordered the cement and tools. During the two following days he had gone to work on the floor and the fireplace, digging the shallow hole which was to become his wife's grave. On December 20, he had swindled the money from his fellow passenger. He had killed and entombed his wife on Christmas Eve, and on December 28 he had defrauded Kilpatrick and Company. On January 2 he had tried unsuccessfully to defraud McLeans.

As they made their enquiries in Melbourne, detectives discovered that Williams had remained busy. He had stayed at six different hotels in two weeks under the names Dobson, Drewen and Williams, and during this time had contacted a matrimonial agency. As a result of introductions received, he had dated two women and had written to seven others, telling them that he wanted to get married immediately. All the women who met him confirmed that he was a charming man of the world, but in retrospect recalled that he had shown a great deal of interest in their financial affairs. Fortunately, none of them were particularly wealthy, and he had dropped them.

Organized

Just how fortunate they were was revealed by Scotland Yard's answer to Considine's cable. The man's name was Frederick Bailey Deeming, a mining engineer who had worked for some time in the South African goldfields. He had turned up in Lancashire the previous summer and had played the role of a rich colonial, giving dinner parties and soirees to which the wealthiest women of the area were invited, along with their husbands and fiancés. He had married one of these girls, a Miss Emily Mather, at Rainhill, and shortly afterwards had booked a passage for himself and his bride to Australia. But this was not the end of the message. In view of the information Scotland Yard had received from Considine, Rainhill police had been asked to look closely at the house Deeming had rented in their neighborhood, particularly at the hearths. Under a newly laid slab of concrete they had found the bodies of a young woman and four children.

The search for Deeming was now even more urgent. He was an habitual murderer, and it became imperative that he be caught before he killed again. Every police station in the country, even those deep in the outback, were issued with a description, and mining towns in particular were placed on the alert.

It was with a sinking heart that Sergeant Considine opened a telegram from the Johannesburg police. Alerted by Scotland Yard, they had traced three former houses used by Deeming. Beneath the fireplaces of each one of them were the decaying bodies of young women.

Aristocrat

Finally, Melbourne police came up with what looked like a lead. A man answering Deeming's description, except that he called himself Lord Swanston, had sailed from Melbourne to Sydney on the coaster *Adelaide* on January 12. A quick check of English and Australian reference books revealed no such

Heiress Kate Rousefell was lucky. She fell victim to Deeming's charms, but not to his deadly habit. She had agreed to marry him, and he was already arranging her final resting place when the police took him away.

title, but a glance at the rest of the passenger list set Considine's blood racing. Also travelling on the coaster had been Miss Kate Rounsefell, a pretty, 18-year-old heiress. She was fair game for Deeming, judging by his past form.

Considine discovered that Miss Rounsefell's parents lived in Sydney, where the *Adelaide* had docked on January 14. When Sydney police called on the parents they were horrified by the news that the urbane aristocrat who had come home with their daughter was a mass killer. 'Lord Swanston' had charmed them completely, and they had gladly given their consent when he had asked if he might marry their daughter, although they had known him for only two days. The prospective son-in-law had told them that he had mining interests in Western Australia, and, after a small, celebratory party, he had sailed on January 16 for Fremantle, on the *Oceana*. Mercifully for Miss Rounsefell, he had suggested that she follow him in two or three weeks when he would have a house near Perth 'all ready for her'.

By the time the police had learned her story, Miss Rounsefell was within three days of embarkation . . . and almost certain death. Perth police were telegraphed and told to arrest

Deeming, alias Swanston, on a holding charge of swindling the jewellers, Kilpatrick and Company. He was a ruthless killer, but like most criminals he had stuck to a rigid pattern in his killings. Considine knew from experience that such conservative creatures had a vastly inflated confidence in themselves and their chances of going undetected. If arrested on the lesser charge, Deeming would probably give up without a struggle.

Unrepentant

The Perth police had little difficulty in tracing their quarry to the small mining town of Southern Cross, about 300 miles inland from Perth. He had taken a job there as a mining engineer, and had rented a house.

When they drove up to the front door, the police saw piles of building materials stacked in the small garden. Deeming opened the door to them, wearing overalls and with a trowel in his hand. The police told him why they were there, and he shrugged and invited them in.

'Doing a bit of building?' asked a policeman.

'Yes,' said Deeming. 'Winter is coming on, and I was just fixing up the bedroom fireplace.'

Deeming, alias Dobson, Drewen, Williams and Swanston, was extradited to Melbourne. He appeared unmoved when the murder charges were laid against him, and during his trial, before Mr Justice Hodges at Melbourne High Court, he showed more interest in the spectators than in the proceedings. He smiled and bowed formally at the young women who crowded the public gallery. Considine had Deeming charged with the murder of Emily Mather, his bride from Rainhill, and he listened quite calmly as the judge sentenced him to death for the killing. He was hanged in Melbourne jail.

It is possible that Deeming was insane. His lack of repentance seemed to indicate that this was so. His crimes had followed a pattern so rigid as to be almost mechanical. It was this repetitive pattern which helped police gradually to track him down. Without such an identifiable *modus operandi*, it is possible that he would have stayed at large, protected by the sheer geographical distances between the crimes in Britain, South Africa and Australia.

Gambling on a hunch

A reckless arrest at Niagara Falls

'HUNCHES' OF THE KIND so familiarly featured in the pages of Dashiell Hammett, Raymond Chandler and the other masters of early twentieth-century fiction, play little or no part in real-life crime detection today. In the late nineteenth and early twentieth centuries, however, when true scientific detection was in its infancy, this was not quite the case. Many a real-life lawman did go along with a hunch, simply because he had nothing better to go on. And some were willing to stake not only their case but also their jobs on the flimsiest of hunches.

Such a man was the great American detective John Wilson Murray, who had become known, long before his death in the early part of the present century, as 'Old Never Let Go'. Born in Edinburgh, Scotland, in 1840, Murray became a detective almost by accident, for his family were traditionally seafarers, and his father was a sailing ship captain on the Liverpool – New York run. It seemed inevitable that young John would follow him. But although the boy loved the sea, he early showed that independence which was to characterize his police work, and sometimes alarm his colleagues. At thirteen he ran away to sea, to make a career of his own, away from his father's influence. He reached New York, but was taken back to his father. Two years later he tried again and reached Washington DC, took a ship to the West Indies, and then sailed for the Great Lakes, where he had a cabin boy's job aboard a coaster. Unfortunately for young John's ambition, his father had asked the ship-owners to look out for him. In 1856, at the age of sixteen, he was sent back again to Edinburgh to finish his schooling.

Fascinated

The following year, however, Murray senior realised that his son was intent on an independent way of life. John Wilson Murray bade farewell to Scotland, travelled back to New York, became a United States citizen and promptly enlisted in the United States Navy, where he served on board the battleship *U.S.S. Michigan* throughout the civil war. In 1865, Murray had a chance meeting with an American Naval Intelligence officer which was to change the course of his career. Murray was fascinated by the officer's tales of

Intelligence life, and applied for a transfer. At twenty-five he became a member of the United States Secret Service, working under its famous boss, Allan Pinkerton.

When he left the Secret Service three years later, Murray joined the police department at Erie, Pennsylvania as a detective. While with the police department he worked for a while as a detective on the payroll of the Canadian Southern Railway. The United States and Canadian police forces along the border shared a great deal in common. When in 1870 he was offered the post of chief investigator to the Department of Justice of Ontario, his career was settled.

By the time Murray was thirty-five, he was Chief Inspector of Criminal Investigation for the Ontario Government. His 'precinct' was huge, 101,733 square miles, and he often 'extended' it. He was known to the Chicago police force, for instance, almost as a colleague, for he often crossed the border to help them out. He was also rapidly earning the nickname of 'Old Never Let Go', for once he got his teeth into a case, he would never close the file until it was

John Wilson Murray (pictured on the left of the group) at Blenheim Swamp. Above: Allan Pinkerton, Wilson's Secret Service boss.

45

solved. If he had no concrete clue to go on, no solid lead to work from, he would resort, often without any reason whatsoever, to his 'hunches'.

No one, not even Murray, could later explain the hunch which helped him solve the Blenheim Swamp murder in February 1890. In the blistering cold of the Canadian winter, two loggers were trekking across Blenheim Swamp in south-eastern Ontario, when they came across a body. It wore an incongruously well-tailored suit, and a neat derby hat had rolled off its head, presumably at the moment that two bullets had entered the brain from behind.

Within hours, Chief Inspector Murray himself was on the spot. In a makeshift log cabin 'mortuary' he and a doctor examined the body. The bullets had entered the head at fairly close range. They were certainly not stray shots from a hunter. It was obvious the man had been murdered, and the murderer had done a thorough job of removing any form of identification. The pockets were completely empty, and the labels and marks had been torn from the suit and hat.

With what would have been a touch of humour in other circumstances, Murray recognized the origin of one item of the dead man's clothing – his underpants. They were of a type made only in England. The suit was also of English cut, and though this did not necessarily prove the corpse's nationality, Murray was willing to gamble that the victim was British. By the soft look of his hands, and the fresh innocence of

Reginald Birchall and his wife Florence.

46

the features, the detective felt able to assume that he had been of good class, and very young. So what was he doing in the Canadian backwoods, frozen to the earth?

Murray sent photographs of the dead face, and details of the man's height and weight to Scotland Yard and to all the American police forces and newspapers. He then set about looking for clues, literally on hands and knees, with a magnifying glass. For two days he crawled over the frozen ground at this backbreaking work, and then, on the afternoon of the third day, he found an elegant amber cigar holder with the initials 'F.W.B.' carved into the mouthpiece. It told Murray nothing at the moment, except that if it had belonged to the dead man he had probably been a cigar smoker. He put the cigar holder in his pocket, abandoned his ground search and began questioning local people, fruitlessly. But back in his London, Ontario office a breakthrough awaited him. A Mr and Mrs Reginald Birchall had seen a picture of the dead man in a Niagara Falls newspaper, and believed they knew him. Murray led them to the morgue and drew back the sheet from the corpse's face. Mrs Birchall blenched and turned away. Birchall nodded solemnly. 'I'm afraid that it is poor Benwell,' said Birchall. 'How ever did this happen?'

Murray questioned the couple about the dead man. How had they known him? Mr and Mrs Birchall were English, Murray learned. On their last Atlantic crossing from Liverpool they had met the young

Below: Niagara Falls in the 19th century, where Birchall said he left the man who became his victim.

man on the ship. His name had been Francis W. Benwell, the son of a good family in the Home Counties. They had travelled on together, after leaving the ship at New York, as far as Niagara Falls. Then they had parted company, as Benwell had said he was heading for London, Ontario. They knew nothing of his future plans, they told the detective, but they would help all they could. They were going back to Niagara Falls. Perhaps Murray would like to meet them there and together they could go over the places Benwell had visited? Murray promised that he would meet them in the town in a few days, and the couple left.

Polished

The interview had lasted less than an hour, and yet during it a hunch had formed itself in John Wilson Murray's mind. He sat alone at his desk for a long time after they had gone, remembering the couple. The elegant speech and accents of both of them, Birchall's tasteful clothes and polished manners, Mrs Birchall's blonde but refined good looks. They were both charming and apparently sincere, and their story made sense. Yet Murray's nose told him that, deep down, there was something phoney about them.

Common sense, on the other hand, told Murray that he was wrong. The initials on the cigar holder were those of the man they had described, Francis W. Benwell. If Birchall had had a hand in the killing, why should he come forward to identify the body,

when the murderer had gone to such pains to obscure all means of identification? Such strange things had been known to happen, but Murray had not a slip of evidence. Acting only on his hunch, he wired a description of the couple to police in Niagara Falls, Canada. 'Shadow this man. Do not arrest him unless he tries to cross the river to the States. I will be there Sunday night.'

It was mid-week, and Murray had a few days to check if Benwell had known anybody in London, Ontario. Almost his entire detective force was put onto the job, as well as local newspaper men. They soon discovered that no one in the town had ever heard of Francis Benwell, and that he had never set foot in the town. So in one respect, Birchall had lied.

On Sunday evening, John Murray entered the town of Niagara Falls and ordered the immediate arrest of Reginald Birchall and his wife on a charge of murder. It was the most unreasonable, reckless act he had ever performed in his life. If his hunch was wrong it would be he, not Birchall, who would be in the dock on charges of false and malicious arrest. He would be ruined. And he knew that he not only had to be correct in his assumption that Birchall was behind the Blenheim Swamp murder, he had to prove it to a judge and jury.

Grimly, Murray began tracking the Birchalls' movements in and around the town, and soon came across a young Englishman named

Pelly who had travelled with the Birchalls and Benwell from England to the United States. The common link between the foursome was quickly explained. Pelly showed Murray a clipping from the London *Times*.

'Canada. University man having farm wishes to meet gentleman's son to live with him and to learn the business with a view to partnership. Must invest £500 to extend stock. Board lodging and five per cent interest till partnership arranged.'

Pelly had answered the advertisement in London and had met Reginald Birchall as a result. Birchall told him of the great opportunities of life in Canada, and when Pelly explained that he would love to go but had only £170 to invest, Birchall agreed to take that sum for the time being. On board ship, Pelly had met Benwell, who had also answered the advertisement, and explained that he, too, was short of the initial £500. Birchall had taken him on as an extra partner to raise the necessary capital.

On arrival in New York, the party had travelled to Buffalo, and then Birchall and Benwell had journeyed on up to Canada to view the farm. Birchall had returned alone. He explained that Benwell had not liked

A grisly piece of opportunism by the undertaker who buried Francis Benwell (right). The 'First-Class Hearse' pictured on the advertising handbill is the one that carried the murder victim to his funeral.

For Elegant & Reliable Furniture call on A. H. Swarts, Princeton, Ont.

TEN   10

A. H. SWARTS,
Furnishing Undertaker and Cabinet Maker.
Caskets —AND— Coffins.
Burial Robes &c.
PICTURE FRAMING
A First-Class HEARSE.
Not to be UNDERSOLD

George Blackstock, QC (left), defended Birchall, but it was Britton Bath Osler, QC, the prosecutor (right) who convinced the jury (below).

the farm and had gone to London, Ontario to visit relatives, before returning to England.

Could Pelly remember the date on which the couple had left for the north, asked Murray? Pelly told him it was early February, which coincided with Benwell's death. And then Pelly reassured Murray by saying that it was he who had spotted Benwell's picture in the newspaper, and had insisted that Birchall travel back to Canada to identify the body. So that was the reason the murderer, if Birchall was the murderer, had come forward. Pelly could have been awkward if he had pressed the matter himself. The hunch, thought Murray with some relief, was paying off.

But the detective was far from home and dry yet. He questioned Pelly about the party's subsequent activities. They had gone over the border to Niagara Falls, said the young man. He had thought then that Birchall's attitude towards him had been odd as they viewed the great natural wonder together. On three occasions, his 'benefactor' had invited him to come right up to the water's edge to take a look at the roaring maelstrom beneath.

All this was more than encouraging, and then the case really broke. Scotland Yard wired new evidence on Birchall and his wife. Birchall had been at Oxford University but had been sent down after some trouble over money. He had married, and had then travelled with his wife around London calling themselves 'Lord and Lady Somerset'. Although nothing could be proved, they were strongly suspected of living by fraud, as they had no visible means of income and yet always had money.

Now that Murray knew the route

travelled by Birchall and his victim
a few weeks previously, he was able
to follow their trail, and fortunately
it had not yet gone cold. Taking the
same train from Buffalo across the
border to Eastwood, Ontario, which
was four miles from Blenheim Swamp,
Murray questioned crews, station
staff and regular passengers. Several
people swore to having seen the pair.
A girl said she had seen the couple
together near the swamp at the
relevant time, and a logger said he
had heard the shots from a mile
away. A farmer identified a photograph of Birchall as a man he had
seen coming from the swamp alone,
and, with a final stroke of luck,
Murray found a girl who had seen a
man getting off the train at Eastwood
Station with Benwell. She had known
him in England as 'Lord Somerset'.

A final piece of evidence came from
the Yard as Murray travelled back
to his headquarters with the two
prisoners. Three days after the
murder, Birchall had callously
written to Benwell's father in
England, asking for the remaining
£100 his son owed on the phoney
farm deal.

Murray was convinced that Mrs
Birchall had played no part in the
murder of Francis W. Benwell, and
she was released. But a few weeks
after his spectacular arrest in the
town of Niagara Falls, Reginald
Birchall went to the gallows.

What it was that had caused him
to throw his highly respected career
so recklessly into the balance over
the Blenheim Swamp case, John
Wilson Murray never knew for sure,
unless it was a deeply subconscious
animal instinct. Certainly, his incredible hunch was totally without
rational basis – but it paid off.

The plodding policeman

...how the Yard caught Dr Crippen

THE PLODDING, dull and rather stupid official police officer, set in sharp contrast to the needle-brained élan of the gifted amateur, is one of the great cliches of detective fiction. Sherlock Homes patronized 'my dear Lestrade' for his slow-moving investigative work, the Saint behaved condescendingly to Inspector Claude Eustace Teal in much the same way, Nero Wolfe and his energetic assistant Archie Goodwin caused Inspector Cramer of the New York Homicide Division to have fits of frustrated rage. The list is endless and the characterization all too familiar.

And yet, if the average real-life police chief were asked what qualities he sought most in an investigating officer, dogged determination, a dedication to routine, and a plodding thoroughness of method would be high on his list. These were precisely the qualities which brought Dr Crippen to justice, in a case which ended with the now-celebrated chase across the Atlantic.

Chief Inspector Walter Dew of Scotland Yard's Criminal Investigation Department was the personification of all these faintly despised virtues, so that even his own colleagues knicknamed him 'Plodder'. Yet, without his patience and

stubbornness, coupled with a sharp intelligence and resourceful brain, Crippen's crime might never have been detected.

The story began on June 30, 1910, when Chief Inspector Dew was summoned into the office of his superior, Superintendent Frank Froest, in the old Scotland Yard building high above the Thames embankment. Already the morning sun had begun to make the office uncomfortably warm, and Superintendent Froest was irritable. He explained that a couple named Nash had turned up to report the disappearance of a friend, and were making thorough nuisances of themselves. They were probably cranks, but could Dew see them? Dew shrugged and walked through into the ante-room where the couple were seated.

Mrs Nash turned out to be an extrovert and a busibody. She did all the talking while her husband sat fiddling with his hat. She explained to Dew that she had come to report the disappearance of a friend and colleague, like herself a vaudeville performer and a member of the Music Hall Ladies' Guild. The missing woman performed as a singer under the names of Cora

Turner and Belle Elmore. She was married to a Doctor Harvey Hawley Crippen.

Mrs Nash produced a sheaf of scribbled notes. 'I have been doing a little investigating of my own,' she told Dew. 'May I tell you about it?' Dew smiled patiently and nodded for her to carry on. According to Mrs Nash's notes, a Mr and Mrs Paul Martinetti had been dinner guests at the Crippen's home the previous New Year's Eve. The party had been mundane, although the doctor and his wife had quarrelled slightly. The marriage had always been tense, Mrs Nash explained.

On February 3, the Music Hall Ladies' Guild had received two letters allegedly from Cora Crippen, stating that she had had to go to California where a relative was seriously ill. But, said Mrs Nash importantly, the letters were not in Cora's handwriting. She had gone around to Dr Crippen's home with one or two other Guild members and had asked about the missing woman. Crippen had been non-commital. About a week later, Mrs Nash had seen Dr Crippen out walking with his secretary, Ethel Le Neve. The young woman had been wearing a fur coat and a necklace belonging to Cora. By March 12, Miss Le Neve had moved into the Crippen home quite openly, and a fortnight after that Dr Crippen had sent out black-edged mourning cards to say that his wife Cora had died suddenly of pneumonia in California. Her recital over, Mrs Nash handed her notes over to Chief Inspector Dew and sat back with a look of grim satisfaction, her duty done.

When his visitors had gone, Dew pondered the notes before him. He had little experience of the flashy world of vaudeville, with its jealousies and scandals. He was the son of a railroad worker and had come to London with his father at the age of ten. After leaving school at thirteen, he had held jobs on the railroads and as a clerk before joining the Metropolitan Police Force, and his world since then had been one of routine. But he had read scandal

Paul Martinetti and his wife, followed by Mr Nash, leave the inquest on Cora Crippen. Right: Ethel Le Neve, Crippen's secretary. She was seen in a fur coat and necklace belonging to her employer's wife. She was later to stand with him in the dock.

The faces of Cora Crippen

The many, repetitive, faces of Belle Elmore, stage name of Crippen's wife, Cora. A failed vaudeville artiste, she vainly sought success on the London stage. Belle demanded singing lessons, but the only notes of any consequence were produced from Crippen's wallet as he paid for the tuition.

sheets, the 'yellow press', and he knew that even in those Edwardian days couples were constantly changing partners, 'living in sin' and running off with lovers. It seemed highly likely that something of the sort had gone on here, and that Mrs Nash was merely revelling in a piece of spicy scandal.

The detective's curiosity got the better of him, however. Instead of assigning the case to the Missing Persons Department, Dew went out and checked with some of the people whose addresses Mrs Nash had given him. Their stories tallied with hers. And so, on July 8, 1910, Dew and a detective sergeant set out for Crippen's home at 39 Hilldrop Crescent, in the North London borough of Islington. The door was opened by a French maid who ushered the two men into a bright and comfortable parlor. A couple of minutes later a young woman appeared, described later by Dew as 'not pretty, but attractive and neatly and quietly dressed'. After introducing himself, Chief Inspector Dew asked to see Dr Crippen, as he had been requested to make some enquiries about Mrs Crippen. The girl appeared to be in no way disturbed. 'I'm afraid Dr Crippen is not at home,' she said. 'He is at his office in Albion House, New Oxford Street.' The Inspector asked the young woman if she was Ethel Le Neve, and for the first time she looked slightly uncomfortable. She blushed as she told him that she was. When Dew asked if she would accompany him to the doctor's office, however, she readily fetched her hat and coat.

The trio travelled down to New Oxford Street in London's West End. Dew had brought Ethel with him to prevent her from warning her lover that they were coming. When they reached the office, she said that the doctor was on the third floor, and then unexpectedly dashed off up the stairs before Dew could stop her.

The two detectives were half way up the stairs when Harvey Hawley Crippen met them. He was about fifty, soberly dressed and small in stature, with a pale face and a large dark moustache. What immediately impressed Dew, however, were his eyes. They were large and protuberant, behind small, steel-rimmed spectacles. The doctor spoke with a soft, pleasant American accent.

Bernard Spilsbury, later to become a world-renowned forensic expert, examines evidence in Crippen's back yard. Right: The ghastly parcel which was discovered in the cellar.

METROPOLITAN POLICE

MURDER

AND MUTILATION.

Portraits, Description and Specimen of Handwriting of HAWLEY HARVEY CRIPPEN, alias Peter Crippen, alias Franckel; and ETHEL CLARA LE NEVE, alias Mrs. Crippen, and Neave.

Wanted for the Murder of CORA CRIPPEN otherwise Belle Elmore; Kunigunde Mackamotzki; Marsangar and Turner, on, or about, 2nd February last.

Description of Crippen. Age 50, height 5 ft. 3 or 4, complexion fresh, hair light brown, inclined sandy, scanty, bald on top, rather long scanty moustache, somewhat straggly, eyes grey, bridge of nose rather flat, false teeth, medium build, throws his feet outwards when walking. May be clean shaven or wearing a beard and moustache, rimmed spectacles, and may possibly assume a wig.

Sometimes wears a jacket suit, and at other times frock coat and silk hat. May be dressed in a brown jacket suit, brown hat and silk hat. May be dressed in a brown jacket suit, brown hat and stand up collar (size 15).

Somewhat slovenly appearance, wears his hat rather at back of head.

Very plausible and quiet spoken, remarkably cool and collected demeanour. Carries Firearms.

Speaks French and probably German.

An American citizen, and by profession a Doctor.

Has lived in New York, Philadelphia, St. Louis, Detroit, Michigan, Coldwater, and other parts of America.

May obtain a position as assistant to a doctor or eye specialist, or may practise as an eye specialist. Dentist or open a business for the treatment of deafness, advertising freely.

Has represented Munyon's Remedies, in various cities in America.

Description of Le Neve alias Neave.—A shorthand writer and typist, age 27, height 5 ft. 5, complexion pale, hair light brown (may dye same), large grey or blue eyes, good teeth, nice looking, rather long straight nose (good shape), medium build, pleasant, lady-like appearance. Quiet, subdued manner, talks quietly, looks intently when in conversation. A native of London.

Dresses well, but quietly, and may wear a blue serge costume (coat reaching to hips) trimmed heavy braid, about 5 inch wide, round edge, over shoulders and pockets. Three large braid buttons down front, about size of a florin, three small ones on each pocket, two on each cuff, several rows of stitching round bottom of skirt, or a light grey shadow-stripe costume, same style as above, but trimmed grey more silk instead of braid, and two rows of silk round bottom of skirt, or a white princess robe, with gold sequins; or a mole coloured striped costume with black moire silk collar, or a dark Vieurose cloth costume, trimmed black velvet collar, or a light heliotrope dress.

May have in her possession and endeavour to dispose of same:—a round gold brooch, with points radiating to edge from centre, each point about an inch long, diamond in centre, each point set brilliants, the brooch in all being slightly larger than a halfcrown, and two single stone diamond rings, and a diamond and sapphire (or ruby), ring, stones rather large.

Absconded 9th inst., and may have left, or will endeavour to leave the country.

Please cause every enquiry at Shipping Offices, Hotels, and other likely places, and cause ships to be watched.

Information to be given to the Metropolitan Police Office, New Scotland Yard, London, S.W., or at any Police Station.

E R HENRY,
The Commissioner of Police of the Metropolis.

Metropolitan Police Office,
New Scotland Yard 16th July, 1910.

'I have come to ask you if you can offer an explanation as to your wife's disappearance,' Dew told him. Crippen sighed and motioned for them to follow him to his office. 'I suppose I had better tell the truth,' he said over his shoulder. 'The stories I have told about my wife's death are untrue. As far as I know she is still alive.' For the next five hours, Dew and his colleague listened to Dr Crippen's calm voice recounting the story of his life and marriage. He had been born, he told them, in Cold Water, Michigan, in the United States, in 1862. He had been educated at the University of Michigan and Hospital College, Cleveland, where he received his doctorate of medicine. Afterwards, he became an intern at the Ophthalmic Hospital in New York, where he began to specialize in eye, ear, nose, and throat diseases. It was while in New York that he met the patient of a friend of his, a singer and dancer named Cora Turner or Belle Elmore. She had used two stage names to get more work playing double bills in off-Broadway vaudeville houses. Dr Crippen fell in love with the seventeen-year-old beauty and married her in 1892.

Money lust

But, Crippen told the detectives, he soon found that he had been a little hasty. His wife's real name turned out to be Kunigunde Mackamotzki, and she was the daughter of a Russian-Polish father and a German mother. The family had been poor, and 'Cora' had developed a lust for money and social position early. She desperately

Captain Kendall, of the *SS Montrose*. His historic cable enabled Inspector Dew to corner the escaping Crippen.

wanted to be a vaudeville star but her singing voice, Crippen commented wryly, was 'not up to it'. He paid for countless singing lessons for her, none of which had any effect on anything but his bank balance.

In 1900 Cora had insisted that they move to London, where the music halls and theaters were the envy of the world. Unfortunately she was able to get only two minor roles, and the result for Crippen was devastating. He was not licensed to practice medicine in Britain, and was reduced to manufacturing and selling patent remedies. Despite the lack of cash, Cora Crippen threw lavish dinner parties in a constant effort to enter the social whirl of London.

Plausible

Finally, when she met a wealthy American named Miller, said Crippen he had let the affair develop in the hope that his troublesome wife would run off with her lover. When she did so, he had invented a story of her death to avoid the scandal and the necessary explanation to friends. In any case, he confessed frankly, he had been having an affair with his secretary, Miss Le Neve, for some time, and Cora had found out, which might have contributed to her decision to run. After her departure, Ethel had moved in to Hilldrop Crescent, and had taken to wearing some of Cora's expensive furs and jewellery.

'I am not going to maintain that my conduct has been proper,' Crippen finished quietly, 'but I feel that I am entitled to some happiness in my life.'

Chief Inspector Dew nodded. The story sounded totally plausible, and the manner in which the doctor had told it convincing. But it did prove one thing. One way or the other Crippen was a liar, even if only over the story he had told his friends.

'I think that it is satisfactory,' he said, closing his notebook. 'But I have to find Mrs Crippen to clear up the matter.'

Crippen nodded in agreement, and when Dew suggested that he might search the house in Hilldrop Crescent for clues as to Mrs Crippen's whereabouts, both Crippen and Ethel

Ethel Le Neve hoped to be Crippen's wife, but she was forced to pose as his son when they fled to Canada. She wore the clothes he bought for her, but was spotted by the captain.

Detective Sergeant Mitchell leaves London to bring back the fugitives.

readily agreed to show him around.

Dew went over the house thoroughly, examining the many drawers and cupboards, and sifting through piles of Cora Crippen's clothing. She had obviously had a taste for flamboyant furs and hats with, as Dew put it later, 'enough ostrich feathers to start a millinery shop.' It did seem slightly odd to the detective that a woman with such a passion for finery should have gone

off taking so little with her. There were no obvious gaps in the racks of garments in her various wardrobes. Dew and his colleague searched the house from the attic to the small damp and unlighted coal cellar without turning up anything in the way of a clue. When he left the house, Dew was more or less convinced of the truth of Crippen's story; neither he nor Ethel had acted guiltily, and there was no indication of what

63

Scotland Yard like to euphemistically term 'foul play'.

The search and the interview had taken place on a Friday. Dew thought about the matter over the weekend, and the more he thought about the aspect of the clothes, the more uneasy he became. Early on Monday morning he went down to Crippen's office to ask further questions. The doctor and his mistress had gone. Dew rapidly questioned the staff of the building. A handyman told him that Crippen had arrived there on Saturday morning, the day following Dew's first visit, and had sent out to a store for a selection of boy's clothing. He had bought a brown tweed suit, brown felt hat, two shirts, two collars and a pair of tan-colored boots.

Dew cursed. His suspicions were now fully aroused, but he had absolutely nothing on which to justify an application for an arrest warrant.

Again he returned to Hilldrop Crescent and the now-empty house. He was convinced that somewhere here must lie a clue to the mystery. He and a colleague began their search again. They went over the attic, and the bedrooms, the servants' room, the bathroom, the drawing and dining rooms, kitchen and coal cellar. But still they found nothing.

'What now?' asked Dew's colleague.

'Now we start all over again,' replied Dew.

The two men examined every inch of the house, finishing in the early hours of Tuesday morning. After a few hours sleep, they came back, and searched for the rest of Tuesday. But by Wednesday evening, even the indefatigable Dew was thoroughly exhausted. 'We might as well have another go at that coal cellar,' he said, 'and then we'll finish for the night.'

The cellar floor was of brick. Dew

Inspector Dew (bowler-hatted) returns to Britain in triumph.

Crippen, escorted by Dew, walks ashore on his way to trial.

had already shovelled out all the coal and had probed the cracks between the bricks, though the cement seemed solid enough. Now he got down on his hands and knees and, using a pocket knife, began probing at the cement fillings. In one place, the cement seeméd a little softer than elsewhere, and after a little prodding the brick came loose. Dew lifted it out. With the removal of the first brick, the surrounding ones seemed to loosen up. Pulling them out one by one, the detectives soon uncovered an oblong patch of earthen floor underneath. The soil was very soft, and by now the detectives were excited. They brought in a shovel and began gently easing layers of the soil out of the hole. A few inches down they came across a ghastly parcel.

Knowledge

It contained a human torso, without arms, legs or head. But it took some time for Dew to recognize the remains as human at all, for the bones had been removed.

The following day, July 14, Dr Augustus J. Pepper, Home Office pathologist, took charge of the grisly parcel at Islington morgue. He discovered that the dismemberment had been done by someone with an excellent knowledge of human anatomy, and considerable surgical skills.

By this time Dew had dug up the rest of the cellar floor and had found pieces of a pair of pyjamas, and friends of Cora Crippen identified them as hers. None of this, however, proved that the body was that of Cora Crippen, or whether indeed it was a woman's body at all.

During his investigation in the morgue, Pepper had found a wrinkled patch of skin measuring five by seven inches on the torso. Although he knew that wrinkling does occur after death, he felt that this might be the remains of an old surgical scar. Dew questioned friends of Cora, and discovered that she had undergone major abdominal surgery in New York.

Chief Inspector Dew now began to question everyone who had dealt

Crowds thronged the streets outside the Old Bailey. Inside the hapless Crippen was on trial for his life. The interest in the case was so intense that minor witnesses, such as Cora's friends, were photographed.

with Crippen in his work, and after interviewing dozens of chemists and chemical suppliers, he discovered what proved to be an important fact. Only one new substance had been added to Crippen's 'shopping list' of chemicals used in his patent medicines recently, and this was grains of the vegetable poison hyoscine, which had been delivered to Albion House in January.

The week had been a busy one for Dew, and it was to become even more frantic. Shortly after the discovery of the human remains, Dew had obtained an arrest warrant, and had immediately put out a description of Crippen and Le Neve, who he assumed would be travelling as a boy in the clothes Crippen had bought on the previous Saturday. The following Friday he received a cable from the captain of the SS Montrose, a transatlantic liner bound for Quebec from Antwerp, Belgium. Not only was it a break for Dew, it was a milestone in criminal history. It was the first time a transatlantic cable had been used to catch a murderer on the run.

The cable said that a man answering Crippen's description, accompanied by a younger 'boy', had boarded the ship at Brussels, identifying themselves as 'John Robinson and son'. The boy looked effeminate, never appeared without his hat, and his clothes were ill-fitting. The captain had seen Robinson squeeze his 'son's' hand in a very tender way, which he had thought hardly fitting to a father-son relationship.

Dew was confident that the couple could only be Crippen and Ethel Le Neve. He booked a ticket on the fast liner SS Laurentic, in a bid to outrace the Montrose across the Atlantic. The whole world was agog by now at the drama which was being played out on the high seas. Bookmakers in New York and London took bets on the result. Would Dew get there first, and arrest his man, or would the doctor slip away?

In fact, there was no chance of escape. Aboard the Montrose the news of what was going on was kept secret. In Quebec, reporters from all parts of the United States and Canada lined the quayside, waiting. When the Laurentic, with Dew aboard, steamed into Quebec several hours ahead of the Montrose, the London detective found himself an international celebrity, and spent the day fending off reporters.

Finally, he managed to board a launch and went out secretly to meet the incoming vessel. Going aboard with the pilot, Dew immediately recognized Crippen, despite the beard he had grown. When he walked up to him he simply said: 'Good morning Dr Crippen.'

The doctor gave himself up immediately, without fuss. But Dew's task was not yet done. Unless he could prove that the body in the cellar was that of Cora Crippen, he had no case to go on, he could not prove that her husband had murdered her.

However, when he arrived back in London on August 10, he found that two medical men, Dr William Willcox, a toxics expert, and Dr Bernard Spilsbury, soon to be renowned for his forensic pathology, had been hard at work. Willcox had proved that the organs taken from the body contained hyoscine, the poison which Dew had discovered to have been bought by Crippen earlier in the year. And Spilsbury had incontrovertibly shown that the wrinkled scar tissue – the skin, hairs, and formation of the cells – was indeed an abdominal scar from the body of a woman of the same age as Cora Crippen.

The trial of Crippen and Ethel began on October 18, 1910, and was by no means an easy one for the prosecution. Crippen's lawyer fought to show that the body had been buried in the cellar before he took the house, but with the weight of Spilsbury's medical evidence, and Dew's detective work, he failed. On October 22, the jury returned their verdicts. Crippen was guilty, Ethel Le Neve was innocent. In mid-November, the doctor walked to the gallows.

It was the medical evidence which clinched the case against Crippen, but it was dogged, persistent and patient detective work on the part of Chief Inspector Walter Dew which had led to the discovery of the crime. The sea race and the historic telegram were the elements most remembered in criminal history and, like his 'plodding' colleagues of fiction, Dew's bulldog tenacity went unrewarded – except for the satisfaction of knowing he had brought a killer to justice. No professional detective would want more.

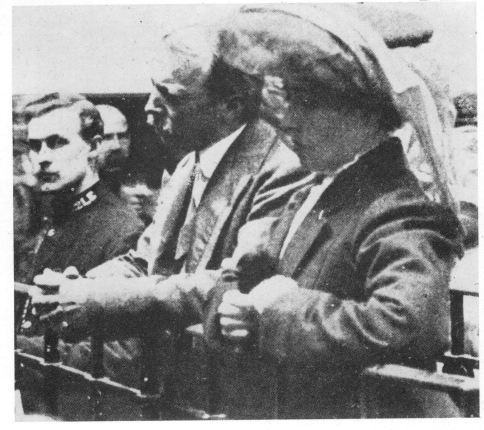

A quizzical-looking Crippen stands with Ethel in the dock at the preliminary hearing at Bow Street Court, London. Together they listened as evidence was given of their arrest (right) aboard the Montrose on the high seas.

A first and final clue

The victim who helped trap her own killer

THROUGHOUT THE recorded history of crime detection, all sorts of odd leads and clues have guided astute sleuths to their quarry. What was possibly the clearest and bravest clue was the description of the murderer, written by his victim, minutes before she was raped and killed.

At around midnight on Monday July 20, 1970, a Suffolk County police patrol car eased over to the side of the Sagtikos State Parkway on Long Island, New York, just outside the fashionable village of East Islip. The driver had been attracted by the sight of an automobile, apparently undamaged, standing on the hard shoulder with its headlights full on. It was a new, blue, Ford Maverick, and as the patrolman approached it he saw that he had been wrong in his first impression, for the wind-screen on the driver's side had been

smashed in, and nuggets of the shattered glass lay on the front seats and under the dashboard. The driver's door was open, and the engine was still turning over in neutral. After switching off the ignition, the officer walked carefully round the car. Not a scratch or dent showed anywhere on the gleaming paintwork. Obviously, this was not an ordinary accident. The patrolman noted the license number, and peered once more into the car's interior with a flashlight. On the front, passenger seat, jammed up against the back, he found a small, spiral-bound notebook, and a tan leather pocketbook which contained 50 dollars, and papers giving the owner's address.

The name and address was that of Miss Adele Kohr, 36, Shinnecock Lane, East Islip, which was only a quarter of a mile further along the

road. The officer radioed to head-quarters with details of what he had found, and then drove to the girl's home. When he rang the bell, the door was snatched open immediately, and an anxious man appeared. He was Francis Kohr, Adele's father, and he had been just about to call the police to report his daughter's non-arrival home. The policeman saw the looks of panic appear on the faces of Mr Kohr and his wife, and he tried to reassure them. 'Maybe she's walked home for some reason,' he suggested. But a glance at the clock told them all that this was unlikely. Adele was working as a nurse at the Suffolk State School for mentally retarded children at Melville, 18 miles away from East Islip. Her late shift ended at 11.00 pm, and the drive, along the fast parkway, took just under half an hour. Her car had been found after midnight, and it was now 1.00 am. If she was walking the quarter mile to her home she was taking her time...

After seeing the girl's parents, the patrolman drove back to police headquarters and placed the personal effects found in the car before the Head of Detectives. They now lay in front of Detective Sergeant Tom Richmond, and as head of the Suffolk County Homicide Squad, he reluctantly agreed that the girl's disappearance was probably a case for his department.

There was nothing in the pocketbook to tell him much more than he already knew, except, perhaps that the motive had not been robbery, for Adele's money was still there. Then he turned to the small spiral-bound notebook. Leafing through the first seven pages, he discovered a neat list of figures and prices. It was a carefully kept record of gasoline bought and mileage covered since January, when the girl had bought her Ford Maverick. On the eighth page, Tom Richmond found something else. It was a series of disjointed words, apparently in the same handwriting that had recorded the small, meticulous figures on the previous leaves, but scrawled and shakey. Looking back, he found that the scrawl began, faintly, on the third page of the book and was superimposed over the gasoline tables. With some difficulty he began to decipher it. It read: 'A man in a car pulled alongside me . . . on the

Sagtikos . . . he wants me to stop . . . he is following me in the same lane and I can't pull away . . . doing 65 . . . he is alongside again . . . beard . . . glasses . . . long hair . . . hippy type . . . blue shirt . . . the car is a Tempest . . . light green . . . T-37 . . .'

Richmond turned over another page. Scrawled shakily across the double spread were two words 'dark pants.' There the message ended.

Judging by the present tense used throughout, and the jittery nature of the handwriting, Richmond guessed that the girl had jotted down her impressions as she drove. She must have steered the car with her left hand while writing in the notebook, which was lying on the seat beside her. But the last two

words 'dark pants' must have been written after she had been forced to a stop, and as the assailant was approaching her. She could not have spotted the color of his pants while he was sitting in his Tempest-37.

Richmond called in Mr Kohr and asked him for a description of Adele. She was 5 ft 2 ins tall, and a pretty girl with light brown hair, green eyes and a fair complexion. She weighed about 120 lbs. Adele was in her early twenties, and, although she had dated a number of young men, as far as her parents knew she had no regular boyfriend. She always wore her blue, nurses' uniform travelling to and from Melville, and on Mondays she wore a yellow bikini under her outfit. That was the

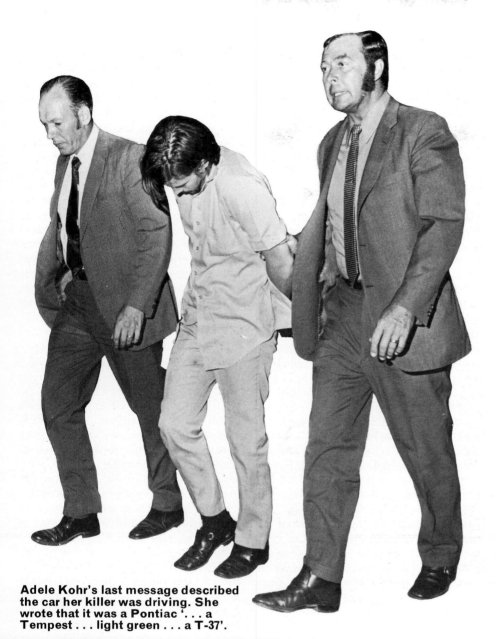

Adele Kohr's last message described the car her killer was driving. She wrote that it was a Pontiac '... a Tempest ... light green ... a T-37'.

day that she taught her young charges to swim, and she usually kept the swimsuit on after the lesson. On her feet she wore moccasins.

Blackened

Tom Richmond also learned a little about Adele's character. She was a serious young woman, and was dedicated to her job with the backward children of Melville. Although not a zealot, she sympathized in general with the Women's Liberation Movement, and felt strongly about the fact that rape had always been difficult to prove.

Sergeant Richmond's hopes that Adele Kohr might have beaten off her mysterious attacker and gone into hiding somewhere, were quickly dashed. At 11.00 am the following day, July 21, he received a call from the village of Patchogue, about 20 miles further east along the parkway from the spot where Adele's Ford Maverick had been found. Some children playing in a small wood at the end of deserted Webb Avenue had stumbled upon the naked body of a young woman.

When he arrived at the scene, the detective trod carefully up to the body in order not to disturb the loose sandy soil on which it lay. Richmond grimaced as he looked at the face, which had been beaten beyond recognition. The eyes were blackened and swollen, the lips and cheeks were gashed and puffed out, and the nose was broken. The light

brown hair was matted with blood. Adele's body lay in the center of a wide arc of tire tracks. A car had been driven across her at high speed and the grid patterns of the tire treads still marked her skin. Richmond's men prowled around carefully, and on the edge of the woods came across a torn, blue, nurse's uniform. A few feet further into the woods they found the two pieces of a yellow bikini, and a pair of white slip-on shoes. To verify the identification, a copper bracelet, a gold cross and chain, and three individually styled rings on the girl's fingers were immediately recognized by Francis Kohr as having belonged to his daughter. When the mobile police laboratory arrived, the medical examiner quickly established the cause of death to have been strangulation, and the young woman had been raped.

Tell-tale tracks

Richmond was most interested in the tire tracks on the ground and the body. Like fingerprints, tires tell a remarkably accurate story to forensic scientists, and these six-tread tires were fairly new. Plaster casts, known as *moulages*, were taken of them, so that a comparison could be made with the tires of a suspect's car. The next job was to find the car, the light green Pontiac T-37 Tempest which Adele had managed to describe in her last few moments. Richmond knew that the color description was not necessarily accurate, for the sodium vapour lamps which lit the Sagtikos State Parkway distorted color at night. The car might be green, beige, blue or any other light color, but not black, deep blue or red. A check at the Riverhead Licensing Authority, where all automobile records were kept for Suffolk County, revealed eighteen Tempests of the type of color Tom Richmond wanted to trace. Richmond detailed four detectives in teams of two to check out the list immediately.

Detectives Thomas Mansell and Richard Dean checked out the first name on their list and found that the owner had an alibi, and did not fit Adele's description of the man who had stopped her. The second name was Linda Meyer, of 185, Hawthorne Street, Central Islip, the next hamlet to East Ilsip where Adele Kohr had lived.

The door of the ground floor apartment was opened by a young and pretty brunette. 'Miss Meyer?' asked Detective Mansell. 'It's Mrs Meyer,' she replied, 'I was married in April.' 'Are you the owner of a light green 1970 Tempest T-37?' asked the detective. She said she was, but that her husband drove it too, and she called him to speak to the detective.

A tall young man came to the door. His long dark hair covered his ears, and he had a beard and glasses. The two officers asked him to accompany them to the Suffolk County police headquarters, and he walked to the car with them without a word.

When Tom Richmond looked up from his desk and saw Mansell and Dean with the bearded, long-haired, bespectacled Robert Meyer standing between then, he said, smiling grimly: 'If it takes more than ten minutes to get a confession out of him I shall ask you both to turn in your shields.' In fact it was scarcely two minutes before Meyer spilled out his story. Tom Richmond, known among his colleagues as 'The Greatest Persuader' because of his patient and delicate handling of suspects, put a hand gently on Meyer's shoulder. Meyer looked up blankly. 'I'm sick,' he said. 'I'm very sick, I need help. . .' 'Well, before we can help you we have to know what happened,' said Richmond. 'It happened last night didn't it?'

Confession

Meyer nodded and began to tell them what had occurred. He had been driving along Sagtikos when he spotted the young woman, had chased her in his wife's high-powered T-37 and finally forced her to a stop. Then he had reversed his car up to hers so that she could not drive off again. She had locked the doors and screamed, so he had smashed the windscreen with a jack and reached in to open the door himself. In the woods near Webb Avenue he had torn off her clothes, beat her unconscious, raped her and then strangled her. Finally, in escaping at high speed in his car, he had run over her body.

Tom Richmond checked through Meyer's criminal record by computer and realized that he had made a timely arrest, although not timely enough for pretty Adele Kohr. Meyer had been arrested three times previously for attacks on women, and each charge was more serious. For the final assault he had served two years of a three-year sentence. Acting on impulse, the detective sergeant made a check on recent, unsolved, sexual attacks in the Long Island area, and one which had occurred a few weeks previously caught his eye. A 23-year-old woman had been kidnapped from the Walt Whitman Shopping Centre at Huntingdon, Long Island, and had been robbed and raped by her assailant before being thrown out of his car. The description of her attacker fitted Meyer exactly. Richmond had the young woman brought down to Suffolk County headquarters, and she immediately identified him.

Surprised

Robert Meyer was put on trial for murder, kidnapping, rape, sodomy and robbery in Queen's County, on the grounds that he might receive prejudicial treatment in Suffolk. Despite a defense plea of temporary insanity, he was found guilty of second degree murder and was sentenced to 25 years or life imprisonment for the slaying of Miss Kohr.

As he left the courtroom, Detective Sergeant Richmond was stopped in the corridor by Linda Meyer, Robert's wife, who was accompanied by her mother and mother-in-law. The pale-faced, somberly dressed young women apparently spoke for the three of them when she addressed Richmond. 'I want to thank all of you for the way you handled yourselves in this arrest,' she said quietly. 'My husband is a sick man, and I don't believe he has any business being free. You have done your duty well.'

Richmond was very surprised, and later told reporters, 'That was the first time I ever heard any relative of a murder suspect, in all the years I've been on this job, actually thank detectives for making an arrest. It almost floored me and the other guys.'

Of course, Mrs Meyer had been right. Tom Richmond and his team had done a swift and efficient job in bringing her husband to justice. But Adele Kohr's courage and foresight in wildly jotting down those details in her little notebook, in the face of what she must have guessed was imminent assault, if not death, meant that Robert Meyer could not go undetected and commit further brutal and hideous murders.

The founding father

Vidocq of the Sûreté

IF ANY ONE MAN can be regarded as the father of modern criminology, then the sobriquet must surely be applied to the founder of the French Sûreté, François-Eugène Vidocq. Not only do Vidocq's exploits survive in the novels of his friend Balzac, they also provide a central theme for the work of today's detectives. Almost all the fundamental techniques of detection were pioneered by Vidocq – the list is astonishing. Some of the ideas which he introduced seem basic enough today, but he was the first man to employ them, much to the surprise of his colleagues and quarry alike. For example, until Vidocq, no investigator had attached any great importance to the apparently irrelevant clues which might surround a crime. He was the first man to build up a picture of the crime as if it were a jigsaw puzzle, and in so doing he also brought to bear his ability to see inside the law-breaker's mind. In that sense, he was the first of many detectives to behave in the manner of a brilliant amateur psychologist.

Not that his understanding of the criminal mind was purely intellectual. On the contrary, this paragon among policemen spent the first thirty-five years of his life as a petty villain. He was born on July 23, 1775, in the township of Arras, where his next-door neighbor in teenage years was also to become something of a celebrity. The neighbor was Robespierre.

Good looks

Vidocq, sharp-featured, saturnine, endowed with an unruly mop of dark hair, was a loner from the start. Nature had given him quick wits, and he used them to skirmish with the society in which he lived.

His father ran a small bakery, but the idea of sweating over hot ovens did not appeal to Vidocq. In his early teens he ran away to sea, then joined the army, and after that took up with a travelling circus, in which he learned something of acting and make-up, a gift which was to stand him in good stead. His surly good looks appealed to women, and it was a woman who first got him into trouble; when she left him for an

The chain gang at the top security La Force prison was the unlikely starting point of Vidocq's career as a lawman. The dubious skills he learned in jail were the basis of the famous Sûreté.

army officer, Vidocq beat up his rival so badly that the man was taken to hospital. Vidocq, on the other hand, was taken to jail, and it was then that his career and fame began.

He escaped three times from prison. The first was while serving his time as the manacled member of a chain gang in La Force prison, France's top security jail, and while 'out' he employed skills he had learned from fellow prisoners, with the significant difference that he was better at them. He became a top forger, he organized smuggling gangs, and he was a master pickpocket.

His last escape took place in 1799; he was twenty-four years old, and already weary of the life of crime into which he had fallen. He was being harassed by the fairly disorganized police *inspecteurs* of Paris, where he now lived, and at the same time preyed upon by the underworld. For more than ten years he lived by thieving, venturing out at night in disguise, and by day posing as an old clothes dealer in a shop near Les Halles. By 1810 he was tired of this life, and one day he went along to the Prefect of Police, Monsieur Henri, to give himself up.

Undercover

Henri had other ideas. Vidocq was by that time a legend, and to the surprise of the criminal, Henri put a proposition to him. The police chief was in desperate trouble. He had a handful of inspectors and twenty-eight justices of the peace, with which he was expected to impose the rule of law and order on Paris. It was an impossible task, and he asked Vidocq to help him. According to his memoirs, Vidocq looked quizzically at the police chief when he made this request, and said: 'I Monsieur Henri? I am one man. You have a police force. How can I help you?'

Henri explained. He already had police informers, he told Vidocq. What he wanted was agents who knew the habits of the underworld, who could move easily in criminal circles, and who could stamp out crime almost before it happened. In short, he wanted a team of plain-clothes policemen. There had never before been such a force. It was a totally new idea, and Vidocq took to it instantly. By forming this force, Vidocq made criminological history and was to go on making it. Over

Sir Robert Peel, founder of London's Metropolitan Police, was a keen admirer of the unorthodox, and he greatly enjoyed Vidocq's memoirs.

the next few months, he travelled around the cafes and bars of Paris, selecting colleagues to help him in his task. First four, and finally twenty, ex-convicts were turned into detectives by the enthusiastic Vidocq. His 'security brigade', the Sûreté, is today the national crime-fighting establishment of France, and it can claim to be the world's oldest detective force.

Within a few years, Vidocq had drastically reduced the crime-rate in the French capital, and he had personally arrested thousands of villains. His methods are comprehensively illustrated by the Fontaine case. Although the villains in this case may today seem to have been less than sophisticated, the techniques which Vidocq used in order to trap them broke new ground at the time. What is more, they have

since been echoed in hundreds of cops-and-robbers movies and TV programs.

Fontaine was a hard-drinking, giant of a man, a butcher by trade, from the town of Courtille. He regularly travelled around the cattle markets on the outskirts of Paris, carrying large sums of money. One day, he had been to the market at Corbeil, and stopped for a drink at an inn near Essons. He had fifteen hundred francs with him, and after buying drinks for all the company, he set off to stagger home. Three men from the inn said that they would accompany him for part of the way.

As soon as the party was on the dark road, Fontaine was knocked down from behind, and all three of his new acquaintances attacked him, using a knife and cudgels. He was stabbed twenty-eight times before his assailants took his purse and left him for dead. Astonishingly, he survived, and as soon as he was able to speak he poured out his story to Vidocq, who had arrived at his bedside.

Fontaine was unable to give a thorough description of his attackers, but he recalled that one of them had a limp and another was very big. Vidocq visited the scene of the crime to see what he could find there. Again, this simple technique was a Vidocq innovation. He found several footprints in the churned-up ground, and had casts made of them. He found a man's coat button, with a rag of cloth still attached, and a piece of torn paper.

On the paper were a few fragmented words, written in ink.

'Monsieur Rao . . .
Merchand de Vins,
Bar . . . Roche . . .
. . . Cli . . .

Vidocq, in addition to his other talents, had an encyclopedic knowledge of Paris and its inhabitants. It did not take him long to deduce that the full address was

'Monsieur Raoul,
Merchand de Vins,
Barriere Rochechouart,
Chaussée de Clignancourt.'

Raoul was a hard man who kept a wine shop frequented by the worst

Robespierre, the French Revolutionary leader, who went to the guillotine, was a next-door neighbor of the teenage Vidocq in the town of Arras.

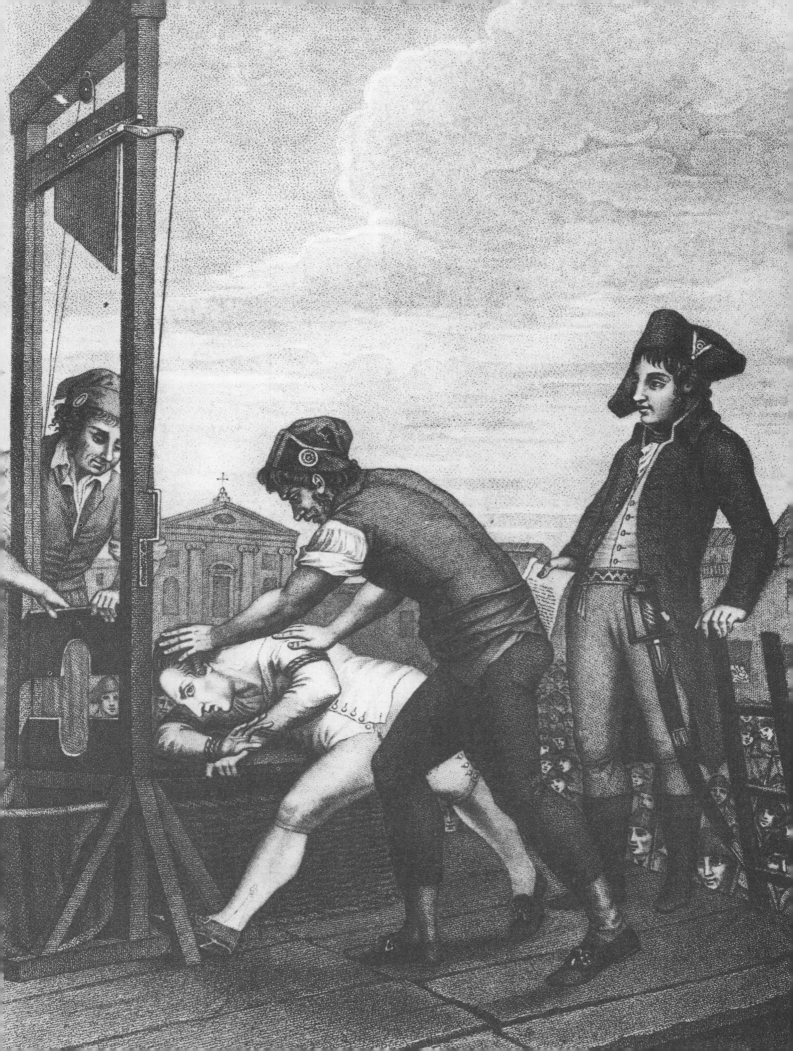

criminals in Paris, on the lower slope of Montmartre. Vidocq had the shop watched, and a list of regular customers was compiled. One of them was a man with a limp, and Vidocq was able to confirm that he was a cut-throat named Court. Vidocq could not afford to alert Court to his suspicions, for the teeming alleys of Paris offered ample cover for any fugitive. So the innovative detective employed what we might today call a 'holding charge', though he was less than scrupulous about its nature. He went to Court's house, and politely told him that he and his wife were suspected of harboring smugglers. He was sure, Vidocq said, that the matter could be cleared up if the couple were to come down to Sûreté headquarters. Once there, they were locked in a cell.

Agitators

With Court out of the way, Vidocq now had to pin down Raoul, who was equally likely to disappear if he knew that he was suspected of attempted murder. The detective called at Raoul's wine shop and feigned extreme embarrassment.

'My dear Raoul,' he told his suspect. 'I know that this is unthinkable, for neither you nor I are inclined to politics, but rumour has it that you are allowing your tavern to be used by political agitators. An informer tells me that you have printed copies of anti-Government songs on your premises. I must ask you if I may search for them.'

Raoul was instantly relieved. He was, of course, not guilty of any sedition, and it was with a clear conscience that he allowed Vidocq to search his quarters. In a writing desk, Vidocq found an old document torn in two, a perfect match for the piece he had found by the roadside bearing part of Raoul's address. The tavern-keeper was arrested and lodged in the next cell to Court.

Vidocq and a colleague then set about interrogating Court. Again, Vidocq pioneered a technique, which is now familiar, of first bullying, then soothing the prisoner. Pretending to know far more than they did, Vidocq and his helper threatened Court with the guillotine for a number of murders, and then hinted that perhaps the justices would be lenient with him if he turned informer. 'All the people you attacked are not dead,' said Vidocq.

'They are willing to come to court and testify against you.'

To the detective's surprise, Court broke down at this point and confessed to the murder of a poultry dealer about which the Sûreté knew nothing. He named Raoul as his accomplice. Vidocq promptly went into the next cell, where Raoul lay sleeping, awoke him brusquely, and told him that Court had confessed to the murder of the poultry dealer and the Fontaine attack, and had implicated him. In the hope of winning mercy, Raoul too confessed. Fontaine the butcher was then brought along to confirm identification.

The third man was still at large, and the wily Vidocq surmised that if the men in custody realized that he did not know their companion's identity, they might well remain silent. Not for the first time, Vidocq organized a sumptuous dinner for three, along with gallons of wine, and had it brought to their cell, where he sat down and joined them.

As the two prisoners became more and more drunk, Vidocq flattered them on their skill and daring in getting away with robbery and murder. 'You were wise to confess, however,' he said. 'Things will go a lot harder with your two companions when we catch them.' 'Two?' said Raoul, slurring his words. 'You know nothing, Vidocq. There were only us and Pons Gerard.' It was classic story-book stuff. Almost as he uttered his indiscretion, the villainous innkeeper realized his mistake, but Vidocq was already on his way out of the room. He knew Pons Gerard, a large man who had been a lieutenant of customs, and now dealt in horses in La Capelle. Apart from his massive strength he was an extremely stubborn man. He, too, would need to be trapped into confession before he could be arrested.

Reassured

Vidocq and two detectives named Goury and Clement set off for La Capelle dressed in the rough country clothes of horse-dealers. Fortunately, Gerard had never met Vidocq. When the detective found him in a tavern, he walked up to him and extended a hand. 'Bonjour, Pons,' he said. The big man scowled. 'The devil take me if I know you. Who are you?'

Reassured, Vidocq told him that

he was a friend of Raoul and Court. The police had arrested them for the attack on the butcher, he said, and Raoul had asked him to come and warn Gerard to flee. Gerard was astonished. 'The butcher is alive? Surely he can't be. All three of us beat him and stabbed him so badly that he could surely not survive.' The three detectives exchanged surreptitious glances. They had their confession. Now the question was how to get this huge brute of a man under lock and key. Again Vidocq resorted to drink, pouring glass upon glass of brandy out for Gerard, who swigged them back as he boasted of his exploits. The police, he swore, would never catch him as they had the other two.

'Perhaps not,' said Vidocq. 'But you must be very wary of them. They are led by the famous Vidocq.' History offers a colorful account of the arrest.

'I am not afraid of this Vidocq,' snarled Gerard. 'If he were here I should crush the life out of him.' He brought his hands together in imitation of a stranglehold, and the detective seized his opportunity. Snapping a pair of handcuffs on to Gerard's extended wrists, he told him, 'You may try, my friend. I am he.'

Confessions

Gerard was so astonished that he accompanied the three detectives speechlessly to headquarters, to join the other two robbers.

A search of Court's house revealed a coat with a button missing – the same button which Vidocq had found at the scene of the crime. He also took boots from all three prisoners, and found that they perfectly matched the plaster cast footprints he had taken. With this evidence, the paper, and the confessions, he took his case to court and won convictions with ease. Raoul and Court were found guilty of the murder of the poultry dealer, and went to the guillotine. Gerard was jailed for life.

The two men asked that Vidocq be present at their executions, and entrusted him with letters to give to their families. Just before he laid his head under the great knife, Raoul told the detective, 'You are the only man we can trust.'

Francois-Eugène Vidocq stayed as head of his Sûreté for eighteen years. Then, in 1828, he was ousted by a

MÉMOIRES DE VIDOCQ

FORÇAT ET CHEF DE LA POLICE

**

MÉMOIRES DE VIDOCQ

FORÇAT ET CHEF DE LA POLICE

*

When the Sûreté went 'respectable' in 1828, Vidocq could hardly claim to fit the new image and was removed from his post. His memoirs were an instant success, but he left behind a more valuable legacy of police procedure.

new prefect of police, who understandably, if misguidedly, objected to having a detective force staffed entirely by ex-convicts.

The later stages of the innovator's career continued to display something of a twentieth-century touch. First of all, he wrote his memoirs, which enjoyed world sales in half-a-dozen languages. A keen reader was Sir Robert Peel, who founded London's Metropolitan Police Force ('Scotland Yard') two years after Vidocq's retirement. After his literary success, Vidocq invested the profits in something which might almost be described as a social-work venture. He founded a business with a staff of ex-prisoners. For all his ability to crack down on criminals, Vidocq was also a pioneer of rehabilitation. Sadly, his business – a paper mill – failed. He then set up the world's first private detective agency, specializing in marital cases. This was initially successful, until his funds were stretched by a series of lawsuits alleging invasion of privacy, another twentieth-century touch in the story of Vidocq. Apparently, invasion of privacy was causing concern long before the era of bugging devices and investigative journalism. Undaunted, Vidocq spent his last years giving lectures on his experiences, but died in poverty in 1857.

He left behind the world's first criminal records department, a whole series of staple police procedures, and the ultimate justification for the maxim, 'Set a thief to catch a thief.'

Into the mind of the murderer...

**Detective Fowler,
and the
brides-in-the-bath killer**

G. K. CHESTERTON's fictional priest-detective Father Brown utilized two principal abilities in solving the almost surrealist crimes in which he became involved: a powerful memory, and a knack of 'thinking' himself into the part of the murderer. Once he had 'become' the killer, looking at the world with the killer's distorted vision, the priest was well on the way to identifying the culprit and pin-pointing his method of execution.

These same two abilities were used in at least one real-life case, that of George Joseph Smith, who became known to British newspaper readers as 'The Brides in the Bath Slayer'. It was memory and dogged police work which led Detective Inspector Arthur Fowler Neil to Smith in the first place, but only a flash of real insight into the arrogant murderer's mind enabled Neil to secure an eventual conviction.

In January, 1915, Inspector Neil was head of C.I.D. in the Kentish Town division of the Metropolitan Police, then a relatively hum-drum lower middle class 'manor' in North London. But if sensational crime in his area was rare, Neil nevertheless liked to spend at least one day a week reading through newspaper clippings relating to coroner's reports, court cases, and anything else which might conceivably have a bearing on his job.

On this particular morning, a clipping from the sensational Sunday newspaper *The News of the World* caught his eye.

'Particularly sad circumstances under which a bride of a day met her death were investigated at an Islington inquest on Margaret Elizabeth Lloyd, thirty-eight, wife of a land agent of Holloway. The husband said he was married to the deceased at Bath. After travelling to London she complained of headache and giddiness, and he took her to a medical man, who prescribed for her. The following day, at 7.30 she said she would have a bath, and she then appeared cheerful. A quarter of an hour later the witness went out, and returned at a quarter past eight, expecting to see her in the sitting room. As she was not there he inquired of the landlady, and they went to the bathroom, which was in darkness. He lit the gas, and then found his wife under the water, the bath being three parts full. The next day the witness found a letter amongst the deceased's clothing, but there was nothing in it to suggest that she was likely to take her life. Dr Bates said death was due to asphyxia from drowning. Influenza, together with a hot bath might have caused an attack of syncope.'

Identical

The death had taken place at 14, Bismark Road, Highgate, in Inspector Neil's area, but what disturbed him about the otherwise straightforward report was that it brought on a distinct sense of *déjà vu*. He was certain he had read of an almost identical death about a year before. A search of his clippings file proved his memory to be correct; he came up with a cutting from a Blackpool newspaper dated December 14, 1913. Blackpool is a sea-side resort on the North West coast of England popular with honeymooners.

'Bride's Sudden Death. Drowned After Seizure in a Hot Bath. Mrs George Smith, of 80, Kimberley Road, Portsmouth, who was married only six weeks ago, died suddenly in a Blackpool boarding house. . . .'

Striking

The rest of the report followed a familiar pattern. The husband, described as being of 'independent means', had met his wife, a nurse, three months previously, and six weeks afterwards had married her. They had travelled to Blackpool on a belated honeymoon, engaging rooms at 16, Regent Road. During the journey the wife had complained of headache, and had seen a doctor on arrival. She had then taken a hot bath, and as she was a long time her husband had entered the bathroom and found her lying dead under the water. A Doctor Billing had said that the heart was 'enlarged and affected' and concluded that the heat of the water had caused either a fit or a faint.

The similarity between the two cases was too striking to ignore, and Inspector Neil immediately set off for Bismark Road, Highgate, where he interviewed the landlady, a Mrs Blatch. The room rented by Lloyd was on the top floor, with a bathroom off the stair landing, one flight down. The couple had arrived, she said, on December 17. The landlady par-

The marriage certificate of John Lloyd, the alias of George Smith, and the doomed Margaret Lofty (right).

ticularly remembered that Lloyd had carefully inspected the bathroom before signing the agreement. She described Lloyd as a medium-sized, athletic-looking man with 'ordinary' features, apart from his keen eyes. He was aged between forty and fifty.

That evening Lloyd had told Mrs Blatch that his wife was not feeling well, and she had sent the couple off to Dr Bates. The following day Mrs Lloyd seemed better, and before setting out for an afternoon walk had asked for a bath to be drawn for that evening. The couple returned at 7.30, by which time Mrs Blatch had drawn the bath and retired to the kitchen. She subsequently heard splashing, and a short time later the sound of the harmonium in the living room, which could only have been played by Lloyd. A little later, the doorbell rang.

When she answered it she found Lloyd, who explained that he had gone out for tomatoes for supper and had forgotten his key. Had his wife come down to the living room yet? Mrs Blatch told him that she had not, and he went upstairs. Immediately afterwards he called for help, and when she rushed up she found Lloyd lifting his wife from the bathtub. He called for Dr Bates but Mrs Lloyd had drowned. Lloyd stayed only long enough to settle the funeral formalities, and then moved out to an unknown address.

Neil inspected the bathroom and was immediately struck by the size of the tub, which was only fifty inches long at the bottom and sixty-six at the upper rim. He found it hard to believe that even a small adult could have drowned 'accidentally' in it.

'Lethargic'

Dr Bates, when interviewed by the detective, could add little, but confirmed his part in the story. Mrs Lloyd had seemed 'lethargic' when she called at his surgery with her husband. The husband, he said, had done all the talking. Bates had decided that the lady was 'feverish' and had prescribed accordingly. The autopsy showed clearly that she had drowned, but apart from a minute bruise above the left elbow there were no other marks on the body. The sudden death might have been caused by a convulsive movement. The inquest had returned a verdict of accidental death. But one final

thing had struck him, the doctor said. Lloyd had shown no sign of grief, and had ordered the cheapest coffin.

Returning to his office, Neil immediately set in motion a hunt for Lloyd and an investigation into the affairs of the dead woman. The response to the second part of his inquiry was prompt. A Miss Likker, who ran another Highgate boarding house, remembered the Lloyds coming to her for a room. Lloyd had examined the bathtub thoroughly and had asked if 'someone could lie down in it'. She had thought his manner so odd that she had turned him away.

Callous

Then a will turned up. Margaret Elizabeth Lloyd, nee Lofty had made it out in sole favor of her husband, George Joseph Lloyd, on the afternoon of December 18, three hours before her death. That same afternoon Mrs Lloyd had gone to a savings bank and had drawn out her entire life savings.

On January 12, Dr Bates contacted Inspector Neil and showed him a letter from an insurance company, asking about the circumstances of Mrs Lloyd's fatal accident. On December 4, 1914, Margaret Elizabeth Lofty, newly engaged to Lloyd, had taken out a life insurance policy for £700, naming her husband-to-be as sole beneficiary.

Inspector Neil needed no further confirmation that he was on the trail of a callous murderer. He asked Dr Bates to delay his reply for a while, until a report came through from the Blackpool police. When that report came it convinced Neil that Lloyd and Smith were one and the same. The names were changed, but the circumstances were almost identical.

Mr George Joseph Smith had arrived with his fat but pretty wife, Alice, in Blackpool on December 10, 1913. Significantly, his first call had been at a boarding house run by a Mrs Marsden, but he had left when she had told him that there was no fixed bathtub in the house. He had finally settled at Mrs Crossley's boarding house in Regent Road, after carefully inspecting the bathroom. Late in the afternoon of the same day he had asked Mrs Crossley to recommend a doctor for his wife. Doctor George Billing, had heard

small and insignificant heart murmurs, and had prescribed a little heroin and caffeine. At six o'clock the following evening Mrs Smith had ordered a bath. At eight she had gone up to her room with her husband. Soon afterwards Mrs Crossley's doorbell had rung and Smith stood outside. He had gone out to buy eggs, he said, and had forgotten his key. After going upstairs he had shouted for help, and asked that Dr Billing be fetched. When the doctor arrived he found Smith holding his wife's head out of the water of the bath where she lay. The two had some difficulty in lifting out the heavy woman, but there was no signs of violence on her. Billing found that death was due to drowning after heart failure. Accidental death had been recorded.

The Blackpool police had done groundwork on the financial status of the dead woman, and had come up with a remarkable fact. Alice, whose maiden name had been Burnham, had had only £27 in cash when she married Lloyd, but she had lent her father £100 some time previously. A day before the wedding the bride had taken out life insurance for £500, and the day after, at the prompting of her new husband, she had demanded the return of the £100 loaned to her father, and she had even threatened legal action to recover it.

Arrogant

Apart from her rather pretty face, Mrs Smith had been an unattractive woman with a bulky body. Like the plain Mrs Lloyd she had seemed doomed to spinsterhood until her whirlwind courtship.

After studying the Blackpool report, Inspector Neil prepared a report of his own for the Director of Public Prosecutions, Sir Charles Matthews. Here, he said, was a plain case involving a man, 'Lloyd–Smith', who had evolved a regular pattern for murdering women and robbing them of their money.

He was either incredibly arrogant or wildly over-confident, and because of this his capture should be easy. Doctor George Billing had heard report to the insurance company on the death of Mrs Lloyd and, Inspector Neil felt sure, the killer would turn up to claim the money.

Sir Charles Matthews was skeptical. 'It is incredible to me that a man could murder two women by

Alice Burnham, the bride. The method of drowning confused the investigators and almost allowed the killer to avoid detection.

The ones that got away

George Joseph Smith had two more 'brides'. Unlike the others, they survived their notorious consort. Caroline Thornhill (below) married him in 1898, but left him two years later. She remained his legal wife, although he 'married' a young woman named Edith Pegler (right). They lived together for varying peeriods between separations. Smith seems to have felt real affection, for he always returned to her.

drowning them in the bath,' he wrote back to Neil. 'I have never heard of such a thing during the whole of my lifelong experience.' But, he suggested, Neil should continue his investigation and try to arrest 'Lloyd – Smith'.

As Neil had forecast, the arrest was no problem. Dr Bates gave the insurance company the all-clear on Mrs Lloyd's death. Lloyd, who had been in touch with them through a lawyer, turned up at the company's office, and Inspector Neil was there to meet him. The arrest took place on February 1, 1915. Neil told Lloyd that from investigations, he had reason to believe that he was identical with George Smith, whose wife had drowned in Blackpool.

'You married Miss Lofty, your last bride, in Bath, Somerset, under the name of Lloyd?'

'Yes,' replied the man. 'But that doesn't prove that my name is Smith.' Neil studied him for a while. There was the beginning of panic in the big sensual mouth and sallow features. 'Very well,' said the Inspector, 'I am detaining you for making a false attestation on oath to a registrar.'

'Lloyd' immediately relaxed. 'Oh,' he said. 'If that's what you're making all the fuss about, I may as well tell you – my name is Smith.'

So Neil had gained his first objective. He had his man under lock and key, and he had convinced Sir Charles Matthew to go ahead with

Bernard Spilsbury had to work against the clock in his laboratory (top) to find a solution, and convince Charles Matthews (above) not to drop the case.

the case. This now involved the exhumation of the body of Margaret Elizabeth Lloyd! Thirty-seven year old Bernard Spilsbury, later to be knighted for his work in forensic medicine, was put in charge of the new autopsy, and his principal task was to discover whether the woman had been drowned by accident or by force.

To Neil's dismay, Spilsbury, like

Bates, could find no sign of violence on the body. To drown a healthy woman by forcing her head under the bathwater would have needed a considerable force, simply because her death struggles would be frantic and convulsive. The murderer would have to grip her hard, leaving scratches or bruising, and there were none.

Nor were there any signs of the woman having been sedated in any way. Spilsbury was forced to the reluctant conclusion that death could only have been caused by a sudden stroke.

Neil refused to be convinced. It had to be murder, but how, in view of the circumstances? He had the Highgate bathtub brought to the Kentish Town police station, and there he conducted experiments, using policewomen of about the same size and weight as Mrs Lloyd.

Whichever way he tried to push them under, they always managed to grab the sides of the tub, or free their hands to claw his face. Furthermore, he ended up soaked in water, and the noise of the struggle was considerable. Yet inquiries showed that 'Lloyd – Smith' had used the same clothing before and after each death, and had been totally dry when seen by the respective landladies before the discovery of the bodies. Apart from the normal splashing noises made by a bather, no violent sounds or cries had been heard.

Epilepsy

It was in a state of frustration that Neil received a report from Herne Bay, a sea-side resort in Kent. Despite precautions, the newspapers had got wind of the Lloyd exhumation, and had pieced the story together. The police chief at Herne Bay immediately recognized the pattern, as a similar death that had taken place in his town on July 13, 1912. A man named Henry Williams had moved into a house with his wife, Bessie. The house had no bath, and on July 9, Williams had bought a tin bathtub from a local ironmonger. On the following day a Doctor French had received a visit from Mr and Mrs Williams. Although the husband claimed that his wife suffered from epilepsy, the wife herself complained only of a headache, and Dr French had prescribed a bromide. Two days later, Williams had called Dr French to report that his wife had had an

epileptic fit, but the doctor found the lady in good health. At eight o'clock on the morning of July 13, he had received a note asking him to come at once, as Mrs Williams was dead.

Dr French found Bessie in the bathtub, her head under water, a cake of soap clutched in her right hand. Her legs hung out over the end of the tub, and an autopsy convinced him that death had been caused by drowning during an epileptic fit.

Subsequently, Herne Bay police investigations had shown that Bessie, nee Mundy, had had money of her own, amounting to £2,700. 'Mr Williams had been the sole beneficiary under her will, and photographs quickly showed that 'Williams' was identical with 'Lloyd – Smith'.

Baffling

Meanwhile, Neil and Spilsbury had travelled to Blackpool for the exhumation of Alice Smith. The body was considerably decayed, but the organs were sufficiently intact for Spilsbury to draw his conclusions. There was no poison in the body, and there was not the slightest evidence of violence. The state of the heart and lungs showed him that the victim had not been drowned by force. Again the investigators were left with the baffling problem. Glib-tongued with women though 'Lloyd – Smith' obviously was, surely he had not persuaded his wives to drown themselves? And yet that was what the evidence pointed to, except for natural causes.

The Blackpool tub was shipped to Kentish Town, to lie alongside the one from Highgate, while Neil and

The happy couple: Mr Williams, the art dealer, and bride Bessie Mundy. Soon afterwards, she was found dead in a tin bath at their home (right). The inquest verdict was misadventure. Bessie left £2,700. Needless to say, her husband was the beneficiary.

Spilsbury made their third melancholy journey, this time to Herne Bay. The evidence there was strikingly similar. The rotting body of Bessie Williams showed every sign of rapid death by drowning, with no wounds, no bruises or marks of any kind. On February 23, her rusty iron tub was taken to Kentish Town to join the other two.

For ten days, Neil and Spilsbury sat around their pathetic collection comparing notes on the respective weight and height of the victims, and the lengths of their individual tubs. If anything, Bessie, the first victim, was the most baffling. She had been five feet seven inches tall, but the tub in which she died was only five feet long, with an almost vertical foot and a sloping head. Assuming that she had had an epileptic fit, the first stage would have contracted her body, but not enough to draw her head under the water. The second stage, that of vigorous thrusting outward of the limbs, would in fact have pushed her head up the slope of the bath, definitely well clear of the surface.

What was absolutely certain was that, on the face of it, force would be needed to submerge the head, and as there was no physical evidence of this, and no one had seen 'Lloyd – Smith' commit the crime, they had no conclusive evidence to bring before a court.

Gullible

However damning the circumstantial evidence might be, without clear method being shown a good lawyer would get the accused man off without difficulty.

Neil studied the record he had obtained on the man he held in custody. His real name was, it transpired, George Joseph Smith, aged 43. He had a record of petty fraud, confidence trickery, and theft.

In each case he used his powers of persuasion to gain his criminal ends and he had never used violence. Most probably, reasoned Neil, he had used flattery and cajolery to persuade his gullible female victims that they had headaches, and that they needed to see a doctor, thus establishing their ill health. He had earlier persuaded

them to part with their money and to make wills in which he was the sole beneficiary. But to persuade them into suicide by drowning? Such a degree of love was unimaginable.

At that moment, Detective Inspector Arthur Fowler Neil had his pure flash of insight. He saw himself as the murderer, standing over his victim as she happily soaped herself in the tub, and perhaps indulging in affectionate love-play.

He rushed to Spilsbury, to find that the pathologist had come to a similar conclusion to his own, though by a different route. What would happen, asked Neil, if Smith jocularly lifted his wife's feet and ever so lovingly *pulled* her under? Would she be able to struggle out without noise? Spilsbury agreed, if Bessie Williams' feet had protruded from her bath, she must have been pulled.

Massive

Excitedly, Neil began his experiments again. This time he used a policewoman who was a skilled swimmer and diver. He told her what he was going to do, as she lay relaxed in the bath, and then he reached for her feet and pulled. Her head, naturally, sank beneath the surface, but to the surprise and shock of both Spilsbury and Neil she made no effort to struggle. She became unconscious almost instantly. For half an hour Neil and the doctor struggled to bring the unconscious woman back to life, and it was with profound relief that they finally saw her stir and open her eyes.

All she remembered was that, as she went under, water had rushed up her nose and she had immediately blacked out. Medically, she had suffered a massive shock to her system despite the fact that she had expected Neil's move, and had tensed herself for what was coming.

In those days of criminal pathology, no one had previously noted such an effect, but after further research, Spilsbury was able to show that when water was forced into the nasal passages while the victim lay on her back, unconsciousness invariably occurred almost instantaneously.

Triumphantly, Inspector Neil handed over his final, damning piece

Smith used the dock to shout abuse at police witnesses. He was still protesting innocence as the hangman slipped the noose over his head.

Crowds fought for a seat in court. Smith told Lord Justice Scrutton, 'You can't sentence me to death.' The judge proved him wrong.

of evidence to the Director of Public Prosecutions. The trial lasted eight days, and the jury was out for exactly twenty minutes.

On June 30, 1915, Mr Justice Scrutton condemned Smith, alias Lloyd, alias Williams, to death by hanging, and sentence was carried out a few weeks later.

In retrospect, Smith had been ridiculously arrogant, yet he had got away with an almost perfect murder not once, but three times. Had it not been for the tenacious memory of one policeman, and that flash of insight, he might have continued to kill, unsuspected, indefinitely.

Solving the

jigsaw puzzle

Ted Greeno and the latter-day Ripper

The **Old Bailey**, where justice was done to the modern Ripper amid the rubble of the blitz.

To DETECTIVE Chief Superintendent Greeno, solving a crime was like solving a jigsaw puzzle. He believed that the evidence of a crime, like the pieces in a puzzle, is always there. It just has to be searched for and pieced together. This is not an uncommon view of detection, but what made Ted Greeno unique was his meticulous insistence that he had the whole picture. It was an attitude which sometimes irritated Greeno's juniors, but it paid off. At the age of 45, having neatly solved 12 murder cases, he was made a detective superintendent, the youngest officer ever to attain this rank. His job was to tackle the spate of wartime crime in London in the 1940s, and it was his attention to minute detail which allowed him to emerge triumphantly from the responsibility. One of Greeno's colleagues said that, had Greeno lived 50 years before, because of his meticulousness, he would undoubtedly have captured Jack the Ripper. It was not an idle statement, for in 1942, Ted Greeno captured a latter day 'Ripper'.

Alarming

One snowy, Tuesday night in February, 1942, the original Jack the Ripper was very much on Ted Greeno's mind as he called at a small, gloomy, apartment in Gosfield Street, off Tottenham Court Road. The naked body of a prostitute named Margaret Florence Lowe lay twisted on a bloodstained, divan bed. Around her neck was one of her own silk stockings, and her breasts and stomach had been slashed with a razor. She had not been able to cry out for help, and her neighbors had not heard a thing. The discovery of Margaret Lowe's body was all the more alarming since she was the third woman to die in a similar manner in three consecutive days. On the previous Sunday night, a respectable, married woman, aged 40, named Evelyn Margaret Hamilton, had been found strangled and butchered in an air-raid shelter, off Montague Place. On the Monday, a 34-year-old prostitute named Evelyn Oatley had been found in a similar condition in her single room in a house in Wardour Street. The first two cases had been initially investigated by Greeno's minions, but now, with the death of Lowe, Greeno decided that he should step in and personally supervise the inquiry.

On Wednesday, Greeno spent the daylight hours putting together the known pieces of his jigsaw, but preying on the back of his mind was the uneasy feeling that a pattern was emerging. Surely the killer would strike again that evening? There was little he could do but keep his men on the 'beat' on extra alert. To his relief, no report of murder came in that night.

The relief was short-lived, however. On Thursday evening, as Greeno stood by the side of a pathologist Sir Bernard Spilsbury, watching the autopsy on Margaret Lowe, a police constable handed him a message. The fourth killing had taken place. This time the victim was a part-time prostitute named Doris Jouannet, the 32-year-old wife of a 74-year-old hotelier in Sussex Gardens. Greeno and Sir Bernard Spilsbury rushed through the blacked-out streets of the West End of London to the scene of the murder. As soon as they were shown the body they recognized the horrible signs. A silk stocking was tied tightly around Doris's neck, and her naked torso was cruelly slashed. Spilsbury examined the deep wounds, and from their direction he could see that the voracious killer was left handed.

While the pathologist examined the corpse, Greeno searched the rather squalid room for clues. On the dusty mantlepiece he found a clean patch the length and shape of a fountain pen, and the unmistakeable outline of a broken-toothed comb. As the fingerprint men arrived and got to work, the superintendent rummaged through the dead woman's bed-side drawers. A roll of elastic tape caught his eye as a small oblong piece had been cut from it.

Comparison

Greeno assessed the facts so far. He had a left-handed killer who apparently had a vendetta against prostitutes. Although the first victim did not fit into this pattern, she had been out at night on her own and could easily have been mistaken for a street walker. The comparison with Jack the Ripper was already evident. He had killed only prostitutes, and he had operated in the ill-lit alleyways of the East End, three miles away from where this present-day counterpart had been at work. The war-time blackout made the visibility conditions almost identical. Speed on the part of the police was going to be essential, for the murderer might strike again at any time. One question particularly puzzled Greeno. To put it rather cruelly: why had the man who had killed on Sunday, Monday, Tuesday and Thursday taken Wednesday off?

The superintendent gave a carefully worded release to the Press on his findings so far. It was calculated to instil caution and a little fear into the West End girls, and thus guarantee Greeno the co-operation from them that he needed.

Muffled

He established his enquiry headquarters at Tottenham Court Road police station, and then he and his men set out through the snow to question the prostitutes of Paddington and Soho. Each one was asked the identical question. Did you ever meet a potentially violent man in the blackout, or do you know a girl who had?

On Friday afternoon came a report that on Thursday night, shortly after the discovery of Doris Jouannet's body, a young girl had been attacked by an airman. He had picked her up and taken her for a drink at the Trocadero Club near Piccadilly Circus. Then he had taken her into an alley by the side of the Captain's Cabin pub, kissed her, and gripped her around the throat. Fortunately, a young man coming from the pub had seen the girl's torch fall to the ground and had heard her muffled cries. When the young man ran towards them the attacker fled, dropping his service-issue gas mask. On it was a service number and the name Gordon Frederick Cummins. The girl had estimated the height of her attacker at about 5 ft 7 ins tall, and his eyes were wide set and green. He had worn the forage cap of an airforce officer cadet.

The police had quickly traced Cummins to a commandeered block of flats in St John's Wood, where a number of airmen were billeted. But instead of going to the flats, the police had telephoned the duty corporal there. They told the corporal what had happened and instructed him to ring them when Cummins returned. This enraged Greeno because Cummins had turned up at his billet at 3.30 am but the Corporal had not reported his presence straight away. Cummins was not

Evelyn Oates, a Soho prostitute, was the second victim of the wartime Ripper. She died because the prying eyes of another girl's 'ponce' frightened the killer away before he could strike.

Colleagues believed that if Ted Greeno (far left) had been at work 50 years earlier, the original Jack the Ripper would never have got away. Greeno certainly justified this tribute when his meticulous approach to criminal investigation trapped the Ripper's latter-day counterpart. Left: Greeno and fellow officers gather outside the air-raid shelter in Marylebone, where Margaret Hamilton (below) was found.

arrested until 5.00 am which gave him an hour and a half to set up an alibi.

On Greeno's instructions, Cummins was booked for 'assault with intent to commit grevious bodily harm', the most serious charge Greeno could bring based on the evidence.

Even so, the examining magistrate was uneasy. There was no evidence to suggest that Cummins had anything to do with the murders of the prostitutes, and he suggested that Cummins may simply have had too much to drink in the Captain's Cabin pub and been rough with only the one girl. Reluctantly, the magistrate had the suspect remanded in custody for a week while Greeno made further enquiries.

Greeno's first call was at Cummins billet where he examined the pass books. He was soon discouraged when he saw that they clearly

showed that Cummins had been in billets when Evelyn Hamilton, Evelyn Oatley, and Margaret Lowe were murdered. In addition, his room-mates swore that they had seen him go to bed early on those nights, and had seen him on parade the following morning. On Wednesday night, the killer's night off, he had been on fire duty at St John's Wood. However, on the Saturday of the same week, Greeno's relentless questioning of over 500 prostitutes began to pay off. A street girl named Phyllis O'Dwyer told him that she had encountered a 'wild customer' on Thursday night, between the time of Doris Jouannet's death and the attack on the girl near the Captain's Cabin. Phyllis had met a young airman wearing an officer's cadet cap, near her place in Regent Street. When they both were in her room she had taken off her clothing except for a large necklace and a

pair of high heeled boots. The airman had began to play with the necklace, and then quite suddenly grasped it in his hand and twisted it against the girl's throat. 'All I could see were his eyes,' she told the superintendent. 'Very wide-apart, green eyes, blazing like a madman's.'

Fortunately for Phyllis she had kept on her 'kinky' boots. As the necklace had tightened, she had lashed out and caught her assailant in the groin with a high heel. He had screamed and fallen off the bed.

'I pulled the necklace off and shouted at him, 'What do you think you're doing?' and then he seemed to become quiet. He said he was very sorry, said he'd sort of got carried away. He'd already given me £5, but he gave me another £5 to show how sorry he was, but I said he'd have to get out anyway, and he went.' Phyllis still had the money – ten £1 notes and two were in series.

Sir Bernard Spilsbury, the pathologist, found that the killer was left-handed.

By now Greeno was convinced that Cummins had been responsible for the attacks on the girl by the pub and Phyllis O'Dwyer, the method of attack, strangulation, was too much of a coincidence when compared with the three murders. He saw Cummins at Brixton jail. Cummins was a nervous man of 5 ft 7 ins, with wide-set, green eyes. He admitted, under questioning, that he had been to the Trocadero on the Thursday night, but said he had not been with the attacked girl. His gas mask must have become mixed up with someone else's. He had a strange one, to prove it. To Greeno's satisfaction, when Cummins signed his statement, he did so with his left hand.

The policeman's nose told him that he had his man. The border of the jigsaw puzzle was complete, but now he had to find the center pieces. He went to the billet in St John's Wood and stripped out all Cummins'

property for examination. The evidence was startling. Cummins' wristwatch was padded with a piece of elastic tape of exactly the same shape as the piece missing from the roll found in Doris Jouannet's bedroom drawer. In the pocket of his best uniform was a comb with broken teeth, and a fountain pen, and both fitted the dimensions of the dust marks on her mantelpiece. Old Mr Jouannet confirmed that they had indeed belonged to his wife, and even pointed out her engraved initials on the pen.

Cummins had admitted that the gas mask case bearing his name had been in his possession until Thursday night. Examination showed that it contained grit and cement dust which closely resembled samples picked up from the air raid shelter in which the first body, that of Evelyn Hamilton, had been discovered. In the dustbin at the billet

was a propelling pencil which Mrs Hamilton had borrowed from a friend, and a pair of rubber overshoes. Greeno took the shoes down to Cummins in Brixton jail.

'He looked puzzled when I asked him to take off his boots,' Greeno wrote later. 'But with the boots in my hand I produced the overshoes I had rescued from the dustbin . . . "Why did you throw these away?" I asked. "Was it because you'd read something in the papers about our finding footprints in the snow?" He didn't answer, but the overshoes fitted perfectly.'

Pressure

Then there was the question of the money O'Dwyer had been given by the man who attacked her. Greeno traced all the airmen who had been on the last pay parade with Cummins, and some of the steadier ones still had a note or two left. From the numbers on these notes, and the position the men had taken in the parade, it was possible to find the man who had drawn the money given to Phyllis O'Dwyer. It was Gordon Cummins.

Whatever the entries in the billet pass book said, and despite the fact that his comrades swore that Cummins had been in bed at the relevant times, the evidence showed that he was the killer. Greeno went back to St John's Wood and questioned the officer-in-charge and his men. Under pressure, one man admitted to having 'filled in' for Cummins occasionally. Another, more importantly, revealed that on Monday night, he and Cummins had crept down the fire escape after lights out and had gone into the West End. He remembered the night, because on Sunday afternoon Cummins had been almost broke, but on Monday he had seemed to be flush with cash and had bought drinks for two of them. Another little piece had slipped into place, because Mrs Hamilton had left home on Sunday evening with £80 in her handbag, but when she was found, it had gone.

Cummins' friend remembered that they had picked up two girls in Soho, and Cummins had taken his girl to her room in Frith Street. They

Doris Jouannet was the fourth victim. She was a part-time prostitute, and when not on the streets, Doris reverted to her more respectable role as wife of a London hotelier.

had arranged to meet later, but Cummins had not turned up and Greeno knew why. But Evelyn Oatley had not lived in Frith Street, so what had happened to the first girl? How had she escaped the killer's clutches?

Greeno went down to Soho and made enquiries. By this time, co-operation from the girls was plentiful, and one of them admitted that she had taken Cummins back with her on Monday night. Greeno went back to her room with her to talk, and discovered what he called 'the most fantastic feature of all'. The room was a tiny one with a blanket strung across one wall to screen off an alcove. As they talked the detective got the impression that they were not alone. Glancing at the blanket he saw a ragged hole, and from it two eyes peered. He leaped to his feet and snatched the blanket away. Behind it was the girl's ponce. 'This was the one case where a ponce did some good,' wrote Greeno. 'I knew that Cummins had seen what I saw – those eyes behind the blanket. That was why he had fled. Otherwise this girl might have died that night instead of Evelyn Oatley.'

Greeno was amazed to discover that Cummins had a rendezvous with a fourth girl on the Thursday night. If he had not met this last girl, he might just have got away with the crime. He had killed Doris Jouannet in Sussex Gardens; an hour later he had tried to strangle Phyllis O'Dwyer, who had escaped by kicking him in the groin; he had then walked down Regent Street to Piccadilly and tried to strangle girl number three by the Captain's Cabin pub; and according to his testimony he had picked up the fourth girl an hour later. This time he had done nothing. He had explained to her that he just wanted company, because he did not want to go back to his billet too early. She had made him cocoa, he had given her £2, and stayed talking with her until just after 3.00 am. If he had not had that cocoa, he might have reached the billet before the duty corporal found that he was not in his bed.

Greeno decided to charge Cummins with the murder of Evelyn Oatley as one conviction was all that was needed on a capital charge. Once convicted, Cummins went to the gallows, still protesting his innocence. After the trial, outside the Old Bailey, Superintendent Greeno was accosted by an elderly prostitute who asked him if 'he had got the right man'.

'You see, none of us have dared to go to work lately. You're certain it's all right now?' The Assistant Comissioner of Police later called Greeno to his office and remonstrated with him for replying in the affirmative. 'Suppose it gets out that you have given these women permission to solicit on the streets?' he asked. 'Well, hardly permission!' was Greeno's retort.

It was the end of another 'jigsaw' puzzle for Edward Greeno, but far from the last. He retired from the force in 1960. As Head of Scotland Yard's Number One district, covering the West End and Soho, he had been known as the 'Governor' to crooks and policemen alike and had 88 special commendations to his credit. He had spent 38 years policing London, and, as the *Daily Express* put it on the day he retired, 'his record of successful murder investigation bears comparison with any force in the world. One thing is certain; the underworld will be celebrating tonight.'

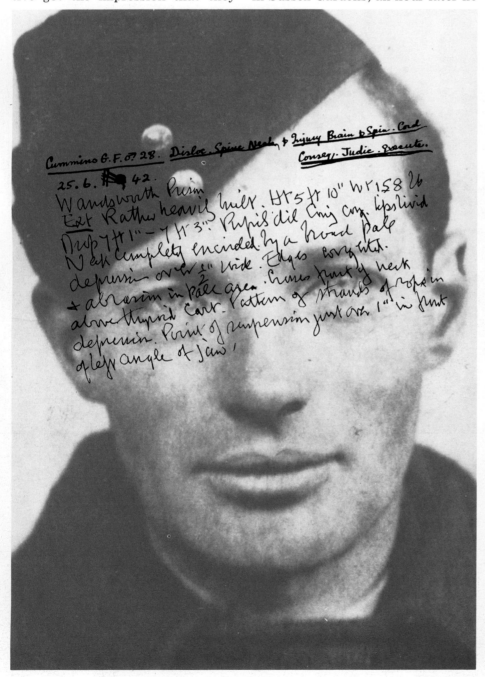

Impersonal and clinical, these words wrote a judicial end to the brief career of Gordon Cummins. A comb, pen and a cup of cocoa helped to lead him to the scaffold where he died still denying guilt. The hanging brought relief to the 'Ladies of Soho'.

A trap to catch a giant

How they stalked Al Capone

IN THE ENTIRE HISTORY of crime and criminals there has perhaps never been a period of sustained and organized lawlessness to match that spawned by the passing of the Volstead Act of 1920. As is well known, the Act had precisely the opposite effect to that which was intended. This paradox was in part due to the law itself being badly worded. For, though it was forbidden to manufacture, sell or transport liquor, it was not illegal to drink it. There were ordinary citizens who may not have taken much alcoholic drink at all prior to Prohibition, but who enjoyed the thrill of frequenting illicit speakeasies. Such delights may even have introduced law-abiding citizens to the pleasures of the brothels and gambling halls because they shared premises with the speakeasies.

Despite the legend that has grown from the 'roaring twenties', the sheer scale of crime is difficult to imagine. In 1926, Chicago alone had 20,000 liquor joints, 3,000 brothels, 200 top gambling houses, and 2,000 illegal bookmaking joints. The famous Capone mob was only one among four or five gangs operating in the city, but its boss was estimated to have an income of $110m from bootlegging, gambling, prostitution and other illegal industries.

Unpunished

The law enforcement activities of the FBI and other agencies were hampered because officials were 'in the pay' of the gangsters. Capone's gang rigged the election of the Mayor of Chicago and the Chief of Police. Many judges, district attorneys and ordinary police officers were also on Capone's payroll. In Chicago alone, between 1923 and 1926, 135 gangsters died in street 'shoot-outs' for which no one was ever charged, and 116 unexplained bomb attacks went unpunished. One solution to the problem was to jail the gang leaders, but there was rarely any tangible evidence to connect them with the crimes. Everyone knew who ordered the St Valentine's Day massacre, but how could it be proved? When seven members of the 'Bugs' Moran mob were shot dead at a garage in North Clark Street on

Dead men tell no tales – and neither did the killers involved in gangster Al Capone's notorious mass murder, The St Valentine's Day Massacre.

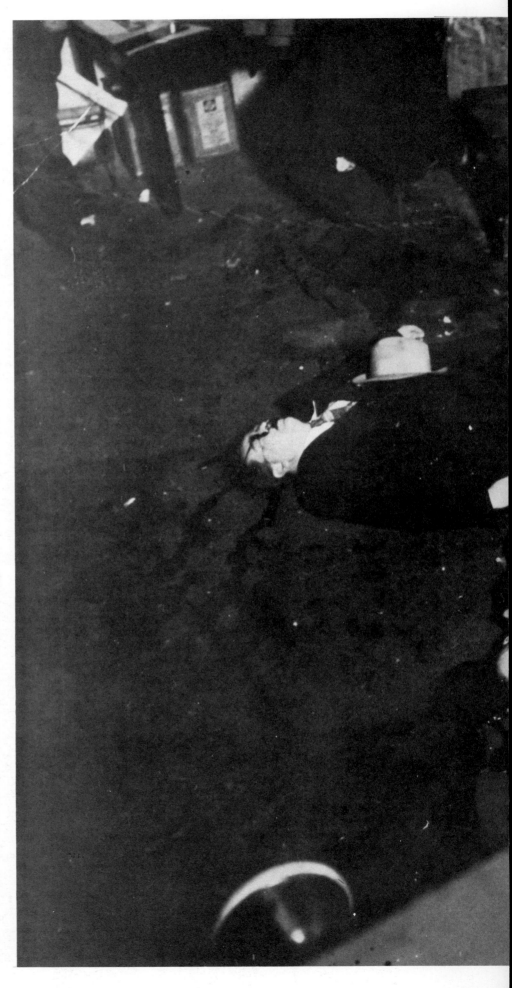

February 14, 1929, Al Capone was 2,000 miles away in his Florida residence. The victims did not live to tell the tale, and the killers would never 'talk' for fear of retribution.

It was unfortunate for Capone that Chicago had at least a handful of responsible citizens left. Six prominent businessmen, who became known as 'The Secret Six', put up a fund of $75,000 and placed it at the disposal of the Federal Government to help nail the man they called 'the millionaire gorilla'. At the same time, President Herbert Hoover issued a memo to his senior law-enforcement officers which said that Capone had to be jailed. At a conference attended by the major law enforcement agencies, a gentle, quiet-spoken man came up with an idea. His name was Elmer Lincoln Irey, head of the Intelligence Division of the Internal Revenue Service. He already had one credit to his reputation. He had jailed Ralph 'Bottles' Capone on a charge of tax evasion, and he thought that it should be possible to get his big brother on the same charge. 'I don't happen to share the fear that Al Capone instils in a great many people,' explained 41-year-old Irey in his soft voice. 'As far as I am concerned he is just a big fat man in a mustard-colored suit.'

Elmer Irey was not a policeman in the strict sense of the word. Born in Kansas City in 1888, he had moved as a child to Washington DC, where he attended Washington High School and Georgetown Law School. After graduation, he had entered the office of the Chief Post Office Inspector, and in 1919, when he was 31 years old, Irey had been chosen, with four or five other postal inspectors, to form the Intelligence Service of the Internal Revenue. The service was set up to track down tax frauds. The system of tax collection in the United States had always been a very open one, where citizens were asked to assess their own taxes and pay them voluntarily. Inevitably, there were a number of cheats and Irey's job was to find them.

Armored

In March, 1930, Irey set out for Chicago for a meeting with Arthur P. Madden, head of the Chicago office of the Intelligence Service. Quietly and surreptitiously, the two men filed a report on the top gangster's life-style. It was not a penny-pinching one. Capone ran a huge house in Chicago, as well as the estate in Florida, both staffed with armies of servants and bodyguards. His seven ton, armored limousine was fit for a president, and his constant parties were held on a royal scale. He spent

a small fortune on clothes alone, wearing only monogrammed silk shirts which he bought in dozens, crocodile skin shoes, and expensive, if vulgar, suits.

Despite all this ostentation, Capone officially earned no money, and spent none. His company accounts, which were highly complex affairs, showed that he was technically poverty-stricken. But the task of proving income tax evasion would be extremely difficult, even for an expert like Irey. What was needed was an undercover man, someone who would be totally accepted by the gangster fraternity, who knew them intimately and had an 'authentic' criminal record, and yet at the same time would be a lawman of the highest integrity. The obvious choice was Michael J. Malone.

Disguised

Malone was one of the most dedicated detectives who ever lived, and yet his true story may never be told in full, for, though he was responsible for infiltrating dozens of underworld circles until his death in the early 1950s, he kept no records, and few records were kept of his activities. Only one or two top Intelligence men knew his real identity. To the others he was 'Pat O'Rourke', and on his rare visits to Intelligence headquarters in Washington he went heavily disguised. Malone had many things in common with France's Eugène Vidocq. He was a good actor, with an ability to blend into any background. He had nerves of steel and a sharp intelligence. His dark, almost Mediterranean looks and his ability to speak Italian made him an ideal candidate for infiltration into the Italian-dominated Capone empire.

Irey and Malone interviewed dozens of informers in Brooklyn, which was an area Capone knew well, as he had served his criminal apprenticeship there. While they were doing this, a well-known gangster was gunned down in the street. The FBI arrested the killer, and kept him under top security. They then put out the word that Malone, or rather 'O'Rourke', had done the shooting.

Equipped with a phoney criminal record, Malone travelled to Chicago along with another agent, Frank J. Wilson, who was later to be head of the United States Secret Service. Wilson set up an office separate from

Big Al liked to be seen as a family man, and often took time off from crime to take his son to a ball game. However, he would only travel in his specially-built, bullet-proof 'tank' (left). His wife Mamie (right) was not quite so fond of being seen in public.

the regular Intelligence Service headquarters and he, Irey and Arthur Madden took great pains never to be seen together, and never to be connected in any way with one another. The telephones of over 50 of Capone's leading colleagues, and those of their girlfriends, were bugged, and the calls monitored on a switchboard which was manned day and night.

Using 'Secret Six' funds, Malone booked into the Lexington Hotel, the hangout of most of the Capone gang, equipped with a costly wardrobe and a healthy bank balance. He drank discreetly in a corner of the main bar, and rarely went out except to buy newspapers, which he scanned as if searching for some particular item. Soon, the Capone boys became curious. One night about a week after he booked in, a 'heavy' eased himself into a seat at Malone's table. 'What's your line, Jack?' he asked. Malone look him over expressionlessly, staring him out. Then he replied, 'I'm a promotor. Know anybody who'd be interested in buying some gold bricks?' The Capone aide laughed, and invited him upstairs for a drink 'with the boss'.

Proposition

When Malone reached Capone's suite, the big gangster began to quiz him. Malone played the part of the taciturn, tough guy to perfection. He told Capone he came from St Louis, and hinted that 'he was on the run'. But he had carefully cultivated a slight Brooklyn accent, and Capone detected it. 'Where are you really from?' he asked. 'O.K.' Malone replied, 'I'm from Brooklyn.' Capone was delighted. Gradually, under his questioning, Malone pretended to relax, spilling out names, gangster hang-outs, and underworld gossip. When he 'admitted' that he was on the run for the shooting, which Capone had heard about, the gangster chief seemed satisfied. 'Hang around', he told Malone. 'We might have a proposition for you.'

For two days, even the normally nerveless Malone was edgy. He knew that Capone would be checking out his 'background' in Brooklyn, and that if one word of it rang false he was a dead man. But eventually

Scarface Capone's headquarters, the Lexington Hotel, at the corner of 22nd Street and Michigan Avenue. It was here that the lord of Chicago crime lavishly entertained his guests.

109

'Scarface Al' was satisfied. He offered Malone a job as a croupier in his gambling club in the Hawthorne Hotel, Cicero, a suburb of Chicago, which was an ideal position from which Malone could keep his eyes and ears wide open.

For some months all went well, although there were tense moments. On one occasion a monitored telephone call revealed that 'Snorky', which was another of Capone's nicknames, was going to 'have that feller living at the S.P. taken care of'. The S.P. stood for the Sheridan Plaza Hotel, where agent Frank Wilson was living. The call could only mean that the Capone gang were on to Wilson, and he went to ground. Nevertheless, despite Irey's protests, he insisted on staying on the job.

Then at a New Year's party in 1931, Malone came up with the first snippet of real information. He had been talking drunkenly with one of Capone's close colleagues, and had carefully brought the subject around to income tax. How did Al get away with not paying up? The gangster laughed. 'The income tax dicks ain't so smart,' he said. 'They've had a record book of Al's for five years that could send him to jail, only they're too dumb to realize it.'

Overjoyed

Arthur Madden had been in charge of various raids on Capone-run premises over the last few years during which numerous record books had been seized, but he could think of no such book. However, he and Wilson began sifting through every ledger they had in their possession. After a few days they found an accounts book labelled 'Burnham Barracks', which was a brothel the gangster ran just outside Chicago. Leafing through it, Wilson soon realized that it related, not to the relatively small time brothel, but to a gambling organization. It noted bets paid in, and the profits of what was obviously a large-scale gambling outfit. What was more, almost every page showed large sums paid out to someone mentioned only as 'Al'. It had to be Capone himself. The ledger, Wilson discovered, had been seized in a raid on the Hawthorne Hotel, the same place in which Malone now worked as a croupier.

Elmer Irey was overjoyed at the news. At last he seemed to have

evidence which, properly handled, could prove Capone's evasion. However, he would first have to find the accountant who had made the entries, and the chances seemed slim. Surely Capone would have had the man bumped off by now. A handwriting expert examined the ledger, and discovered that not one but two different hands showed in the writing. Carefully he compared the writing in the ledger with that of every known underworld accountant and many of Capone's top men, but there was no comparison. There

was only one chance left. Could Malone discover the names of the two men who had compiled the accounts? At enormous risk, for it was extremely unwise of any member of the mob to become too nosey about the boss's business, Malone questioned his original source of information, over a few drinks. Had the boss taken care of his accountants? 'No,' said the mobster. 'Les Shumway and Fred Reis went to ground. The word's been out for them for five years, but we haven't caught them.'

Armed with the two names, Irey

Capone signs a $50,000 bail bond (above). He is flanked by State prosecutors already claiming a watertight case. Below: Their confidence was justified as a worried Capone (hand to face) leaves court during an adjournment. The smile is back in place as Capone (left) leaves for jail in a first-class Pullman car.

sent his agents poking through the seedier rooming houses of Chicago. The job of accountant, even to Capone, would have been a fairly ill-paid one, with lots of personal risk, and a man would have to be desperate to take it. Finally, after a week of slogging, one of them found Shumway's old lodgings. But, said the landlady, he had gone south to Miami in 1925. That posed a problem. Capone's estate was in Miami, the town was crawling with his gunmen, and the only agent Irey had suitable for the tracking job was Frank Wilson, who had been recognized by Capone's mob. After careful consideration of the risks, Irey agreed to let Wilson go, heavily disguised. Once in Miami, Wilson began the wearying footwork of checking out rooming houses, small hotels and gambling joints for news of the missing man. The nearest he got was a tip that a 'guy who might be Shumway' was working at the Hialeah Race Track. Wilson winced. Hialeah was a favorite haunt of Capone when in Miami, and his bodyguards would be thicker on the ground there than anywhere. Nevertheless armed with a description of his quarry and a pocket camera, Wilson went to the track, narrowed down the possibilities to three men, and took photographs of them all. He sent prints back to Irey in Chicago, and Irey showed them to Shumway's ex-landlady. She identified one as her former lodger.

Now Wilson had a delicate task to perform, which was to persuade Shumway to talk. He tracked the ex-accountant to his hotel room and asked about the ledger. Naturally, Shumway was terrified. Capone didn't know him personally, he said, so he was able to work at the track. Most of the men who had known him had been 'eliminated' in gang warfare. He had been safe until now, and he wanted no trouble. Right, said Wilson. We will subpoena you into appearing, in person, before a jury at Capone's trial. Then we leave you to the mercy of Capone's thugs. The alternative, the agent pointed out, was for Shumway to co-operate with the Federal Government and

In spite of his humble origins, Capone took to wealth and the good life with the ease of a duck to water. However, as he smilingly prepared for a swim at his mansion at Palm Island, Florida, the taxmen were ready to close in.

allow the Treasury agents to protect him until the conviction of Al Capone was clinched.

Shumway took little persuading. Within a matter of hours, Wilson had whisked him back to Chicago, to Irey's office. Irey's gumshoes, meanwhile, had tracked down the second accountant, Fred Reis, to a small town in south Illinois, where he had been hiding in fear since leaving Chicago. The same argument was used on him. Testify in secret or be subpoenaed. Reis also agreed to co-operate.

After intensive questioning, the two ex-accountants testified before a federal grand jury about Capone's receipts entered in the ledgers. The jury indicted Capone for failing to pay taxes and for failing to file income tax statements. He was released on $50,000 bail, and his first act on leaving the court room was to place a similar sum on the heads of Shumway and Reis. Elmer Irey had been expecting this. He planted information that Reis was in Los Angeles, and Shumway in Baltimore. While Capone hoods raced off to both towns, Reis was shipped to South America to await the trial, and Shumway and an agent took jobs in an Oregon lumber camp.

By now, Capone was seriously worried. In September, one of his men offered Irey a million dollars to drop the case against the gangster boss, which was one of the largest bribes ever offered a lawman. Characteristically, Irey had the messenger thrown out of his office. Capone tried a new tack. He offered to pay a certain amount of back taxes to stay out of jail, but this too was totally unacceptable to Irey.

Malone was still working under cover, and he was able to report to Irey the two, last-ditch attempts by the gangster to stay free. He had arranged for four New York gunmen to travel to Chicago with orders to kill Irey, Arthur Madden, and Frank Wilson, as well as the two witnesses. Irey staked out armed agents at every window overlooking Chicago's Post Office Building, where the Federal Court was to be held. The New York killers did not appear.

Gorilla

Malone also reported that Capone had got hold of the list of the 100 prospective jurors for the trial, and had sent his men to each of them in turn to either buy or frighten them off. But Irey contacted Judge James H. Wilkerson, the presiding judge. Wilkerson secretly drew up another list of jurors, untouched by Capone, and twelve of these were empanelled.

Finally, Malone heard that a Capone gunman had got into court. Irey had him arrested, and Capone was finished.

The trial lasted eleven days. The jury deliberated for ten hours, and found the 'millionaire gorilla' guilty as charged. He was fined $50,000, ordered to pay $30,000 in court costs, and jailed for eleven years. Capone died in seclusion in Miami. Paresis from an early syphilis attacked his brain, and he died, mentally deranged, in January 1947.

The team of Elmer Lincoln Irey, Wilson and Malone went on to even bigger and better things. Their technique of jailing criminals for income tax evasion paid off time and again, particularly in the famous cases of Boss Pendergast in Kansas City, and Huey Long in Louisiana. It was the most deadly and dangerous of all forms of detective work, but despite all odds the three men survived until the big gangs were broken. By the time Irey died in July, 1948, as head of all Treasury and Secret Service agents, he and his team had justly earned the newspaper title 'The Giant Killers'.

In death, Capone becomes just a weight to be humped across a graveyard.

Frozen and forgotten, Capone's vault at Mount Olivet cemetery.

The tailor-made clue

Half way across the Atlantic, Franz Muller was trapped by his hat

THE VICTORIAN DETECTIVE, and indeed the detective up until World War II, had at least one advantage over his more modern counterpart. He lived in the heyday of the personal trademark. Every tailor, for instance, stitched into the suits he made his individual label, which often included the name of his client. Each umbrella maker stamped his name on the ferrule or handle of his product, and there was never much trouble identifying a 'getaway' vehicle, since all carriage makers had their own styles and idiosyncracies.

Small keys

It was a hat which trapped Franz Muller in 1864, in Manhattan, and led him to the gallows in London. The case was widely reported, and it had one interesting repercussion on both sides of the Atlantic.

The story started one summer morning, when Inspector Michael Kerressey of London Metropolitan Police 'K' Division was notified that a murder had been committed on his 'patch'. An old man had apparently been beaten to death in a railway carriage, and his body thrown from the moving train. The body had been identified as that of Thomas Briggs, a chief clerk in one of the City of London banks.

Inspector Kerressey set about the routine of establishing the events leading up to the death. Mr Briggs, he discovered, had been a neat and meticulous 69-year-old man, who still worked, and was a highly valued member of his firm. On Saturday night, according to his custom, he had gone down to Peckham, in South London for supper with his niece and her husband, a Mr Buchan. They had eaten early and at eight o'clock, Mr Briggs had stood up, taken out a large gold watch and chain, and announced that it was time for him to go home. Mr Buchan later remembered the watch and chain. There were two small keys tied to the thick links of the chain with a piece of string, which was an incongruous detail in view of the old man's passion for neatness of dress. Mr Buchan had walked Mr Briggs as far as the horse-bus stop in the Old Kent Road, where Mr Briggs had bought a ticket to King William Street. From there he had walked the short distance to Fenchurch Street railroad station, where he bought a

Murder on the tracks (top). Samuel Briggs was found dying by a train-driver and was taken to a pub (above), the victim of 'good boy' Franz Muller (right). Everyone who knew Muller thought he was innocent.

first-class ticket to Hackney Wick. The ticket inspector did not remember seeing him on the platform that night, but knew that his usual habit was to go to the front of the train, to a first-class carriage near the engine. There were, in those days, no corridors between the carriages. At 9.50 pm, the train had pulled out.

By sheer coincidence two young men from Mr Brigg's bank, Harry Verney and Sidney Jones, got on the train the same night at Hackney Wick station, Mr Briggs' intended destination, and entered the same compartment. Dusk was falling, and there were no lights in the compartment. Sidney Jones sat down heavily and then jumped up again in annoyance. A wet patch on the seat had soaked his trousers. He rubbed the stain with his fingers, and held them up to the light from the station outside. Even by the flickering gaslight, he was certain that the stain was fresh blood.

Verney suggested that they call the guard, and they leaped to the platform just as he was about to blow his whistle. They told the guard what they had seen, and he fetched a kerosene lamp. By its light they saw that Jones had been right. The seat was stained with blood, and a smear of it covered the door panels. On the luggage rack was a black leather briefcase and hat, while on the floor of the compartment lay a heavy stick, its handle daubed with thick blood and hair.

At about the same time as Verney and Jones were making their grim discovery, a train of empty carriages was wending slowly down the track in the opposite direction, going from Hackney Wick to Bow. As the engine passed over a bridge which crossed a canal, the driver saw a dark shape huddled by the parapet. He put on his brakes, and the steam engine hissed to a stop. He and the guard got down and walked back to investigate. The shape was the body of an elderly man who was unconscious and breathing shallowly. The side of his head was bleeding profusely.

The two men carried the body to a nearby pub, the Mitford Castle, and sent for a local doctor, Francis Toulmin. Dr Toulmin took one look at the victim and was shocked to see that it was one of his own patients.

The pub landlord sent for the police. As Dr Toulmin worked busily to clean up and stitch the savage wound he shook his head. 'I can't hold out much hope,' he said. 'He's an old man and someone has hit him very hard about the head.' Dr Toulmin was right. Thomas Briggs was carried to his house in Clapton Square, Hackney, where he died the following evening without having recovered consciousness.

Savage wound

Inspector Kerressey spoke to Mr Briggs' son, who had identified the body, along with the briefcase and walking stick. But the hat on the train had not belonged to his father, he said. The old man liked to wear rather old-fashioned hats with a high 'bell' crown. The hat in the train was about one and a half inches shorter than his father's, with a jauntily curled brim, and a distinctively striped lining. The victim's gold watch and chain were missing, but nothing else had been stolen, despite the fact that he had been wearing a diamond ring and had four gold sovereigns in his trouser pocket – a considerable sum of money.

The detective had little to go on. Somewhere between Fenchurch Street and Hackney a second person had got into the compartment with Mr Briggs. This person had battered Mr Briggs about the head with his own stick, had snatched the watch chain and then thrown the body from the compartment. But he had made one mistake. In the dark, and the heat of the moment, he had taken the victim's hat instead of his own.

Inspector Kerressey turned the hat over in his hands. The label showed that it had been made by a firm named H. Walker of Crawford Street, near Baker Street, in the West End of London. Kerressey went to see Mr Walker, but was disappointed. The style was very popular with 'young men about town' said Mr Walker. The striped lining had extra appeal for fashion-conscious wearers, and he had sold a great many of them.

Disappointed

The trail seemed to have gone cold, but the detective had one remaining hope. Three rewards had been announced in the newspapers, each of £100. One was from the Government, the second was from Mr Briggs' employers, and the third was from the railway company. The first response came early on the Tuesday morning following the attack, when a hansom cab driver named Matthews came to the police station.

Matthews told Kerressey that he had had a hat identical to the one found in the railway compartment. 'I remember it because it was admired by a young German tailor named Muller,' he said. 'He used to work for a friend of mine. He told me that if I could get him one like it, he would make me a waistcoat in exchange. I went around to Walkers and bought him one for fourteen shillings. What made me think of it was that young Muller called at my house only yesterday. He gave my little daughter this box to play with. I thought it a bit sinister because it has the word 'Death' on it.' Matthews handed Kerressey a small, square, cardboard box. The inspector smiled as he read the inscription. It was not 'Death' but 'De Ath', a name well known among foreign jewellers in Cheapside.

It so happened that the firm De Ath not only sold watches and jewellery but ran a pawn-broking business. The proprietor readily remembered serving a young man with a German accent; once on Monday, the first time some weeks previously. 'The first time he came to pawn his watch and chain. We couldn't give him much for it – £3 altogether. But on Monday he had a rather good gold watch with him which he wanted to pawn. We gave him £3.10s. for it. He redeemed his own watch and chain, and, after paying the five shillings pawnbroker's commission, he had five shillings left which he spent on a ring.'

De Ath took out a gold watch and chain from one of his drawers. Tied to the chain with a piece of string were two small keys. It was Mr Briggs' watch. Now Inspector Kerressey asked the vital question. Did De Ath know the name and address of the young German? 'I don't know his address,' was the reply, 'but his name is Franz Muller.'

Despondently, the inspector went back to see Matthews, the cab driver. Surely he had a clue as to where Muller had lived? Matthews shook his head. It had been some time since Muller had worked for his friend, he said, and he knew that the German had moved his lodgings since then. He thought that Muller had lived in North London, but couldn't be sure. There was one other thing though. On Monday he had lent the young man seven shillings and sixpence.

'Good boy'

Friday arrived, and Inspector Kerressey felt that too little progress had been made. North London was a vast area, heavily populated with immigrants, including many Germans. The murder had been committed between Bow and Hackney Wick, but even that did not significantly narrow down the field. Then in the afternoon a call came through from the City of London police, which was a separate force, more local than the Metropolitan. A German named Repsch had called and asked to see an officer about the Briggs case. Eagerly, Kerressey took down the address, which was near

The misfortunes of Muller, like those of many murderers, presented opportunist printers with a chance to make a quick profit, and point a moral.

Lamentation of Franz Muller

Within a dark and dreary dungeon,
  In grief and anguish now I lie,
For a base and dreadful murder,
  In youth and vigour I must die.
Far from home, and far from kindred,
  In grief and sorrow I deplore,
Unhappy man, on a foreign land,
  I die at the age of twenty-four.

When I had done that dreadful murder,
  I sailed across the raging main;
Justice followed poor Franz Muller,
  For the murder in the railway train.

That fatal night I was determined,
  Poor Thomas Briggs to rob and slay,
And in the fatal railway carriage,
  That night, I took his life away.
His crimson gore did stain the carriage.
  I threw him from the same, alack!
I on the railway left him bleeding,
  I robbed him of his watch and hat.

When I poor Thomas Briggs did murder,
  I went across the briney sea,
And I was fully then determined,
  To reach New York, in America
My guilty soul was pierced with anguish,
  When the stormy winds did roar,
And justice ready was to seize me,
  Before I reached Columbia's shore.

Poor Briggs's goods was found upon me,
  Sufficient evidence, you see,

To bring me to the bar of Newgate,
  And hang me on the fatal tree;
Oh! was there ever such excitement,
  Or will there ever be again,
As there has been with poor Franz Muller
  For the murder in the railway train.

My noble counsel pleaded for me,
  And done their best my life to save,
A British jury found me guilty,
  I must lie in a murderer's grave;
Numbers thought they'd not convict me,
  When at the bar they did me try,
Oh! God above, look down in pity,
  My fate is sealed, and I must die!

Oh! I must die a malefactor,
  In front of Newgate's dismal door,
In the midst of health and vigour,
  Aged only twenty-four.
I never thought the law would take me,
  When I sailed o'er the raging main,
All my courage did forsake me,—
  A murderer in the railway train.

Swift the moments are approaching,
  On the gallows I must die,
The cruel hangman stands before me,
  On the wretched tree so high,
I am full of grief and anguish,
  Full of sorrow, care, and pain,—
A warning take by poor Franz Muller,
  The murderer in the railway train,

H. Disley, Printer, 57, High-street, St. Giles.

Moorgate, and called for a cab.

He found Mr and Mrs Repsch living in one large, spotlessly clean room in an old building. Mr Repsch took in small tailoring jobs and did not seem to earn much money.

Mr Repsch explained about Muller. He was a 'good boy', he said, and a fine tailor. He had come to England from his home in Saxe Coburg two years previously, but things had not gone well for him in the new country. He had held three jobs, and had lost each of them, not because of anything he had done, but because the tailoring trade had become depressed. His last job had been with a gentleman named Hodgkinson in Threadneedle Street, close to the Bank of England. When that position fell through, Muller had decided to go to America, the land of opportunity. But the fare was £4, even by slow sailing packet, and he had no savings. He had pawned his watch and chain, and the Repschs had loaned him ten shillings and sixpence towards his fare. 'But on Monday last,' continued Repsch, 'he came to see us looking prosperous. My wife teased him about it. He had on a new hat, taller than his old one, and a gold watch and chain. He said that he had bought them cheaply from a sailor down at the docks.'

Impossible

Kerressey produced the hat which had been found in the train from a hat box he had brought with him. 'Do you recognize this?' he asked. 'Ja ja, that is Franz's old hat,' said the German. 'The brim is curled, you see? He always wore it like that.' When had Repsch seen Muller before the Monday visit? 'On Saturday night between seven and eight,' was the reply. 'He was going to see a girlfriend, I think. He was going to Fenchurch Street Station, where he caught the train to Hackney Wick. He had lodgings there, near the station at Victoria Park. His landlady was a Mrs Blyth.'

Hardly pausing to thank the tailor, Kerressey ran out to his cab and ordered the driver to whip up his horse and head for Hackney. Mrs Blyth's house was a neat, semi-detached villa, and she herself was trim and neat. Yes, she said, Muller had lodged with her. He was such a nice young man. But he had left for America yesterday, Thursday, on the sailing packet *Victoria*. 'Mrs Blyth,'

said Kerressey, 'do you not know that we want Muller in connection with a murder?' Mrs Blyth's honest face was a mask of horror. 'Murder!' she exclaimed. 'Franz could never murder anyone. It is impossible.'

The inspector calmed her. What had Muller done on Saturday night? Why, he had gone to see his girlfriend as usual in the early evening, she said. He had come in at about 11·00 pm, and she had heard his footsteps on the stairs. Poor Franz. He had had a hard time, what with cash difficulties. That was what puzzled her, she said. How had he got the money to go to America?

The answer to that question was soon clear beyond doubt. When Kerressey returned to his office, he found his sergeant waiting for him. After an exhausting day trooping around the London pawnbrokers, the sergeant had finally come across a shop where Muller had pawned a watch and chain on Monday for £3. So, Muller had first gone to De Ath's shop, and pawned Briggs' watch and chain. He had redeemed his own property, and then pawned it again at the other shop. If he was such a 'nice young man', and the murder had been unpremeditated, he must have devised these needlessly complicated transactions in some kind of desperate daze. In any case, the result was that he had £3, plus the seven shillings and sixpence from Matthews, the cab driver, and the ten shillings and sixpence from Repsch. That made a total of £3.18s., just two shillings short of his fare to America.

There was only one thing to be done. Kerressey had to get to New York before Muller. The United States were racked with Civil War and in the turmoil Muller would vanish without trace if he ever set foot in New York. Fortunately, the shipping lists showed that a fast steamer named the *Etna* was leaving Tilbury dock next day. The inspector booked a passage, and set out across the Atlantic after his quarry.

Stunned

The *Etna* made the transatlantic run in near-record time, and when the *Victoria* sailed up to Manhattan docks a few days later, the British policeman was on the quay to meet it. He stepped on board and spoke to the captain, who pointed Muller out to him. Despite the protestations

by Mrs Blyth and the Repschs that Muller was a 'good boy', Kerressey was still surprised at the quiet-spoken, well-mannered German who confronted him. Muller seemed to be stunned when the detective arrested him for murder. Then he flatly denied the charge. Unfortunately for Muller, he was wearing on his head the evidence which would hang him.

The New York authorities were co-operative, and immediately gave Kerressey an extradition warrant. The two men returned to England on the *Etna* a few days later. On the way, Muller continued to deny that he had been implicated in the slaying.

Too low

The hat had been made by Dignance and Company, of the Royal Exchange, London. The manager of the shop denied that it was one of his at first, saying that they dealt only in the old-fashioned 'bell crown' hats, and the crown of this hat was too low.

But the Dignance label was his, and so he carefully examined it and found that the hat had been altered. One and a half inches had been taken off the top, he explained. But the work was not done by a hatter. A hatter would have done it with a flat iron and varnish. The crown of this hat had been cut down and stitched back very neatly. It was the work of a skilled tailor. The label bearing the name of the original owner had been removed, pointed out the manager. But Mr Briggs was an old customer of theirs, and there was something very special about Mr Briggs' last hat. 'When he came to try it on,' said the manager, 'he found it was slightly too big. One of the assistants stuffed the lining with strips of silver paper to pad it out.'

'You mean that if silver paper is found in the lining of this hat you will be prepared to testify that it belonged to the dead man?'

'Yes, inspector,' replied the manager, who deftly slit the lining – and withdrew a strip of silver paper.

Had he not unwittingly picked up that hat, it seems unlikely that Franz Muller would have been convicted, for the rest of the evidence was purely circumstancial. Instead, there was the widely-reported court hearing, a convinced jury, and a hanging that November, just before Muller's twenty-fourth birthday. He protested his innocence throughout.

The dedicated detective

Sergeant Igii and the Tokyo poisoner

A BLIND AND SELFLESS dedication to duty has always been a characteristic of the Japanese people. It was this dedication which drove the samurai to die for their ideals, and inspired the kamikaze 'holy wind' pilots of World War Two to turn themselves into human dive bombs for the sake of their country and their Emperor. It was this same idealism and sense of duty which enabled Police Sergeant Tamigoro Igii to pursue relentlessly Japan's most notorious, post-war, mass murderer, despite opposition from the general public and his own superiors of the Tokyo Metropolitan Police Department.

The case began on the afternoon of January 26, 1948, as snow drifted down on American-occupied Tokyo. The doors of the Teikoku Bank in the district of Shiina-machi were just closing when a man stepped in and politely presented his calling card to the chief clerk. It gave his name as Dr Jiro Yamaguchi, and he quite credibly presented himself as an official from the medical department set up by the Americans. Over his brown suit he wore a white, doctor's coat, with an arm band bearing the word 'Sanitation', and a pair of surgeon's red rubber boots. The clerk ushered him into the bank manager's office, where he was greeted by the Acting Bank Manager, Takejiro Yoshida. Yoshida apologized for the absence of the regular manager, Senji Ushiyama, who, he explained, had gone home that morning with stomach pains.

Emergency

The doctor nodded sagely. That, he explained, was why he had come. He was attached to General Douglas MacArthur's Occupation Headquarters as a civilian doctor, and had orders to immunize the bank's employees against amoebic dysentery. A sudden outbreak of this disease had been reported in the Shiina-machi area. This was an emergency measure, he explained. The American military would send medics to look into matters more thoroughly later on.

Mr Yoshida was most grateful to Dr Yamaguchi, and ordered his 15 employees, including cleaners and

The Japanese compulsion to dedicate themselves to duty was horrifyingly demonstrated by the kamikaze (right). As relentless was Sergeant Igii's pursuit of Sadamichi Hirasawa (left).

maintenance men, to step into his office for treatment. Dr Yamaguchi bowed politely to them all. He extracted two large bottles from his bag, along with a syringe which he filled with liquid from the first bottle. He asked employees to hold out their drinking mugs, and then squirted a dose of the liquid into each. 'Now,' he said. 'This medicine is very potent and may burn your throats a little. Gulp it down when I give the word, and I will then give you a dosage from the second bottle. You will then be immune from dysentery.'

Obediently, Yoshida and his 15 people raised their cups to their lips and drank. The doctor moved down the line administering the second liquid, and again they drank. A few seconds later, an accountant,

Hidehiko Nishimura, clutched at his throat, choked a little, and then fell to the floor. Yoshida stared from the fallen man to his visitor in sudden, awful doubt, before he too collapsed. Within seconds the entire staff were unconscious or semi-conscious. The 'doctor' stepped over to the tills, picked up 164,400 yen in cash, an uncashed check for 17,405 yen, and stepped out of the bank into the swirling snow. The total haul was the equivalent of $600, a very poor return for the sacrifice of so many lives.

An hour after taking the drugs, Miss Masako Murata came round and managed to press an alarm switch. The police arrived and frantically called for ambulances. But only Miss Murata, Mr Yoshida

and two others survived. The other 12 employees were dead or dying by the time they reached the hospital. Autopsies quickly revealed that the victim's stomachs contained fatal doses of potassium cyanide.

The next day, police questioned the survivors and began to investigate the crime. As they were doing so, a man calmly walked into the Yasuda Bank at Itabashi and cashed the stolen check for 17,405 yen. He had endorsed it in the name 'Toyoji Goto'.

'Rehearsal'

The mass poisoning was as horrifying as anything a fiction writer had ever produced, and turned out to be the biggest single crime post-war Japan was to experience. To investigate it, Homicide Chief Horizaki appointed a crack team of detectives which included Sergeant Tamigoro Igii.

Initial inquiries revealed that what looked suspiciously like a 'rehearsal' for the crime had taken place on two previous occasions. On October 14,

1947, a man whose card announced him as 'Dr Shigeru Matsui' of the Welfare Ministry had entered the Yasuda Bank at Ebara, a suburb at the other side of town. He had told the manager that he was from General MacArthur's headquarters, with orders to immunize the staff against dysentery. In this case, nothing had happened, though the staff had drunk liquid from the bottles which 'Matsui' produced. On January 19, seven days before the fatal raid, Dr Jiro Yamaguchi had made his first 'immunization' at the Mitsubishi Bank at Nakai. In both of these cases, when the promised military follow-up medics did not appear, the managers had notified the local police, but as no crime had been committed, and no motive was immediately apparent, they had done nothing.

Sergeant Igii had several hobbies and interests outside his police work, and one of them was the study of traditional Japanese calling cards, or *meishi*. The cards are still widely used in Japanese professional circles,

both as a token of respect and as a convenience. Even when businessmen meet briefly and casually they exchange cards, and usually file them away for later reference. In view of his keen interest it was not unnatural for Sergeant Igii to begin his investigation with the clue of the calling cards.

Valuable

Dr Jiro Yamaguchi's card bore the tiny logo of a specialist card printer with a shop in the Ginza area of Tokyo. Igii went to see the specialist but without much hope, for there are thousands of 'Yamaguchis' in Japan, and 'Jiro' is a popular first name. He was right. The printer identified his own logo, but said that the card had been mass produced, and he had no means of knowing which of hundreds of Dr Yamaguchis had bought this particular one.

The other card was to provide a valuable clue, however. Igii was mildly surprised when a visitor, Dr Shigeru Matsui, was announced at his office a few days after the poison-

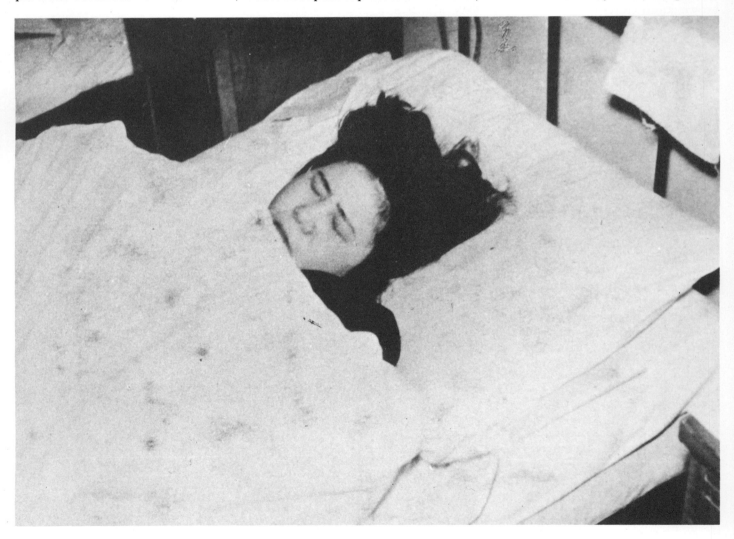

ing incident. Matsui's name had figured in the first 'rehearsal', and the doctor explained that he had read about the case in the newspapers. 'This is one of my cards,' he agreed. 'But I have never been into the Yasuda Bank, and I was at home when the murders were committed. The cards were printed locally in Sendai, in northern Honshu where my practice is. I had 100 delivered but I have only four left. Eagerly, Sergeant Igii asked if he kept a file of *meishi* which he had received in return for his own. 'But of course', smiled the doctor, and gladly gave the sergeant permission to visit him in Sendai to examine them.

At Sendai, Sergeant Igii made a list of the names and addresses in the doctor's file, and painstakingly checked out every one. They were all respectable, professional men such as doctors, lawyers, business-

The survivors of the most notorious mass murder in post-war Japan. Musako Murato (left) and acting bank manager Takejiro Yoshida recover in hospital following the poisoning.

men, and people from the arts world, for Dr Matsui was a keen student of Japanese art. None of the 96 people seemed likely to have callously poisoned the twelve bank employees.

Sergeant Igii returned to Tokyo to try to unearth fresh leads. During the next three months, he and his colleagues questioned over 8,000 people who vaguely fitted the description of Dr Yamaguchi and the fake 'Dr Matsui'. The witnesses had not given the detectives much information, except that the suspect was middle-aged, with greying, cropped hair, a mole on his left cheek and a scar under his chin. There was an astonishing number of people with all of these characteristics.

Pessimistic

Late in April, Japanese police chiefs and American criminal advisers gathered in Tokyo to discuss the case. The mood was pessimistic, and not merely because of the enormity of the task which had so far beaten them. Since the occupation of Japan by the Americans at

the end of the Second World War, some Western philosophies of social organization had influenced the previously imperialistic, Eastern state. One such influence was the concept of 'civil rights'. The team investigating the bank mass murder had been faced with accusations from the Japanese liberal press of having infringed personal liberties through the protracted interrogations. Senior police officers were becoming embarrassed, and many of them at the discussions wanted to quietly forget the affair by allowing it to remain an unsolved case.

Sergeant Igii did not share this view. He was a policeman of the old school. Somewhere there was a callous murderer at large, and Igii felt that at some point in his investigations he had probably interviewed him. If all else failed, he would go back to grass roots and start all over again.

He began sifting through his files on Dr Matsui's *meishi* presenters again, this time looking for something slightly out of the ordinary.

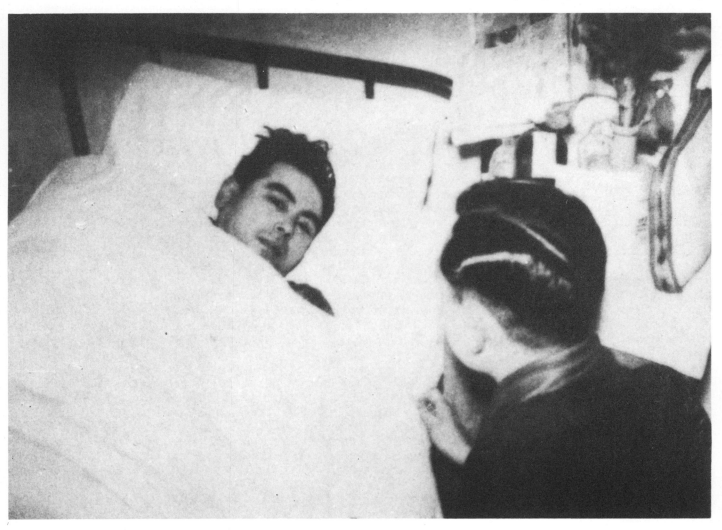

After a great deal of thought he came up with a short list of names, and one of these was Sadamichi Hirasawa of Otaru, Hokkaido. Hirasawa was an artist with whom Dr Matsui had been very impressed. They had met on a ferry travelling from Hokkaido, Japan's northern principal island, and the doctor had commented on a picture the artist was carrying. It was entitled *Spring is Near* and Hirasawa had proudly announced that he was travelling to Tokyo to present it to the Crown Prince. He had told the doctor that he had painted the picture himself, and had shown other paintings all over Japan. He was now president of several leading art societies. The two men had cordially exchanged cards.

Sergeant Igii turned up what he had on the artist from his initial investigation. The Otaru police, at the request of the Tokyo Homicide Department, had checked out Hirasawa thoroughly, and found him to be a mild, quiet-living man in his 50s. They had cleared him completely.

Several of the people on Dr Matsui's list lived on the island of Hokkaido, so the detective decided to go and interview them himself. Before setting out, he telephoned the studio which Hirasawa kept in Tokyo both as a workshop and a second residence. Hirasawa's wife answered, and told Sergeant Igii that he would find her husband in Hokkaido at the main house, as he was tending his sick parents there.

Elaborate

On arrival in Otaru, Igii made enquiries about Mr Hirasawa and, to his surprise, was directed to a dairy. He had been wrongly directed to the artist's brother, who ran the dairy. The sergeant explained the reason for his routine visit, and said that he hoped he would not be disturbing Sadamichi. 'No,' the brother replied. 'He is at home doing nothing.'

At the house, the artist greeted Igii with the customary Japanese courtesy and offered him tea. The sergeant was introduced to Hirasawa's parents, and he noticed that both of them looked extremely well. Some warning chord also jangled at the back of his mind when the painter, with rather elaborate casualness, indicated that the room next door was his studio. There was a

Police Chief Horizaki, seen answering Press questions, gave Igii a deadline.

painting on an easel, brushes were lying around, and several palettes had blobs of paint on them. But the paint on the picture, the brushes and the palettes was dry. Why should Hirasawa pretend to be busy, when he was not? Why should he tell his wife that his parents were sick when they were quite well? None of this had anything to do with the case, Igii told himself, except that it showed Hirasawa to be devious.

Igii's suspicions were aggravated, however, after he had told the artist the reason for the visit. Hirasawa, without being prompted, poured out a detailed account of his movements on the day of the murders. He had been in Tokyo attending a United States and Japan Goodwill Watercolor Painting Exhibition at a major department store in the Nihonbashi area in the morning. In the afternoon he had gone on a visit to his son-in-law, at Marunouchi. Both districts were a good distance away from the bank at Shiina-machi. Therefore, Hirasawa said, he could not have been near the bank at the appropriate time. He added that he had heard about the robbery on the radio.

Sergeant Igii continued his tour of Hokkaido visiting the other people on the list, but he could not get the artist out of his mind. The artist's looks fitted the description of the poisoner. There was a mark like a

mole on his left cheek, and a small scar on the point of his chin, but that alone, as the sergeant knew, was not enough.

Before he left the island, Igii called on Hirasawa again and invited him out to dinner on the pretext of returning his hospitality. Hirasawa sipped saki and chatted quite freely to the detective about his work. Igii appeared to be impressed. 'Perhaps I could have a signed photograph of you?' he asked. Hirasawa was a celebrity in his field, but he said that he had no pictures of himself. To Igii, it was like a Hollywood filmstar making the same claim. Igii asked if he might photograph Hirasawa instead, and the painter reluctantly agreed. Then Igii casually asked about the painter's meeting with Dr Matsui. The artist said that he remembered it well. When asked if he still had the doctor's card, he said, 'I'm sorry, but the card was in a wallet which was stolen from me in Tokyo. It was annoying, for the doctor had written his address with a fountain pen on the back for me, and I intended to call on him.' With a fountain pen? It was an odd sort of detail to inject into a story, the sergeant thought, but then Hirasawa seemed keen on meticulous detail. But there were further surprises in store. The artist expounded on a wide range of subjects during the

Hirasawa faces a court. He has now been under sentence of death for 30 years.

rest of the evening, and these included his knowledge of chemicals, including potassium cyanide. Was he playing an elaborate cat-and-mouse game?

On his return to Tokyo, Igii telephoned Dr Matsui and told him of Hirasawa's account of their meeting. When he came to the detail of the fountain pen, the doctor was surprised. 'I never carry a fountain pen,' he said, 'and I certainly didn't write my address on the card.' This was enough for Sergeant Igii. Triumphantly, he presented his superior, Homicide Chief Horizaki, with the photograph he had taken of his suspect and his report, but his success was short lived. There was to be no further investigation into Hirasawa, said the chief firmly. He had been officially cleared by his local police, and he was a well-known personality. Already, public opinion was bubbling with indignation at the number of arrests and subsequent releases undergone by suspects in this case. If Igii wanted to pursue the matter he would have to do so on his own, and take full reasponsibility. Furthermore, he would have to pay his own expenses. Igii was outraged. 'Very well,' he snapped. 'I will sell my house to pay my expenses, and public funds can reimburse me later.'

Something about Igii's stubborn

confidence made the chief pause for thought, and when a few days later, he discovered that Igii had put his house up for sale for 350,000 yen (about $1,000) he relented. Calling the sergeant to his office again, the chief told him that he could have 70 days in which to wrap up the case, and 70,000 yen for expenses over that period. If there were no results after that time, then the case must be dropped. Igii agreed.

This time the sergeant decided to concentrate on Hirasawa's Tokyo establishment, particularly on his wife, Masa. He also traced friends of the artist and began to piece together details of the artist's life. Hirasawa had presented himself as a busy and successful artist, but the detective established that this was not the whole truth. Either the artist's talents were fading, or fashion had ceased to favor him. It was true that he had once been lionized, but since then the better salons and galleries had begun to reject his work, and he was rapidly going broke. One of his best patrons had been Uzo Hanada, President of the Iino Industrial Company. This man had died during the previous August, and virtually the last source of Hirasawa's income had been cut off.

Igii then discovered two important facts about the artist's private life.

The first was that he kept two mistresses in Tokyo, and they were constantly demanding money. The second was that Masa Hirasawa had paid 44,500 yen into her husband's account on February 9. However, on January 26, the day of the murders, he had been unable to meet an outstanding bill of 150 yen. His membership of most of his art societies had lapsed by that date because of nonpayment of fees. When questioned by Igii, Masa Hirasawa told him that her husband had given her 69,000 yen to deposit, in three separate installments. It was from Masa that the detective obtained a letter written by the artist. When the handwriting was compared with that on the check cashed after the robbery by the phoney 'Mr Toyoji Goto', experts swore that the two were the same.

Chief Horizaki did not ignore Igii's new evidence, and on August 20, the sergeant set out again for Otaru to arrest Hirasawa. A search warrant also enabled him to enter and search Hirasawa's premises. In the Tokyo studio he found a brown suit, white coat, red rubber boots and a black, medical-style bag. In October, the artist was charged with robbery, attempted murder and premeditated murder.

Disease

At his trial, which opened before three judges on December 10, 1948, the court heard that Hirasawa's talent had been sapped by a brain disease called Korsakov's syndrome, after he had been injected with an anti-rabies serum in 1925. Over the years, his painting ability had declined, and finally he had fallen back on deceit to maintain his social position.

Despite the plea of partial insanity, Hirasawa was sentenced to hang. But the sentence was never carried out, and, now in his 80s, he is still incarcerated in Sendai jail under sentence of death. This is said to be the longest-delayed execution in history.

Tamigoro Igii retired from the Tokyo Metropolitan Police Department in March, 1964, from the rank of Inspector. The case of Hirasawa and the cyanide murders had become almost a legend by that time, and, unlike most of his Western counterparts, Igii was recognized in the street as a celebrity.

The motivated detective

**Sergeant Murtaugh,
and the
Chicago nurse murders**

ONE OF THE MOST important things a detective learns early in his career is the need for objectivity. In the ugly face of murder, rape, and kidnapping he must keep his emotions in check, and the most foul scenes of violence must be viewed with clinical detachment. For this reason, many veteran cops cultivate an air of apparent cynicism and hardness, an attitude which sometimes shocks the naive layman caught up with crime as an innocent bystander. Yet sometimes even the toughest policemen are unable to control their natural, human reactions when, for instance, a colleague is shot down on duty, or a small child is sexually molested. Despite what the textbooks say, this can arguably be a good thing. The extra surge of adrenaline induced by anger may give the investigator just that edge of sharpness which means doom for the criminal. In July, 1966, Chicago-based Sergeant of Detectives John Murtaugh discovered this incentive for himself when eight, pretty, young nurses, some of whom he knew by sight, were callously slain in what the papers described as 'the most bestial crime in Chicago's history'.

Just after 6.00 am on Thursday, July 14, as a warm and humid dawn began to break over Chicago's South Side, Patrolman Daniel R. Kelly was called to block 2300 on East 100th Street, in the Jeffrey Manor area. As his car squealed to a stop outside the block he saw a young woman standing on a ledge ten feet above the sidewalk. She was hysterical. 'Help me!' she screamed. 'Help me! They're all dead. I'm the last one left alive.' A bystander, a nurse who had made the emergency call, quickly explained to Patrolman Kelly that the girl was 23-year-old Corazon Piez Amurao, a Filipino nursing trainee who lived in the block with eight girl colleagues. They all worked at the South Chicago Community Hospital.

Former date

The officer radioed for extra assistance, shouted to the girl to stay where she was, and dashed up the steps to the building with his Smith and Wesson ·38 in his hand. The front door was locked, but the back door stood open. A ground floor window was also open, its screen lying on the ground nearby. Dashing through the empty kitchen into the living room, Patrolman Kelly stopped suddenly. By the left-hand wall, on an orange divan, was the naked body of a girl, lying face downwards. Kelly thought he recognized her, and when he turned her over he saw she was Gloria Jean Davy, a 23-year-old nurse. He had once dated her, and the sight of her strangled with a strip of cloth, which was still tied around her neck, sickened him.

While his colleague, Patrolman

Lennie Ponne, tried to soothe the still-screaming Corazon Amurao, Kelly dashed wildly up the stairs to the second floor, the revolver cocked in his fist. He found the second girl's body, naked except for panties, lying in a bathroom doorway. She had been stabbed to death and slashed about the breasts and neck.

To his right was a door leading to the front bedroom. Three more bodies lay there, two on the floor, and one on the bed. The two girls on the floor lay one on top of the other, their wrists tied behind their backs, and strips of cloth wrapped around their throats. The top girl had been gagged. The lower girl was still bleeding slightly from a stab wound in the neck, but, like the others, she was dead. The girl on the bed was bound at wrists and ankles and a gaping wound showed where her throat had been cut. There was one more bedroom, and in it were three more corpses. One had been bound and strangled, the second had been stabbed in the left breast and strangled, and the third had knife wounds in the back, the neck, and the left eye.

Bloody mayhem

Miss Amurao's hysteria had died a little by this time, and Kelly and Ponne began to question her gently. They needed a full description and information as quickly as possible. One man, said the girl, had done all this. He was about 25 and weighed about 175 lbs. He had short, brownish hair, and had worn a dark jacket and trousers with a white T-shirt.

Again, the wail of police car sirens drifted up from the street outside. Soon the two patrolmen were joined by Commander Francis Flanagan, head of Chicago's homicide division, Detective Sergeant John Murtaugh, and Detectives Bryan Carlisle and Jack Wallenda, from the Homicide and Sex Crime Unit. As they looked over the bloody mayhem, Flanagan realized that he was dealing with the biggest mass murder in Chicago's violent history. The famous St. Valentine's Day Massacre had accounted for seven mobster victims. The eight victims here were innocent nurses.

Flanagan and Murtaugh called in the Cook County Coroner, Dr Andrew J. Toman, and returned to Detective Area 2 headquarters, which the Commander had decided

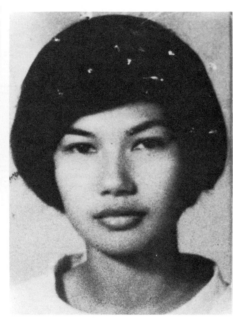
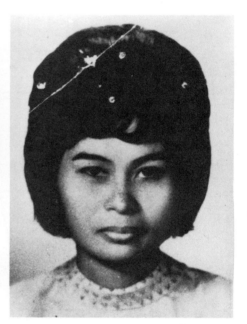

The eight nurses who were the victims in Chicago's biggest mass murder, a crime surpassing even the notorious St Valentine's Day Massacre. From the top, left to right they are Patricia Matusek, Mary Ann Jordan, Nina Schmale, Pamela Wilkening, Merlita Gargullo, Valentina Pasion, Suzanne Farris and Gloria Davy. Facing page: Corazon Amurao, the sole survivor of what was described as the 'most bestial crime in the city's history', is seen leaving the court at Peoria with her mother.

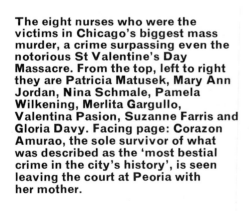

This newspaper illustration shows
where the nurses were murdered.
Right: Mary, Suzanne, Nina, Valentina
and Pamela are pictured in their room
chatting to Nurse Judith Dykton.

would be the centre from which the crime would be investigated. By 8.00 am, less than two hours after the call to Kelly, 140 detectives from all over the city were assembled there for a briefing. Flanagan split them into five teams of 28 men, with orders to comb every bar, rooming house, restaurant and gas station within the city limits, in an effort to find someone whom might have noticed an agitated young man answering the killer's description.

At the same time a telex message was sent out to police forces throughout Canada, the United States and Mexico. Based on further information from the lone survivor of the attack, Miss Amurao, it gave a description of the wanted man, with the additional information, 'Stated that he wanted money to go to New Orleans. May be armed with revolver or knife.'

Extra telephones and a portable exchange were installed at Number 2 Area headquarters to cope with the calls which, hoped Flanagan, would soon be pouring in.

Meanwhile, at the scene of the crime, Dr Toman, the coroner, along with six police pathologists and a team of experts manning mobile crime laboratories, had been carrying out the gruesome investigations. A male porter from South Chicago Community Hospital had identified the victims. Besides Kelly's ex-girl-friend, Gloria Davy, there were Suzanne Farris, aged 21, found in the bathroom, Merlita Gargullo, a beautiful 22 year old who was also Filipino, and her friend Valentina Pasion, aged 23. Merlita, Valentina, and Miss Amurao, who had given the alarm, were exchange students from Manila who had worked in Chicago for just a year. Valentina Pasion's body had lain under that of 21-year-old Nina Joe Schmale, an ex-beauty queen who was specializing in psychiatry.

Permission

The last three corpses, in the second bedroom, were Pamela Wilkening, aged 24, Patricia Ann Matusek, aged 21, whose father kept a Chicago Tavern, and another Chicago girl, Mary Ann Jordan, aged 20. Through tragic irony, Mary Ann, who normally lived at home with her parents, had been out late with her friend Suzanne Farris, and had telephoned her parents to ask their permission to stay with the other nurses just for that one night. Her brother was engaged to Miss Farris, and her parents had agreed.

While the police technicians worked at dusting the room for fingerprints, searching for minute clues, and examining the bodies of the victims, Sergeant Murtaugh, who had been appointed head of the investigation team, returned to Miss Amurao. She had been sedated, and was relatively calm in the manner which often follows shock. Her only physical injuries were the scraped marks on her wrists and elbows. These had occurred while she struggled to free herself of the strips of bedlinen which the killer had tied around her wrists.

She told Sergeant Murtaugh that at around 11.00 o'clock the previous night she and five of her rooming-mates, Patricia Matusek, Pamela Wilkening, Nina Schmale, Valentina Pasion and Merlita Gargullo were in the house together, all upstairs. Four of the girls were in the front

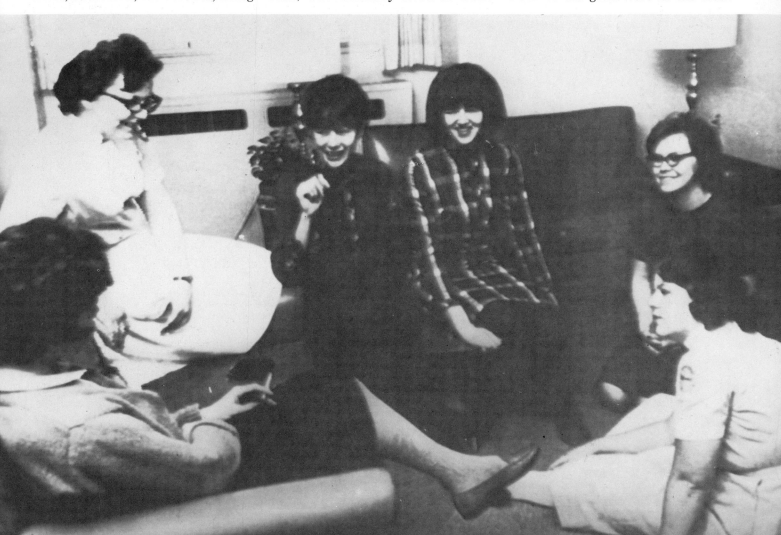

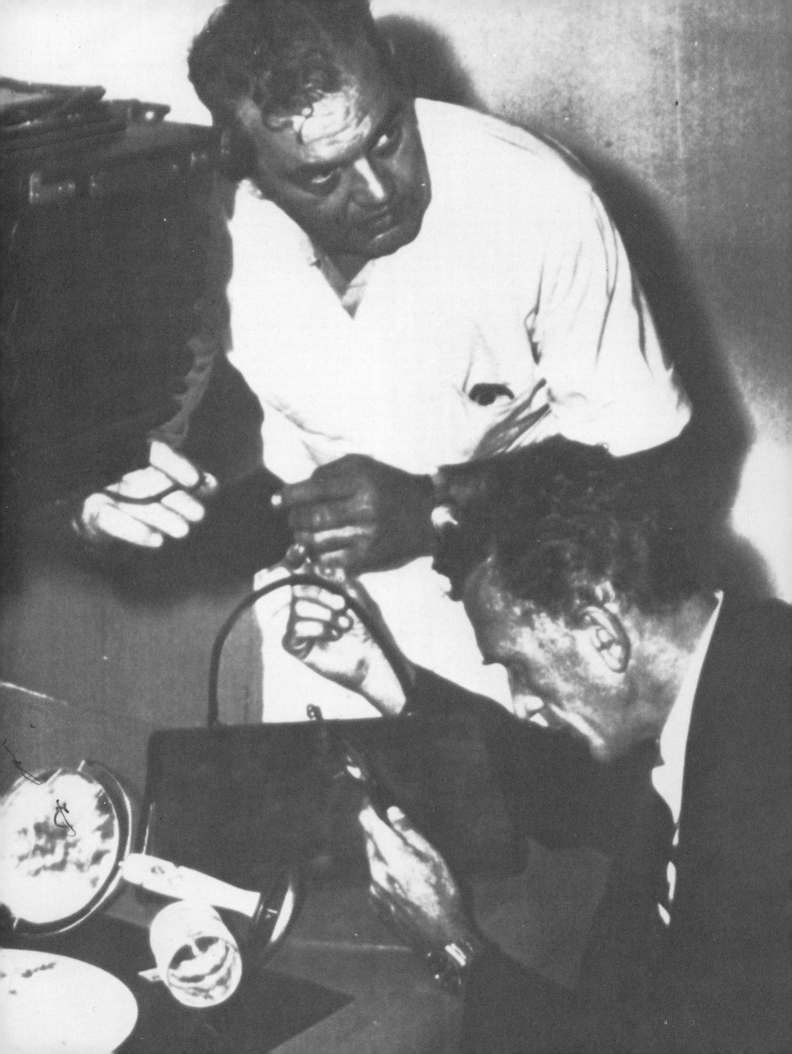

bedroom talking together, while she and Miss Gargullo sat in the back bedroom, which they shared.

Suddenly, there was a knock on the backdoor. Miss Amurao thought it was one of the other girls who had forgotten her key, and went down. On the back step was the young man she had described, holding a pistol in one hand and a knife in the other. 'I'm not going to hurt you,' he had said. 'I need your money to get to New Orleans. I'm not going to hurt you. I just want your money.' The young nurse noticed that he smelled very strongly of alcohol. Waving the pistol at her, he motioned her upstairs, ordered Miss Gargullo out of the back bedroom, and assembled all the girls in the front room. There they were told to lie face downwards on the floor. The intruder slashed a sheet to strips with his knife, and tied their hands behind them. Then he gagged their mouths.

As the man finished the job of tying the girls, Gloria Jean Davy came in downstairs and dialled the number of the house-mother, Miss Bisone, who lived in an adjacent block. This was standard practice for all the girls, and as they telephoned, Miss Bisone logged them in a book. Her records showed later that Gloria's call came at 11.20 pm. Unsuspecting, Gloria finished her call, went upstairs, and bumped into the young man with the gun. He ordered her into the room with the rest and bound her wrists.

Unconvinced

Throughout the proceedings, Miss Amurao recalled, he kept talking to the girls in a soft, slow voice, reassuring them that he was only there to steal their money, and not to do them any harm. Between 11.30 pm and 11.45 pm, the last two girls, Suzanne Farris and her friend Mary Ann Jordan came in, and made their statutory call to Miss Bisone from the kitchen telephone downstairs. When they reached the bedroom the intruder treated them like the rest, even down to repeating his assurance, that money, and not sex or murder, was all he wanted. Whatever the others thought about the young man's claim, Miss Amurao was unconvinced. After tying and gagging all the girls, he spent about half an

Chicago police forensic experts, Ray Heimbuch and William Scanlon, hunt for tell-tale clues at the murder scene. The team photographed prints.

hour rummaging through the house, presumably in search of cash. Then he came back and announced that he was 'taking them all out of there.'

First he took Miss Davy out of the room, and Miss Amurao listened to their footsteps going downstairs. About 25 minutes later he came back alone and escorted Miss Pasion out. Miss Amurao's fears were mounting, and by wriggling and rolling over she managed to squeeze herself right under one of the bunk beds and out of sight against the wall.

She heard the other girls being led out of the bedroom, one by one. She heard no screams, and after a while no further noise at all. Luckily for her, the intruder did not seem to have counted the girls as they came in. At 5.00 am she heard an alarm clock go off, and began to struggle with her bonds, guessing that it was safe to move. Half an hour later she was free, and shouting from the window ledge for help.

Strangled

Sergeant Murtaugh and his colleagues listened to her account in grim silence. Unlike Patrolman Kelly they had not actually dated any of the dead girls, but their work in the Homicide and Sex Crimes Division meant that they frequently went to the South Chicago Community Hospital, and they had shared coffee and jokes with all the victims.

Dr Toman made his report on the initial examination of the bodies. Only Miss Davy had not been stabbed. Several others had been both strangled and stabbed, while in most, the stab wounds themselves had caused death. Vaginal and oral swabs showed that none of the girls had been sexually assaulted.

Detectives Carlisle and Wallenda made a thorough survey of the nurses' quarters. They were able to report that none of the girls' purses contained any money, and Miss Amurao was able to tell them that 31 dollars in cash was missing from her own pocket book. The killer could have lifted 200 dollars or more from his gory haul. Carlisle added that he had watched Dr Toman's team removing the girls' bonds. 'They were good square knots,' he said. 'Their hands had been tied behind them with the backs of the wrists against each other and the palms facing outwards, exactly as the police handcuff prisoners. If you tie the

hands together with the palms facing inwards, the prisoner might be able to work his fingers to the knots.' Therefore, the killer was a man who knew how to tie knots, and it was also very possible that he had been arrested, in handcuffs, in his time. The obvious implication was that he was a seaman, which was particularly interesting to Murtaugh as, only half a block away from the scene of the murders, at 2335 East 100th Street, was a branch of the National Maritime Union.

One of the investigating teams discovered a further lead. He had described the killer to Richard Polo, who ran a gas station near the Indiana State Line. Polo said that he had seen a man answering the killer's description on Tuesday afternoon, the day before the murders. He had carried a small tartan flight bag and an overnight suitcase. He had been in Indiana, looking for work, but was now after a place to stay.

'He had a soft voice and a Southern accent,' said Polo. 'He told me he had slept on the beach by Lake Michigan on Sunday night, and in a rooming house on Monday, but the place was let when he got back on Tuesday. He asked if he could leave his bags with me, and I told him that it was O.K. Then he came back yesterday, Wednesday, to pick them up, and told me he had found a room at the Ship Yard Inn.'

Sergeant Murtaugh knew the Ship Yard Inn well. It was a cheap lodging house overlooking the Calumet Dry Dock, and was used mainly by seamen. At the Ship Yard Inn, the owner recognized the description immediately as that of a young man who had paid nine dollars for a week's rent. He had made a phone call, apparently to a sister in Chicago, and had checked out again. The owner had thought it very extravagant and strange at the time that it happened.

'Pay dirt'

Now the detectives were convinced that the trail was hot. Down at the Maritime Union Hall they 'hit pay dirt' as Murtaugh put it. The hiring agent at the hall remembered the young man, and added that he had been looking for a berth on a ship heading for New Orleans. That had been on Monday, and the agent, William O'Neill, had told him that the only job going was on a Great Lakes boat due to sail from Indiana Harbor. On Tuesday he had returned to say that the berth had been filled. O'Neill told him to come back Wednesday, and he had done so, but no jobs were available. 'The trouble was, he hadn't much experience,' said O'Neill, 'at least not judging by his application form.'

Sergeant Murtaugh almost leapt over the agent's counter, and reached for the application form. He quickly scanned it. 'Richard F. Speck. Description: Age 25; Height 6 feet; Weight 170 pounds; Color of hair, brown.' But the real bonus was the statutory passport-style photograph of the applicant.

Suspicions

By 2.00 pm on Thursday afternoon, almost every detective in Chicago's South Side had a copy of the picture. Murtaugh had run a computor check on the suspect, but he had no police record in Chicago. The Ship Yard Inn was staked out, as was Speck's sister's house, which had been traced from the telephone call Speck had made. The detectives had been careful not to let the sister, Mrs Martha Thornton, know about their suspicions towards her brother, in case he tried to contact her. A trap was cautiously laid. Sergeant Murtaugh's men moved into the Maritime Union in shirt sleeves and open collars. They were to pose as hiring agents. Then the trap was carefully baited. At 2.30 pm Mrs Thornton was telephoned and asked if she knew where her brother was. She said she had no idea.

'Well tell him to get to the hiring hall as soon as he gets in touch,' said the detective on the other end of the line. 'We have a job for him.' Forty minutes later the phone on the hiring hall desk rang. It was Speck. A union official took the call, and told Speck there was a job for him. 'On the Sinclair Great Lakes. Where are you now?'

'Downtown at Ruthie's,' came the reply.

'How long will it take you to get here?'

'About an hour,' said the caller, and hung up.

Twenty extra detectives were quickly stationed around the hall, but to Murtaugh's chagrin, Speck failed to show up. Presumably, he was being extra wary. In the mean-

time, the detectives had spoken to a number of seamen who filled out the picture. On the Monday, before the murder, Speck had been seen to arrive at the hall in a car driven by a woman. Another seaman had seen him on the Tuesday afternoon sitting in Luella Park, half a block away. From there Speck had a clear view of the back of 2319, East 100th Street, where the murdered nurses had lived. He had gone back from the park to the hall and then to Polo's gas station, to leave his bags. Then he had walked back to his rooming house, a run-down place called Pauline's. He had accepted the offer of a couch in the hall for Tuesday night as no rooms were available. On Wednesday morning he had picked up his bags, booked into the Ship Yard Inn, and had spent the day drinking in the downstairs bar.

The police now needed witnesses to Speck's movements immediately before and after the murders. They found William Kirkland, a 22-year-old laborer who had known Speck

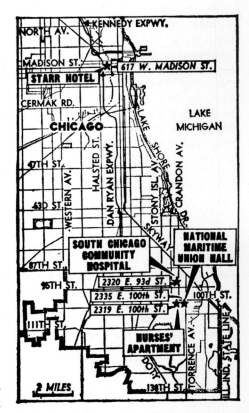

136

for some months, and he said that he had been drinking with their suspect at 7.00 am on Thursday morning at Pete's Tavern on Ewing Avenue, 11 blocks from the nurses' apartment. Speck had been drinking whiskey and beer chasers, and at one point had pulled out a hunting knife with a shiny, 12-inch blade which he said he had bought in Vietnam, while out there as a mer-

A deadly demonstration. Crawford, a barman at Pete's Bar, told police that Speck tried to show him how to kill with a knife. He told Crawford that his knife had already killed several people. Left: A police expert determines the truth of the claim.

chant seaman. 'I asked him if he wanted to sell it,' said Kirkland. 'I offered him a dollar and he gave me the knife.' Kirkland handed over the knife to the detectives.

The barman at Pete's, Ray Crawford, had a startling story to tell of Speck's Thursday morning session there. Speck had been joking around the bar buying drinks for people, spending around eight dollars. Suddenly he had pulled out the knife, grabbed Crawford from behind with one arm and put the knife to his throat. 'He was trying to show me how to kill a person,' said Crawford. 'I remember he said that the knife had killed several

people, and that was how he liked to kill them.'

Speck had left Pete's with another seaman, 'Red' Gerrald, who talked to Murtaugh's men. 'We hit three or four more bars,' said Gerrald. 'In one of them the radio gave out the news of the murders. Speck said it must have been a maniac who had done it.'

Amazing

At 7.45 am, said Gerrald, Speck had driven off in a cab for the Ship Yard Inn, and that was the last he had seen of him.

It was now late Thursday evening, but already the detectives were making steady headway. None of them felt like sleeping for the vision of the mutilated girls drove them on. All through the night the search went on for the cab driver who had driven Speck to the Ship Yard Inn and early on Friday morning he was traced. He had dropped Speck at North Sedgwick Street, where the suspect had paid him $5·90 cab fare.

North Sedgwick Street was a district of high rise apartment blocks. All morning, teams of investigators toiled up and down the lifts, knocking on doors, interviewing early risers who might have seen Speck. Again they had an amazing stroke of luck. Mrs Jo Holland lived on the twelfth floor of the 1300 block, where she spent most of her time sitting at a window, scanning the street below with a pair of high-powered binoculars. She had seen a young man get out of a cab at about 8.00 am the previous day, and had watched him turn south into Dearborn Street. She had even been able to make out the tattoo on his left arm, which was a serpent with the words 'Born to Raise Hell'. The tattoo was one of several identifying marks listed by a Coast Guard who, in response to Chicago police requests to all government departments, had discovered that Speck had once applied to join them. Furthermore, Miss Amurao had recovered sufficiently to identify Speck's photograph. Now all they had to do was find him, and find him fast before he killed again.

Relentless

Murtaugh's team combed the saloons and dives off Dearborn Street, relentlessly carrying on their inquiries. At the Twist Lounge a bouncer remembered seeing Speck

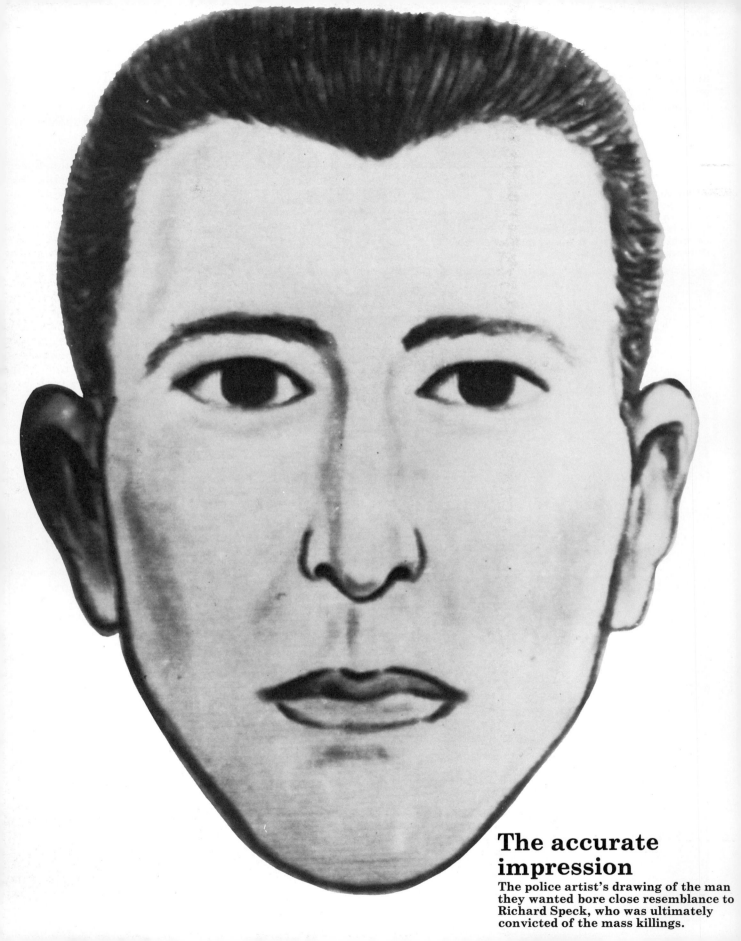

The accurate impression

The police artist's drawing of the man they wanted bore close resemblance to Richard Speck, who was ultimately convicted of the mass killings.

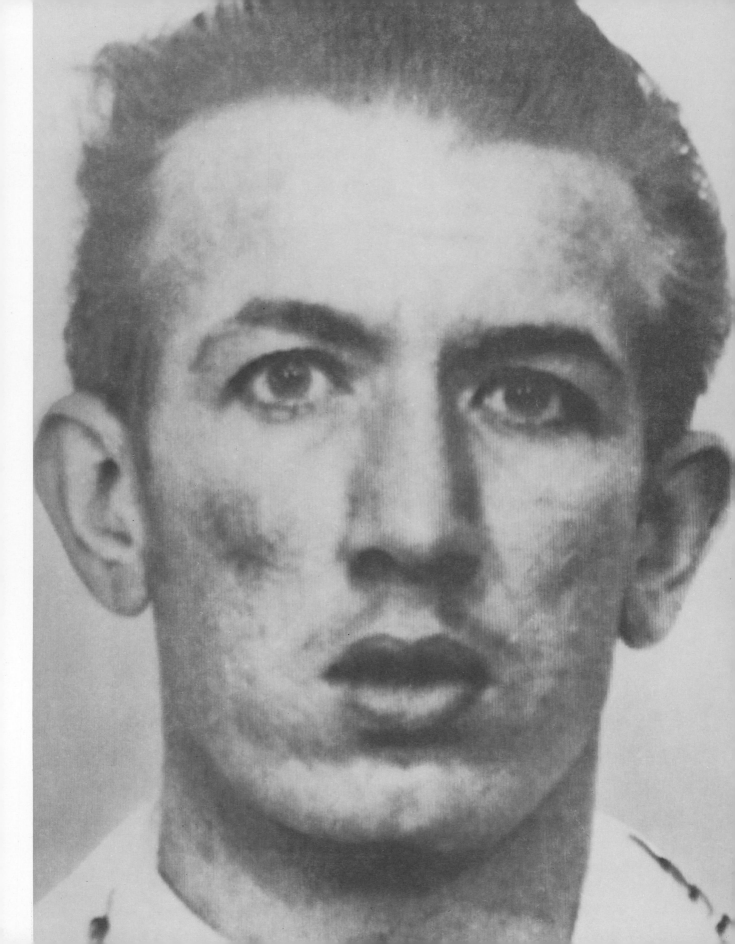

This unpleasant room in the skid row Starr Hotel was where Speck was found in a pool of blood. He had slashed his wrists with a broken bottle. He was taken to hospital, where a doctor recognized his face.

the previous night. Speck had left with a prostitute named Mary at about 3.00 am, and when detectives found her she confirmed that Speck had been with her. He had paid her a miserable dollar and left to go back to the Twist Lounge. The detectives found that he had met another prostitute there who had been with him at the Raleigh Hotel until 7.00 that morning. This time he had paid five dollars, and he had shown the girl a gun.

Murtaugh and his team raced the six blocks to the Raleigh, another seedy flop-house, and to their relief found that Speck was still registered. His room was searched and the detectives found a black jacket, some pants and a T-shirt, which fitted Miss Amurao's description of what the killer had been wearing. They had been freshly laundered. But there

was no gun, and when Murtaugh asked the clerk about it, he received a shock.

'He had a gun,' said the clerk. 'The girl who was with him reported it. I keep a legal house here, and I called the Chicago Avenue Police station to report it.'

Murtaugh called his colleagues at Chicago Avenue with a sick heart. He discovered that two patrolmen had actually interviewed Speck about the gun. Speck had told them that the prostitute had left it in his room, and they had believed him and let him go. However, they still had possession of the weapon, a ·22 caliber revolver.

Blunder

It soon became clear that Speck had taken fright, for by 10.00 o'clock on Saturday morning he had still not returned to the Raleigh.

Murtaugh had given the picture of the wanted man to his detectives only, to avoid the possibility of civil action should Speck be innocent. But there was now no need for

caution, as FBI fingerprint experts had found that Speck's prints matched those found in the blood-stained home of the victims. The wanted man had a long record of trouble. His most recent conviction had been for forgery, and he had drawn three years in a Texas penitentiary. Paroled in January 1965, he had been convicted again of assaulting a woman and threatening her with a knife, but due to a legal blunder he had escaped further imprisonment. His home was in Dallas, Texas although he had been born in Monmouth, Illinois, not far from Chicago.

On Saturday morning, the Chicago Police Department called a press conference, naming Speck for the first time as their main suspect, and publishing his picture. It appeared on posters, in the press and on TV that afternoon, and it got results, though not in quite the way Murtaugh expected. Shortly after midnight, the ambulance service got a call to the Starr Hotel, on West Madison, in Chicago's North Side. A young man

141

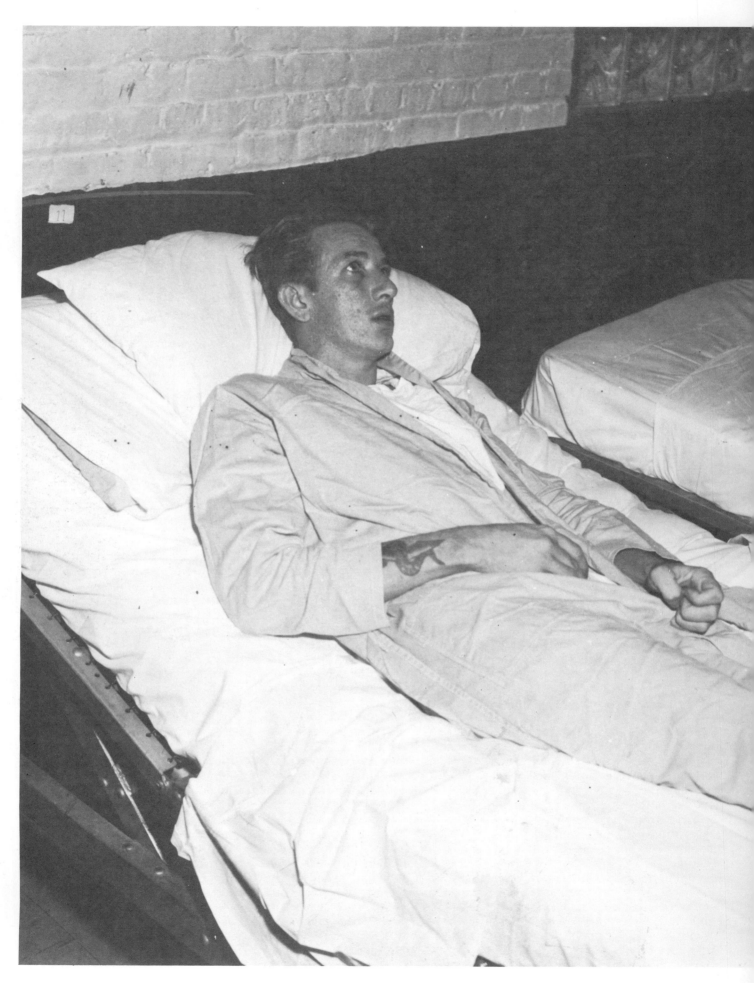

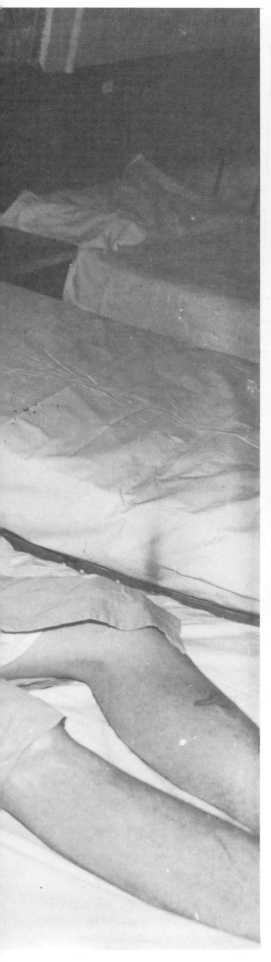

Speck recovered from his suicide attempt and was soon fit enough to go to court (above). The trial was switched to Peoria to guarantee him a fair hearing. He was convicted and given the death sentence, but this was commuted to life imprisonment.

who had registered earlier in the evening as 'B. Brian', had slashed his wrists with a broken bottle. He was rushed to Cook County Hospital's emergency department, where he was treated by Dr Leroy Smith and Dr Smith was just putting down a copy of the *Chicago Tribune* when the injured man was wheeled in. As the doctor washed the blood from the man's left forearm, a tattoo appeared: 'Born to Raise Hell'.

One glance at the pale face on the stretcher convinced Dr Smith, and he called the police. At 12.45 am on Sunday July 17, 67 hours after Miss Amurao had raised the alarm, Sergeant John Murtaugh formally charged Richard Franklin Speck with the first degree murder of the eight girls.

In April, 1967 a jury in Peoria, Illinois, found Speck guilty. He had been tried outside Chicago because his defense attorney pleaded that he would not get a fair trial there. The sentence was death, which was commuted to life imprisonment.

Sergeant Murtaugh and his team had solved Chicago's most bloody mass murder in record time. Few of them, from Patrolman Dan Kelly to Commander Flanagan, had slept a wink during those anxious hours, for not only had they been seeking a murderer, they had been avenging eight friends.

The

monster-hunters

Their only law is justice . . .
and their quest is international

AT THE END of World War II a special kind of investigator came into being. These men are dedicated and qualified in a way that no other group of lawmen have ever been before. It is the hope of the civilized world that they will never be needed again. Each man combines the qualities of the guerrilla fighter and the ace detective, and is, of necessity, anonymous. Unlike his counterpart in a normal detective force, he is ready to flout local laws to further the ends of a wider justice. And, unlike other investigators, he is driven by deep, personal motives. His job is to hunt down those members of the Nazi party who were responsible for killing six million people in Auschwitz, Buchenwald and Belsen. Like the six million dead, he is a Jew.

The first Nazi-hunters to dedicate their lives to the task of bringing to book their former persecutors were two very remarkable men. Simon Wiesenthal and Tuvia Friedman were both former inmates of the concentration camps. In the 1950's, their operations were spearheaded from the headquarters of the Israeli Intelligence Service in Tel Aviv. In 1958, the West German government set up the Central Office for the Prosecution of National Socialist Crimes in Ludwigsburg. The West Germans and the Israelis pooled information and gathered evidence to convict former Nazis of their crimes against humanity. One of their greatest triumphs has been the capture of former SS Lieutenant-Colonel Adolf Eichmann, which involved painstaking, patient, detective work, a hunt across many countries, and an extraordinarily dramatic finale. One of the hunters said afterwards, 'We set ourselves a prodigious task. It was like looking for a needle in a haystack – and finding it.'

Methodical

Eichmann was tall and bony, with large, protruberant ears and sparse black hair scraped back from his high forehead. He went about his monstrous tasks methodically, calmly, and with no more emotion than the manager of a string of abattoirs. In April, 1945, with the war rapidly nearing its end, Eichmann realized his danger and, like hundreds of other Nazi war criminals, he slipped under cover to avoid the Allied dragnet. His in-

Tuvia Friedman found the 'needle in the haystack'.

nocuous appearance made it possible to melt into the crowd.

He visited his home in Linz, Austria to say goodbye to his family, and to smack his eldest son as he said farewell. His wife explained later, 'He told me that he thought that this was the best way to part with the child, to implant some discipline in him.'

For a while, until the surrender of Germany, he went into hiding, helped by the head of the Austrian Gestapo. Then, disguised in the uniform of an airman, second class, in the Luftwaffe, and carrying the papers of 'Adolf Karl' he hitchhiked back to Germany and was captured by American soldiers. Conditions in Germany, however, were chaotic, and after resting for a while, Eichmann casually walked out of the prison camp in which he was being held, and escaped. He managed to obtain a new uniform, this time that of a Lieutenant in the 22

Cavalry Division, and the name 'Otto Eckmann', but was captured again. He then bought some civilian papers, in the name of 'Otto Heninger', escaped once more, changed into civilian clothes and began to look for work. He became the manager of a chicken battery farm and stayed there for a few months, while all around him Allied Intelligence officers searched for the real Adolf Eichmann and his ex-colleagues.

After establishing an identity for himself, Eichmann felt it time to make his next move. He contacted ODESSA, the *Organisation de SS Angehoerigen*, an organization which, run under the cover of a legitimate welfare group, helped former Nazis escape their fate. Eichmann was sent along one of its underground routes, through Austria and Italy to Genoa, where he was lodged as a simple 'refugee' at a Franciscan monastery.

On July 14, 1950, he received a

Simon Wiesenthal, the world's leading Nazi-hunter, regards himself as advocate on behalf of 11 million dead.

passport in the name of Ricardo Klement, and papers which described him as an Italian-German mechanic, whose home had been Bolzano, Italy. Four weeks later he escaped to Buenos Aires.

For two years he worked for a construction firm which employed a number of ex-Nazis, in the township of Tucuman, at the foot of the Andes. Eventually, his wife and three sons were able to join him there. In 1956, he became an employee of the Mercedes Benz company in Buenos Aires, and settled down in a little house in the suburbs.

Eichmann felt completely safe. He had covered his trail sufficiently well for the United Nations War Crimes Organization to admit that they had no idea where he was. Ricardo Klement was confident that Adolf Eichmann had disappeared from the public eye for good.

Meanwhile, in Austria, Wiesenthal and Friedman had Eichmann very

much in mind. As early as 1950 they had begun to try to trace him. Their principal lead was his wife, still at that time living in Linz, and according to one rumor, a friend of Mrs Eichmann acted as go-between for the woman and her missing husband. Wiesenthal and Friedman planted a girl agent as a housemaid in the friend's home, and the agent carefully steamed open letters and monitored telephone calls for months. But she found no mention of the former SS man. Gradually the girl struck up an acquaintance with Mrs Eichmann herself. Vera Eichmann, left alone with the task of bringing up her three sons Klaus, Hans, and Dieter, was only too glad of feminine company, and the children took to their mother's new friend. The agent took the children for walks and told them stories – and every evening she telephoned Wiesenthal. Depressingly, each night the story was the same. Adolf Eichmann seemed to be

totally out of touch with his wife. When Vera Eichmann moved out of the area to a smaller house, Wiesenthal reluctantly admitted that that part of the trail seemed to be a dead end.

Meanwhile, Tuvia Friedman was correlating reports of sightings from all over the world. Eichmann had allegedly been seen in Egypt, Kuwait, Syria, Turkey, Spain, Damascus and even Germany. Each claim was meticulously checked out and each found to be false. Eventually, Friedmann, now working from Israel, had to admit like Wiesenthal that all leads seemed to have been played out.

Then in 1959, the West German Nazi-Hunters in Ludwigsburg contacted Tel Aviv with a tip which they had received from a 'usually reliable' foreign source. Eichmann was working at the Mercedes Benz plant in Buenos Aires, under the pseudonym Ricardo Klement. The hunt was on again.

The first problem the Israeli Secret Service were faced with was that no extradition treaty existed between the Argentine and Israel, particularly where war criminals were concerned. The Argentine Government had overtly turned a blind eye to the presence of a number of ex-Nazis in their country. If Klement did turn out to be Eichmann, he would have to be spirited out of his new country without the authorities knowing, and there would be no diplomatic immunity for the agents if they were caught.

A skilled Hungarian-Jewish agent, himself a former concentration camp inmate, was flown out to Buenos Aires. Quite apart from the diplomatic problem, there were other troubles that faced him. So far no one had a clear photograph of Eichmann in his heyday, for he had gone about his tasks for the Fuehrer in what in other circumstances would have been decent obscurity. So how was the secret agent to know whether Klement was indeed the missing Nazi?

Recognition

Matters were made only marginally better when the agent tracked down the address of the Klement's home from casual enquiries among Benz workers. He recognized Vera Eichmann easily. Wiesenthal had had photographs taken of Mrs Eichmann and her first three children in Linz. She had had another child since leaving Austria. However, it was perfectly possible that the original informant had just assumed, on recognizing Vera Eichmann, that the man she lived with was her Nazi husband. The man could be a perfectly innocent Argentinian. If it was Eichmann, the agent would have to be very careful not to alarm him in any way. He had already shown his ability to slide through the finest nets like a grass snake.

Fortunately, the agent found a room in a house overlooking the Klement home, and spent some days watching the family. Then he decided to take a more positive approach. He had mentioned in the neighborhood that he was a representative of the Singer Sewing Machine Company, and one day he called on a neighbor of the Klements with a cover story. His company, he told the lady that

With one signature (right) Eichmann could send thousands to their deaths, but in the evenings he preferred his other role, that of the loving father to his son Horst.

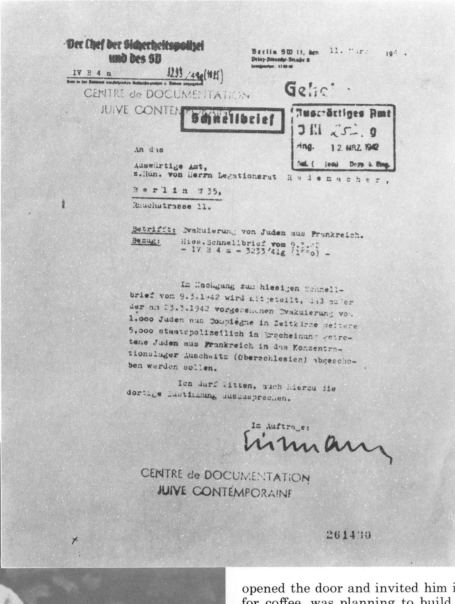

opened the door and invited him in for coffee, was planning to build a factory in Argentina, and felt that this locality was excellent as a site. Would she be willing to sell her house? She said that she supposed so, if the price was right.

'I wonder how your neighbors would react,' the agent asked. 'Klement, I believe they are called?' To his alarm, the woman said; 'That's right. I don't know what they would think. I'll phone Mrs Klement and ask her.'

Before he could stop her or think of an excuse, she had picked up the phone and dialled Vera Eichmann's number. It was natural, of course, that a Singer representative should make enquiries if his company were planning to build a factory, but any hint of suspicion might send Eichmann running for cover.

When she returned from the telephone the woman told the agent that Mrs Klement had promised to talk to her husband about it. 'I don't know what he'll say,' she volunteered. 'The Klements don't mix with the rest of us very much. They're not very forthcoming. They used to be German, I believe. He works at a car plant in the city.'

The agent did not pursue the matter directly with the Klements. Instead he concentrated on getting a good photograph of the car plant worker. One bright Sunday he looked out of his window and saw Klement digging his garden. Using a tele-photo lens, the agent took a whole reel of film of the man from various angles. Then he paid his rent and flew back to Tel Aviv.

'Good old days'

The photographs were quite clear and showed a fair likeness to the missing man. The prominent ears, the bony, big-nosed face, the sparse black hair going grey, all fitted the wartime descriptions. Few concentration camp survivors had been near enough to Eichmann to look at him closely and he had been fastidious in keeping away from the more unpleasant aspects of his work. A West German agent was given the job of combing through old wartime magazines, and finally came up with a faded, blurred shot which showed Eichmann at an early Nazi rally. An Israeli photographic specialist compared the two pictures, detailing particular features, and was able to announce that they could be of the same man, but more than that he could not say with certainty.

An agent named Molnar was rather more positive. He had seen Eichmann briefly in Budapest in 1944, and though the Argentine pictures were of a thinner, older person, he was convinced that Klement was their man. Molnar and a team of assistants were dispatched to the Argentine. Molnar, like all the best undercover men, was an excellent actor. He posed as a German businessman with right-wing political views, and mingled easily with the expatriate German community in Buenos Aires. One night at a cocktail party when most of the guests had had a good deal to drink, he brought the conversation around to the 'good old days' of the Third Reich. To his amazement, his ploy was immediately successful. One of his drinking companions said: 'Yes,

I was only thinking about those times the other day while I was up at the Mercedes Benz plant. Eichmann is working there now you know. What a come-down it must be for him.'

Molnar passed on the information, and then sought confirmation. First he watched at the factory gates as Klement left for home. As far as he could be, Molnar was sure that this was his quarry. To make absolutely certain, he began to drink in bars frequented by officials of the Argentine Government.

One of them, in the visas office, was short of money. Molnar offered to help him if he could identify the man named Klement, and find out Klement's previous name. The following night the Argentine official returned. 'His name was Eichmann,' he said.

Years later, the Israeli Secret Service were to use 'hit squads' in their campaign against terrorists, to the eventual embarrassment of them-

Eichmann (above right) sails to safety in Argentina. The plan was arranged by ODESSA, who also saw to it that Ricardo Klement, as he was known, had proper identification documents.

selves and their supporters. In this case, the Israelis felt that summary 'execution' on the spot was unthinkable. Eichmann had carried out plans for mass murder without trial. It must be seen that his captors were not afflicted with the same disregard for justice. He had to be brought back to Israel and given a fair trial before the whole world.

The big difficulty was how to remove him from his new home. The Argentinian Government obviously knew who he was, and did not seem to care. There would be no assistance from that quarter. It was at this point that the giant, years-long operation departed from normal 'police' procedure, and the Secret Servicemen in Tel Aviv planned the 'big-snatch'.

Meticulous

There was one local factor which might help them. During the official May celebrations, which mark the anniversary of the first Argentinian Government, public offices and banks were to be closed, and there would be feasting and dancing and a general wild air of carnival in the streets. In order to let customs men enjoy themselves like anyone else, the government traditionally relaxed their immigration and emigration controls. It was obvious to the Israelis that their men must strike in May.

In April, 1960, four crack Israeli commando officers landed in Buenos Aires. For a fortnight they tailed Eichmann to and from work, and discovered that his meticulous habits had not changed. He went to work and returned to his home at the same time each day. He took the same buses, and he always alighted in the evening at the local bus station and walked the last few hundred yards to his home.

On the evening of May 11, Eichmann reached the bus station and buttoned up his raincoat against the drizzle which was steadily falling. Away from the streetlamps, which lit the road to his house, were parked two black saloon cars, their engines idling. As Eichmann drew level with them, two Israelis stepped out and blocked his path. The astonished German reached in his pocket for the hand-torch he always kept there. Thinking that he was reaching for a gun, one of the men stepped forward and, with a chop to the neck, knocked him unconscious. Then

Vera Eichmann and her son Haas return to Buenos Aires after the execution.

Two years after the hanging, Horst Eichmann joins the Argentine Nazi Party.

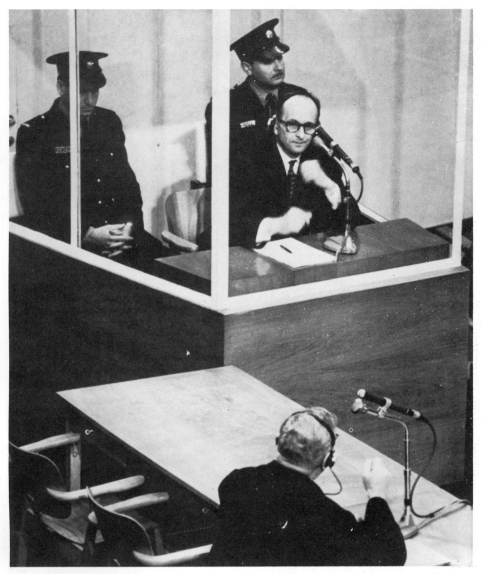

Man in the glass booth . . . Eichmann consults his counsel Robert Servatius.

Eichmann was bundled into the back of one of the cars and driven to a small farmhouse which was to serve as a hide-out.

During the next few weeks, Eichmann shared the house with his captors. He was not physically ill-treated, but the cold intensity of their questioning began to wear him down. Finally, he said, 'Very well. I am Adolf Eichmann. I am willing to stand trial either in Argentina or West Germany.' The four commandos laughed. 'You do not have very much choice in the matter, my friend,' one said softly. They insisted that he sign a paper stating that he was leaving Argentina of his own free will, and was prepared to be judged publicly according to Israeli law. Eichmann complained that his head was aching, and for some time he sat with his large brow buried in his hands. Finally he sat up. 'All right,' he said. 'I am prepared to proceed to Israel for trial.'

Celebrations

On May 24, a Bristol Britannia airliner touched down on the almost deserted tarmac of Buenos Aires airport, and disgorged a number of stern men who told the skeleton staff of officials at customs that they were a charter flight, and had come to see the celebrations. The customs men waved them through. At midnight on May 25, the men returned with five companions. As the customs people had not counted the original number of passengers, the extra number was not noticed. A day later, the big Britannia rolled to a halt at the end of a Tel Aviv runway, and the search for Eichmann was over.

Eichmann's trial was, as the Israelis had intended, observed by reporters and officials from all over the world. Throughout, the thin-faced killer stood in a sound-proof, bullet-proof glass case, listening to the proceedings through earphones which flattened his protruding ears. He was tried on fifteen charges of superintending the deaths of six million Jews.

Eichmann's only defense was that the number should be five, not six million, and that, in his words 'Befehl ist Befehl' – orders are orders. The nature of those orders had never seemed to trouble him. The panel of judges found him guilty, and he was hanged in 1962, after 17 years of dodging the hangman's noose.

The end of the long hunt. Crowds in Jerusalem read of Eichmann's execution.

The curious cat-burglar

Whose fingerprints were in the Count's bedroom?

THE USE OF FINGERPRINTS for identification purposes was first suggested in 1823, by Professor J.E. Burkinje, at the Physiology Department of the University of Breslau (then in Prussia, now in Poland). Yet it was not until the turn of the century that the technique was considered to be sufficiently reliable to be admissible as conclusive evidence in the courts. Even then, fingerprint evidence has its uncertain moments. The oddest case in point was that of the Parisian cat burglar. As things turned out, 'cat' burglar was perhaps less than an appropriate description.

This bizarre case was recounted by the distinguished criminologist H. T.F. Rhodes in his book *Clues on Crime*, published in 1933.

During the summer of 1910, a series of daring jewel robberies took place in Paris, delighting the press and baffling the police. The *modus operandi* in each case was the same. They always took place late at night or in the early hours of the morning, and the victim was always someone who lived completely alone. What was most odd was the fact that front door locks had been forced or smashed, and safes had been burned open with acetylene torches, all without the sleeping owner waking or hearing a thing. Had there been servants on the premises, or someone else who could have administered a drug, the police might have thought that they had the answer, but the facts were that on the night of each theft the occupier had been sleeping alone on his premises.

Burned open

At eight o'clock one morning in September, the police were telephoned by the wealthy bachelor Count de Commercy; his elegant apartment on the top floor of a building near the Tuileries had been broken into, and some valuable family heirlooms stolen. Fifteen minutes later, a Detective Superintendent, a finger print expert and two other officers were greeted in the hallway of the flat by the Count, still clad in his silk pyjamas and dressing gown. He looked tousled and drowsy, and as they walked in the policemen noted that his front door had been forced open from the outside with a jemmy. A tall vase near the Count's open bedroom window had been broken, and the wall safe in the study had been burned open. Otherwise

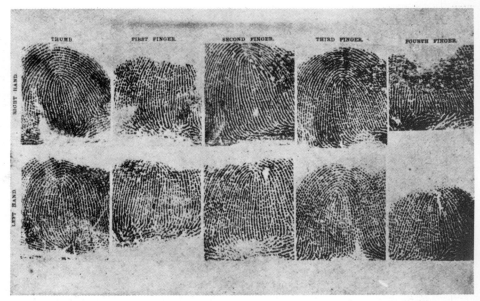

The fingerprints of a chimpanzee (above) are similar to a human's (left).

nothing else was touched.

The Superintendent asked the Count if he lived alone, although he guessed the answer before it came. The Count confirmed that he was the only person resident on the premises. His housekeeper came early every morning to clean and make his lunch, and left in the afternoon. He usually dined out with friends in the evening, as he had done the previous night.

He usually dined out with friends in the evening, as he had done the previous night.

The Superintendent put the next obvious question as tactfully as possible. Had the Count perhaps had a little too much to drink the night before? The Count shook his head with a smile. 'I have never been a heavy drinker,' he said. 'I never drink before dinner, and then I have perhaps half a bottle of wine or less, with a cognac to go with coffee. That's all I had yesterday evening.'

In answer to further questions, the Count confirmed that he had returned home at about 11.00 pm, and had opened the front door with his own key. The door had been firmly locked and intact. He had gone to his study for some papers, which he kept in the safe, and that too, had been undamaged.

'But there is one odd thing,' he added. 'Normally I am a very light sleeper, and I usually awake at six o'clock. This morning I awoke at eight after having slept very heavily, with a slight headache and a bitter taste in my mouth.'

Did the Count think that he could have been drugged, asked the Super-

intendent? It certainly seemed so. 'But I can't see how,' was the reply. 'I ate with my usual small group of friends, all of whom I know well, at our usual restaurant, and felt all right then. When I came home I had nothing to eat or drink but a glass of water from the jug which I always keep beside my bed, I began to feel drowsy and dropped off to sleep about half an hour later.'

Dizzy drop

The Superintendent indicated the open bedroom window, with the broken vase beneath it. Was the window open when the Count came in? 'Yes,' he confirmed, 'I opened it myself. I like plenty of fresh air. But I doubt very much whether anyone could have got in that way to drug my drinking water.'

When he looked out of the window, the Superintendent saw the Count's point. The apartment was four stories up, and a dizzy drop of 50 feet lay between the window and the street. True, a drainpipe ran close by, but it was smooth and slippery to touch. No one but an expert climber could have scaled it in order to get into the bedroom.

By now the housekeeper had arrived, and the fingerprint expert had taken her prints and those of the Count for comparison with any found in the apartment. The police left, with a promise to keep in touch.

Back at headquarters, the fingerprint man went to work with his microscope and a few hours later had his report for his chief. Most of the prints taken from the flat were

Arches

Loops

Whorls

Composites

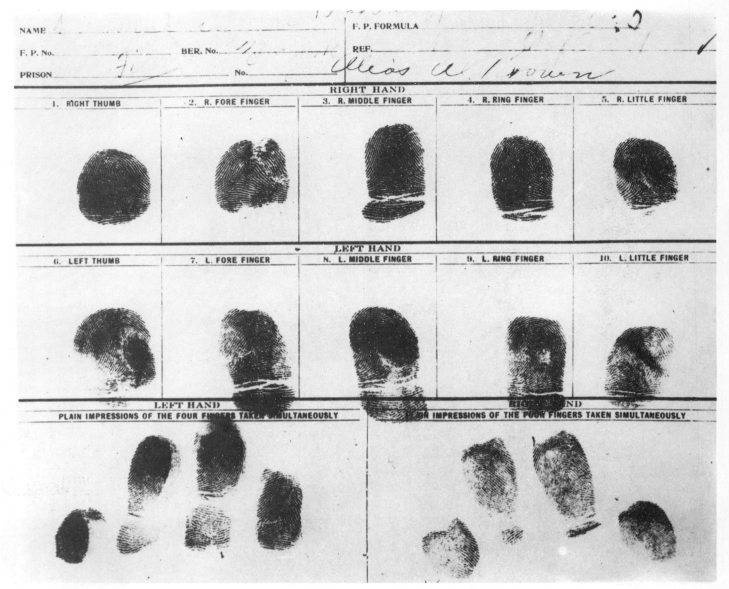

The world's most notorious fingerprints – those of Al Capone, in the Chicago Police Department.

made by either the Count or the housekeeper, but there were further prints, in the Count's bedroom. They were rather unusual, very small, perhaps of a boy, and of what the fingerprint officer described as 'belonging to a criminal and degenerate type'. In those days, there was a popular notion, long since repudiated, that hand shapes indicated the type and state of mind of the owner. However, there were no records of the owner of these prints on police files.

The Superintendent put his men to search underworld haunts, looking and listening for news of villains who employed a young boy without a criminal record. The search was fruitless. Sometimes young people had been used by the Paris criminal fraternity, but none of them had the spectacular climbing ability needed

in a case like this. Meanwhile the police laboratory had analysed the water taken from the Count's bedside jug. It contained traces of a powerful sedative which would hardly register on the palate, particularly as the Count was a cigar smoker.

Back at his office, the Superintendent laid out his problems on paper, in the form of notes for himself.

1. While the Count was at dinner, somebody entered the apartment and put a drug in the water by his bedside.

2. The front door had not been forced at this time. If they had managed to get into the flat to drug the water, why had they bothered to force open the door later on?

3. Whoever put the drug into the

water must have entered the flat through the window as there was no other way in. (Or could the drug have been administered by the housekeeper before she went off duty? Remember to ask the Count how long the woman had been in his service.)

4. The intruder's fingerprints were found only in the Count's bedroom. Why only there? There must be a connection between these prints and the drug.

Again the Superintendent called on the Count and asked him about the housekeeper. The answers to his questions were depressingly unpromising. She was unmarried, had a few highly respectable friends, and had worked for the Count for 12 years, during which time she had

As the Paris case proved, chimpanzees can perform acts of dexterity.

proved to be an able and extremely conscientious servant.

Pondering the series of blanks and dead ends which faced him, the Superintendent called in the fingerprint man again, in near despair.

Unlikely theory

'Look,' he said. 'This boy's fingerprints were found in the Count's bedroom, and no boy could surely have climbed that distance up the drainpipe. The physical strength needed, apart from the climbing skill, would make it impossible. Have you nothing else at all which might be of assistance?' The fingerprint officer pondered a little, and then said that there was something, but it seemed as unlikely as the other theory. 'I told you there was something unusual about the prints,' he said. 'They could have belonged to a degenerate boy: they *might* have belonged to a chimpanzee.'

Then the Superintendent realized what the shape of the hands, with their peculiarly-placed thumb prints, had reminded him of. He had done some research and discovered that in certain members of the chimpanzee family the loops and the whorls of the prints were very similar to those of the human hand. Was it possible that a chimp could be trained to climb a drainpipe, tip a drug into a jug of water, and then climb back down again? It seemed extremely unlikely, but it was the only remaining lead. He made inquiries to find out if any Paris criminal owned a chimpanzee.

It was then that one of those lucky breaks, which have often aided even the most astute law officers, occurred, in the form of a knife murder. A woman criminal was found with a dagger of oriental design sticking in her back, and evidence suggested that her killer had thrown it rather than stabbed her with it. The evidence also pointed to an Egyptian woman, a criminal associate of the victim, who had been a skilful knife-thrower in the circus world. The police called on her in an attempt to bully or cajole a confession out of her. While in the woman's apartment, a detective heard a strange scuffling noise coming from an adjacent room. Throwing open the door, he found a large male chimpanzee.

Experiment

The animal and his mistress were taken back to headquarters, where the Superintendent waited eagerly. With the woman in the cells he called for a jug and a small bottle of water. He placed the jug on the desk, and then, as his colleagues watched, agog with interest, he gave the small bottle to the chimp. The creature gripped it tightly for a few moments, and then bounded across the room, swung up onto the desk, uncorked the bottle with its teeth, and tipped the contents into the jug. Then, with the cork and bottle clutched in its hand, it hopped down and shambled across the room again.

'I think we have found the culprit,' the Superintendent said.

Fingerprint checks quickly revealed that the prints at Count de Commercy's apartment had been made by the same monkey which the Superintendent held in custody. Further checks in the Count's apartment revealed the presence of a form of lice which never attach themselves to humans but are found in monkeys of various types.

So the method by which the crime had been carried out was solved, with the animal virtually proving its own 'guilt'. Unfortunately, despite stringent efforts by the Superintendent, no conclusive evidence could be found to link the woman who owned the animal with either the knife murder or the series of robberies. The animal could obviously not be brought to trial, and the two were reluctantly released. When the woman was arrested on a serious charge some days later, however, and sent to jail, the jewel robberies ceased. So the Superintendent had proved to his own satisfaction that he had solved the mysteries.

Murder without a motive

The San Francisco 'Paper Bag' killer

THE APPARENTLY MOTIVELESS psychopathic killer is the criminal that experienced police officers dread more than any other. The psychopath whose illness shows itself in sex crimes, is at least predictable. His attacks stem either from distorted lust or, occasionally, from a puritanical hatred of sexuality. His victims, too, usually follow a pattern. They may be young girls, prostitutes, or homosexuals, but this at least gives detectives some sort of line to work on.

In his widely studied book *Crime and the Sexual Psychopath*, Dr J. Paul De River says of the sex killer, 'The disregard for all law, whether made by man or God, in (the psychopath's) striving to gain his will for power, and the fantasy, actual or imagined, of the torture and pain of his helpless victim, throws (the psychopath) into a state of clouded consciousness ... he ... often is very clever in carrying out his crimes and covers his tracks so that he will not be apprehended.' The disregard for civil or moral law, and the cunning and stealth, are also part of the make up of the 'non sexual' psychopath. Like his sex-motivated counterpart, he is only 'mad' sporadically and for the rest of the time he might lock the details of his acts out of his consciousness. With no immediately obvious pattern or motive to his killings, the psychopath's crimes may not be linked together. As a final obstacle, most demented murderers do not, contrary to the evidence of horror films and crime fiction, look particularly different from their fellows. Indeed, a high percentage of them tend towards great personal charm, lulling their victims into easy familiarity with them. It is only then that they strike.

Sharp pain

For all these reasons, the San Francisco Police Department can be forgiven for not realizing that they had a pyschopath on their hands when a stabbing was reported to them in December, 1972. A plump, balding businessman from Phoenix, Arizona had walked into the men's room of the Greyhound bus depot near Market Street, San Francisco, aiming to freshen up.

He was aged 54, quite successful, and walked with a slight limp as the result of an accident in his childhood. As he leaned over the basin to splash

water on his face, an arm came over his shoulder, and as he straightened up he felt a sudden sharp pain in his chest.

He had been stabbed, and as he slumped to the floor, bleeding and fast losing consciousness, he heard only the sound of his attacker's feet running across the tiles. He had seen nothing. Fortunately the wound was not serious, and after a couple of days he was able to leave the hospital and resume his affairs. Six weeks later, however, the same man was walking along Powell Street, two blocks away from the scene of the assault, when a young man with long, blond hair ran towards him with a knife in his hand. This time the businessman was ready. He was stockily built and, despite his age, he aimed a punch at the young man's head and almost downed him. The youth dropped the knife and ran back up the street, straight into the arms of two patrolmen. 'You sure have one hell of a city here,' said the businessman, as he made out his statement at the San Francisco Hall of Justice. 'I'll be glad to get back home.'

Too busy

The young man was charged with attempted assault with a deadly weapon, and the case against him looked water-tight. Just before the trial was about to come up, the San Francisco District Attorney's office contacted their main witness who had gone back to Phoenix. Weeks had elapsed since his visit to California, and the businessman had a major deal to attend to on his home territory. He was sorry, he said, but he could not spare the time to come back to San Francisco to give evidence. As the potential victim refused to testify, the case had to be dropped, and the blond, young man was released.

The waterfront city of San Francisco has more than its fair share of murders and attempted murders. Its undermanned Homicide Department consisted of eight, two-man teams of officers, who worked on a rota basis, and the department was manned at all hours of the day, every day. Because of the pressure of the amount of work, the routine report of the assaults on the visiting businessman was perfunctorily read and filed.

On Tuesday, October 16, 1973,

patrolmen Alex Barron and Tom Burns were cruising in the Market Street area when a message crackled over their car radio. They were to proceed immediately to 345 Third Street, where a shooting had just taken place. Slamming his foot on the throttle, patrolman Barron threw his car around into Third Street, just as the ambulance raced away with its siren wailing.

The place where the wounded man had lain was marked with a chalk outline and a wide patch of sticky blood.

Gun shots

Barron and Burns interviewed the shocked bystanders. A parking lot attendant had seen the incident. According to him, an elderly man, who was short, stocky and balding, had been limping up the street when a young, blond-haired man had come chasing after him. The youth had held a small brown paper bag, which looked as if it might contain sandwiches, in his right hand. But the bag did not contain sandwiches. As the youth came up behind the old man he held it out at arm's length and the parking attendant had seen the bottom blow out as three gun shots hit the limping man in the back of the head, the neck and the shoulder. Before anyone quite realized what had happened the gunman had carried on running north towards Market Street and had vanished into the crowds.

The ambulance took the victim to the San Francisco Mission Emergency Hospital, where doctors began to clean up his wounds, but there was little they could do. One bullet had shattered his brain and lodged in the frontal bone of his skull. He died without regaining consciousness.

'Starsky'

The team 'on call' at the Homicide Division that day consisted of Inspector Frank Falzon and Detective Jack Cleary. Inspector Falzon was a remarkable young man. He had been assigned to the Bureau of Inspectors in 1969, when he was scarcely 26 years old, becoming one of the youngest police officers ever to achieve such rank in San Francisco. Since graduating, he had worked in the black ghetto area of Fillmore, and then in the ironically-named Tenderloin district as a vice squad officer. Now 33, with dark, good looks and curling hair, he bore a passing resemblance to 'Starsky' the fictional TV detective. His partner was more prosaic but totally reliable. He was a bulky, balding, 40-year-old cop who chewed cigars and had a reputation for thoroughness.

When Falzon and Cleary arrived at the scene, little was left to mark the spot except the chalked body outline, the sanded bloodstain, and a folded copy of that day's *Racing Form*, a gambling newspaper which the victim had apparently been carrying.

Valuable

Falzon scouted the gutter and sidewalk, looking for spent cartridge cases; their absence meant that the pistol had been a revolver, rather than an automatic, which ejects empty shells. Using the list of witnesses compiled by patrolmen Barron and Burns, the two detectives began to build up a picture of the scene. The killer was a white, male adult, aged between 18 and 22, height 5 ft 9 ins, 130 lbs in weight, with shoulder length blond hair. He had been wearing a pair of faded jeans and a yellow shirt. None of the witnesses remembered having seen the killer before. Most of the witnesses had known the old man by sight, though not by name. He had often been up around the gambling and betting houses in Market Street, buying form sheets for the horse races at Bay Meadows track, which was a regular venue of his.

One witness was rather more valuable than the others. Anthony Miller lived in a third floor apartment at the corner where Third Street was interrupted by a parking lot. He had heard shots, and had looked out in time to see the killer running away from his prostrate victim. Miller had watched the blond man, with the gun still in his hand, run into the parking lot and tear off the yellow T-shirt he was wearing. Underneath he had another, green, shirt. He had run back to Third Street and then walked rapidly to a white van parked some distance away from the scene of the shooting. He got into the van and drove off. Miller had been unable to see the license number.

Back at headquarters, Falzon and Cleary discovered that the Mission Emergency Hospital had traced the man whose corpse lay in their morgue. He was 70-year-old Lorenzo Carniglia, and his address was 525 Texas Street, a respectable, working class area in the Potrero district. The immediate cause of death had been the bullet through the head, although a second bullet had penetrated the chest cavity and lodged in his clothes. The bullets were fired by a ·22 caliber pistol.

When the two sleuths started checking into Carniglia's background, they found several possible leads. He was described as being a house painter, but he had been far from that. Since coming to the United States from his native Italy many years before, he had by careful wheeling and dealing acquired eight residential buildings on the San Francisco Bay side of the city, as well as several houses on Texas Street. Despite his age, he was a drinker and a womanizer. He gambled at Bay Meadows whenever races were being run there, and though a rigidly honest businessman, he was reputed to keep a check on every dollar. Falzon discovered that he actually toured each of his apartment blocks in person every week, collecting the rents himself.

So there could be several reasons why people wanted him 'rubbed'; women, gambling, or money. Falzon and Cleary exhaustively checked the first two possibilities and found nothing to go on. His family were convinced that the third alternative might yield the truth, and for a while Falzon agreed with them.

T-shirt

On a tour of the man's properties they came to Hunter's Point, a block which was largely populated by blacks. One of the tenants laughed when they told him what they had come for. He was a big man, and he made no bones about the fact that he was not shedding tears over Carniglia's death. If he had been the killer, he said, he would have made a protracted job of it. Falzon checked the black man out and got nowhere.

Two weeks after the killing, the detectives had no further lead on old Carniglia's sudden death on Third Street. But they had one possible clue. They found the yellow T-shirt on the parking lot. The detectives called a press conference and pictures of the shirt's curious, tie-dyed pattern were shown on TV and in the papers. Again there was no result. The trail of the blond gunman seemed to have come to a dead end.

Over the following weeks, Falzon and Cleary dealt with numerous other killings in the violent city. And then, on Thursday, December 20, a freezing-cold day, Homicide received notification of another shooting. At 8.50 am, a hobo in a long, ill-fitting and ragged overcoat had been picking about the trash cans outside the Life Line Mission on Market Street, where it met Fifth and Folsom Streets. His weary-looking back was turned to the gas station on the corner. The Reverend Ralph Eichenbaum, minister at the Life Line, who knew the scavenging man by sight, was sitting in his car thinking out the short sermon he would give before handing out free breakfasts. He guessed that, as he had been present for the last few weeks, the man in the long torn overcoat would be there listening to him again this morning.

Similarities

Suddenly, Mr Eichenbaum saw a slim young man wearing a blue hooded anorak and a knitted wool cap over long blond hair walk briskly from the gas station and up towards the man by the trash cans. Under his arm he held a long Safeways supermarket bag made of shiny, stiff paper. Three feet away from the scavenger, the young man stripped off the paper bag to reveal a single barrelled shotgun. The man by the garbage bins straightened up and turned, his jaw sagging.

Without showing a sign of emotion, the young man pointed the gun straight at him and pulled the trigger. The ragged man's features disintegrated into an oval of torn flesh, and he fell without a sound to the sidewalk. The young man turned on his heel and walked quickly back to the gas station, still holding the shotgun in his hand. He climbed into a white van, threw the gun onto the passenger seat and drove off.

Falzon and Cleary were on the scene within minutes. Although they were not 'on call' at the time, the paper bag concealing the gun, the blond killer, and the white getaway van linked this shooting with that of Carniglia. There were other similarities too. The hobo was short, stocky, and balding and, according to the Life Line staff, he had walked with a slight limp.

There were few clues to be found on the body. A razor blade and scissors, carefully wrapped in paper, a pair of spectacles, a comb, a ball point pen and eleven cents were all he had. According to the Reverend Eichenbaum, the man had attended at the morning, free breakfast sessions at the Mission for three or four weeks, and although he had given no name the minister thought that he lived nearby. Falzon and Cleary began checking out neighborhood rooming houses. At a broken down hotel on the corner of Sixth and Howard Streets the description was recognized. The victim's name was Ara Kuznezow, and in his otherwise bare room the detectives found a New York City welfare card.

The New York authorities had little to add. Kuznezow was 54 years old and a native of Russia. He had trained as an architect in his youth, but had no recognized American qualifications.

Final clue

Falzon compared his notes on the two cases. Both victims had been immigrants, elderly, with bald heads, stocky figures, and both had walked with a limp. They were gunned down suddenly on the street by a young, blond man who had carried his weapon in a paper bag. Paper is notoriously difficult where fingerprint lifting is concerned. Most surfaces do not preserve prints at all, or, if they do, the prints are not good enough to be used. In the case of the Safeways bag, the detectives were lucky. The gunman had left it lying by his victim, and its stiff and shiny exterior yielded several fingerprints. The San Francisco forensic technicians lifted these and compared them with their files, but they reported to Falzon that they had nothing comparable on record. They were wrong. Whether through haste or inefficiency, they had made a mistake. The final clue left to the homicide team was the white van. No one had seen the license number, and there were thousands of white or light colored vans in the San Francisco area, but it was the only lead left to the man the newspapers were now calling the 'Paper Bag Slayer'. The detectives tried to narrow the hunt down a little. As both killings had taken place on weekday mornings in the Market Street area, perhaps the killer was a van driver who worked in the vicinity. Over the next few weeks police officers interviewed nearly 400 owners of white vans in the Market Street area, and over 100 van drivers. They were looking for someone young and slim, but not necessarily blond, for hair can be dyed.

A month went by, and they seemed to be getting nowhere, when, on January 25, 1974, they received an anonymous telephone call. The caller sounded extremely nervous. He asked to meet Falzon because, he said, he had information about a white van and its driver. The young inspector had dealt with dozens of crank calls since he started his investigation, but he had nothing else to go on. He agreed to meet the caller, who turned out to be a man in his early 20s. The young man insisted that his name be kept out of the matter. He had a friend, he explained, a guy named Daniel 'a real good guy, straight and level'. But he had an idea that his friend was going mad. Dan had shown him two guns one day, and had said that he was going to use them on 'a man who kept raping young girls'. 'He told me he had killed this man a couple of times, but he kept coming back from the dead,' said the informant. 'He said that he had stabbed him once, had tried to stab him again, and had shot him at point blank range twice, but still the man kept coming back.'

It fitted. Falzon was dealing with an obsessive psychopath. He ran Daniel's name through the computer which kept San Francisco's criminal records, and the computer came up with the details of the stabbing at the Greyhound depot and the attempted knifing of the same man six weeks later. The Phoenix businessman had not suspected that he had been attacked by the same man twice, and neither had the police. This time, Falzon checked the fingerprints on the file with the fingerprints on the Safeways bag himself, and found they were a perfect match. As final corroboration, it was discovered that Daniel worked on Tehama Street, near Market Street, as a delivery van driver, and of course his vehicle was white.

On the afternoon of January 26, 1974, Falzon and Cleary walked up the neat gravel drive to Daniel's home in an expensive San Francisco suburb. It was an area of lawns and swimming pools, where each house cost around $150,000. It was not the sort of area which normally spawns a killer, but the psychopath can spring from any environment.

Welcome

The man's parents were polite but incredulous when Falzon told them the reason for his visit. They showed him up to Daniel's room, where he was lying on the bed, his long, blond hair spread on the pillow around him. He smiled and welcomed them in, and almost eagerly showed them the Browning pump-action shotgun which had killed Kuznezow. He had thrown away the pistol used for the earlier killing, he said, but had another one ready for use. He handed it over to Falzon and Cleary and willingly went with them to the Hall of Justice, where he made a full statement and was charged with the two murders.

Once at the Hall of Justice, Daniel's calm cracked and he began to weep. He had, he said, a girlfriend who had been raped in 1972 by a short, elderly man with a bald head, stocky shoulders and a limp. The man had never been caught. Falzon checked out the story and found it to be true. After the rape, Daniel had begun to have day dreams in which he caught the man and killed him, but the man always came back, and always haunted him.

Insanity

'It actually sent chills up my spine hearing him talk,' said Falzon. 'He said the man tried to disguise himself by wearing different size ears or a different nose, or having sometimes thin fingers and sometimes fat fingers, but Daniel always knew him because he could never change his height and weight, the shape of his face and, in particular, his peculiar walk.'

On May 16, at San Francisco Superior Court, Daniel was found not guilty of the murders by reason of insanity, but was ordered to be detained indefinitely in Atascadero State Hospital for the Criminally Insane. To Inspector Frank Falzon the relief at the verdict was far greater than that he normally felt when putting away murderers, for Daniel's mental instability had made him almost undetectable.

The psychic detective

A student of Freud . . .
and a murder at the ranch

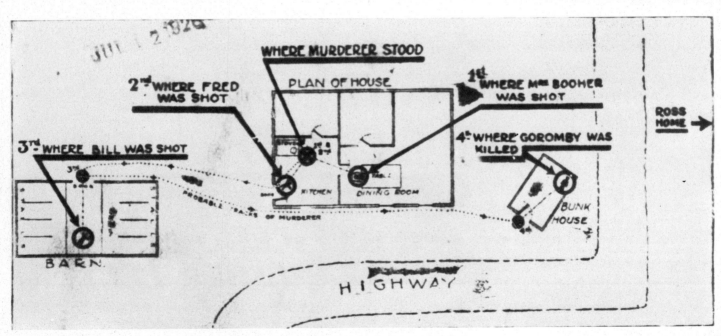

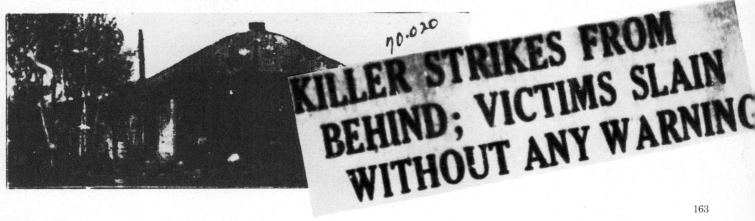

AFTER MOST MAJOR CRIMES, whether murder, robbery or kidnapping, the police department dealing with the case is inundated with telephone calls and letters. There are the inevitable 'confessions' from deranged sensation-seekers, who are quickly weeded out. There are cranks with grudges who try to incriminate innocent people, and there are sick hoax callers. Surprisingly often, there are also calls from people who believe that they can help police by using 'psychic' methods, and not all of these people are deluding themselves. The Russian police are reported to have experimented with people with telepathic powers in solving crime, although few details of the results have ever been made available in the West. Nearer home, the famous Dutch clairvoyant Gerard Croiset, has been called in from time to time by both European and American police forces, with varying degrees of success.

Urgent call

One 'psychic detective' who has gone down in the history of criminology was Dr Maximilian Langsner. The doctor had studied under Freud, and he perfectly filled the stereotype of his profession, with his shock of white hair and slightly shabby dress. An account of the doctor's work is entered in the official records of the Police Headquarters in Edmonton, Alberta, and such recognition is a part of his achievement. His methods, after all, were not those of a conventional detective. He is further celebrated because of the sheer speed with which he solved a murder case which had completely baffled the police.

In the evening of July 8, 1928, the police at Mannville, Alberta, received an urgent telephone call. A country doctor named Heaslip was reporting a mass murder at the isolated ranch belonging to the Booher family. Constable Olson drove quickly to the ranch and found Henry Booher, a man in his middle 50s, with his youngest son, Vernon, and a neighbor, Charles Stevenson. In the kitchen of the house, slumped over the table, was the body of Rose Booher, the rancher's wife. She had been shot three times in the back of the neck from close range. In the next room, sprawled on his back, was the body of Fred Booher, the eldest son of the family. He had been shot in

the mouth, again from point-blank range. In the bunkhouse across the yard was a third victim, Gabriel Cromby, who had emigrated from Austria to Canada the previous year. He had died from wounds to the head and chest.

Constable Olson took the three survivors out on to the porch for questioning. The rancher's son, Vernon Booher, said that he had been working out in the fields some distance away when, at about 8.00pm, he had heard the sound of shots, apparently coming from the ranchhouse. He had hurried back and found the body of his mother in the kitchen, and that of his brother, Fred, in the next room. Running to the bunkhouse for help he had fallen over Cromby. He had then driven to a neighbor's house and telephoned Dr Heaslip without touching anything. 'Was there anyone else on the ranch?' asked Constable Olson. 'Yes,' replied Vernon. 'There was another hand, Rosyk. I've been unable to find him. Perhaps he is the killer, though why he should do such a thing beats me.'

Olson, the Boohers and Stevenson spread out and began to search the remaining buildings, and within a few minutes the missing Rosyk was proved not guilty. Olson found his body lying behind a bale of hay in one of the barns. He had been shot twice in the chest. As far as Olson could discover the killings had been totally without motive. A diamond

ring belonging to Mrs Booher had not been touched, and money in a cash box in the kitchen was still intact.

The country constable telephoned Edmonton Police Headquarters for assistance. Police Chief Mike Gier and Detective Jim Leslie travelled the 80 miles to Mannville the following day, and questioned the survivors again. They dusted the house for fingerprints, but found only those of the family and helpers. The murder weapon had been a ·303 rifle, but Henry Booher said that he had no

such gun on the ranch. He possessed only a ·22 rifle and an old twelve-bore shotgun, neither of which had been fired for some weeks. A close search of the house and grounds revealed no trace of the ejected ·303 shells. The murderer had methodically picked them up and taken them away with him. There were no strange tire tracks or footprints. There was nothing at all.

In despair

After three days of methodical hunting for some kind of lead, Police Chief Gier was in despair. He was under pressure from his superiors to find the killer, who was obviously insane and might shoot more innocent people if not found quickly. Yet Gier, a detective of considerable experience, had done everything he could. It seemed that only some stroke of fate could solve the case now.

Gier then remembered Dr Langsner. Some years before, as a sergeant in Vancouver, British Columbia, Gier had been involved in a jewel robbery investigation where the thief was caught but the missing property had not been recovered. The case had been widely reported, and, as a result, a white-haired man with a foreign accent had turned up at Vancouver Police Headquarters. He had announced that he was Dr Maximilian Langsner, and that he would be able to help the police if he could be allowed into the suspect's

cell. Something about his confident manner had convinced the police to let him try. After half an hour of standing motionless, watching the prisoner, he had walked out and announced, 'You'll find the jewels behind a picture in a yellow painted room.' There had been no such room in the thief's apartment, but when they located his girlfriend they discovered that her sitting room was yellow. Behind a picture, taped to the wall, were the missing jewels.

Gier had spoken to the doctor afterwards, fascinated by his ap-

Gerard Croiset, the Dutch clairvoyant, has been called in to assist police on both sides of the Atlantic.

parent telepathic ability. Langsner had told Gier that he had studied psychology with Freud in Vienna after the First World War. He had then gone to India, where he had studied the ability of yogis to control the mind. He had come to Canada to live with the Eskimos near Fairbanks, Alaska because, he explained, they were a relatively unspoilt people, with a powerful, innate ability to hunt and navigate by means of telepathy. Now, the hard-pressed Police Chief felt that Langsner might help him with the Booher mystery. He sent a cable off to Fairbanks, and received word that Dr Langsner would do all he could.

The Doctor arrived in Edmonton on July 15, the day fixed for the inquest. He was driven to Mannville, and given a seat at the Press table, where he watched and listened to the proceedings with apparent interest. He was hearing the evidence for the first time, but very little emerged that the police did not already know.

Mrs Booher had been in the kitchen making strawberry jam. The killer had entered the house and shot her from behind. Fred Booher, Rosyk and Cromby were killed at intervals during the two hours that followed Mrs Booher's death. Neighbors reported hearing shots at intervals between 6.30 and 8.00 in the evening, but had not paid much attention. Almost every farmer owned a gun, and a marauding fox had been

reported in the area. One witness, Robert Scott, testified that he had stopped on the road leading to the Booher ranch at about 6.30 pm and had exchanged a few words with Vernon. While they were talking, Rosyk had arrived and asked for instructions on what work needed doing next. Vernon had asked him to feed the cattle in the barn.

Vernon Booher took the stand and said that, thinking back on things, he might well have heard the earlier shots almost subconsciously. He had known that Charles Stevenson, the Booher's nearest neighbor, was going out after the fox and so, like everyone else, he had not paid attention to the sound of gunfire. It was only the later shots, which seemed to come directly from the house, that had sent him running across the fields.

Charles Stevenson, called as a witness next, looked embarrassed. 'I think there is something I ought to tell you,' he said. 'It's been troubling me. I own a ·303 Lee Enfield rifle which I keep in a closet. This morning I looked for it and couldn't find it. I think maybe some-

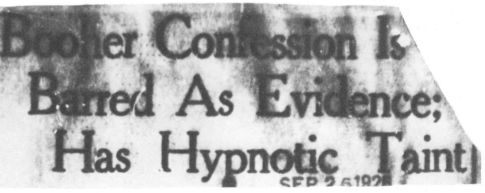

one stole it.' He added that he had last seen the gun on Sunday morning, shortly before setting out for church. He had not reported the theft because he thought that perhaps someone had borrowed it. 'Neighbors around here all know each other and if you want to borrow something, and there's no one around, you just take it, and tell them afterwards. I've borrowed the Booher's shotgun many a time like that.' He added that he did not think the borrower could have been one of the Boohers, for they too were at the church service on Sunday.

With the inquest over, Gier, Detective Leslie and Inspector John Longacre of the Mannville police went into conference. Dr Langsner sat silently by while they talked. Gier

recalled afterwards that nobody seemed very talkative, so to get the ball rolling he said, 'It seems to me that three people could have committed these murders – Henry Booher, Vernon Booher or Charles Stevenson. What puzzles me is the motive. Maybe we shall find the killing was done by a lunatic. Our first and most important task is to find the gun. It may tell us all we want to know.' Dr Langsner was looking at Gier steadily and Gier said that he was half joking when he asked him, 'You look as if you know something. Could it be the name of the killer?' The doctor solemnly replied, 'The rifle is not important. There are no suspects in this case, only the murderer, and I have recognized him.' Gier asked him to name the person he thought was the killer. 'Vernon Booher,' he replied.

Inspector Longacre was skeptical and asked him if he had any proof. Dr Langsner snapped his reply, 'Of course I have no proof. How is that possible? I am sure though, and yet I cannot tell you why I am sure. I can tell you, however, what one or two

people were thinking about in court today.' The detectives looked puzzled, and Dr Langsner explained his theory. 'When a man commits a crime, and it may not necessarily be murder, he knows that he has offended against the social code. He seeks for ways to protect himself. In his mind he plays with the details of the crime so that he can have an explanation prepared, should it be necessary to defend himself. The problem is much more acute, naturally, when he has killed someone, and often the persistence of thought becomes too great to bear and the criminal confesses, because only by so doing can he find relief from an intolerable burden. When Mr Stevenson told the court about the missing rifle, Vernon began to think intently about it. He knew where it was.' The doctor closed his eyes and was silent for a moment. Then he continued, 'It is in a clump of prairie grass at the back of the house. It is to the west, because I can now see the sun in that direction.'

Intolerable

The following morning, Gier, his two colleagues and Dr Langsner drove out to the Booher spread. It was a neat and well kept place, and the two-story house and out-buildings stood in the shade of tall linden trees. To the west stretched a vast field of pasture. If the rifle is out there, thought Gier, it is going to take some finding. The police had already searched that area.

Under security

Dr Langsner walked slowly round the house with a glazed look on his face. The detectives followed him, fascinated. Then for 20 minutes, he walked around in circles, apparently deep in thought, while the lawmen became increasingly impatient. Suddenly he stopped, wiped the sweat off his forehead, and exclaimed, 'I have it now. If you will take ten big steps forward.' Detective Leslie began pacing forward, counting as he went. He had just reached nine when he stumbled, bent down into the long long grass, and straightened up again. In his hand, held by a looped handkerchief, was a ·303 Lee Enfield rifle. 'You can handle it,' said Dr Langsner. 'Vernon wiped it very clean of fingerprints, and thinks a good deal of what he did.'

Dr Langsner was right. Back at the fingerprint department at Edmonton, technicians were unable to find any prints. Nevertheless, Gier felt that he would prefer Vernon Booher to be under his scrutiny. He booked Vernon as 'a material witness' and held him in Edmonton jail, officially for his own protection.

Now, Dr Langsner behaved in exactly the same way as he had in the case of the Vancouver jewel thief which Gier remembered so well. For half an hour he stood in Vernon's cell, staring silently at him. Then he returned to Gier's office, and began to talk in a matter of fact tone. 'Vernon is guilty. There is not a shadow of a doubt about it. He killed his mother because he had

away and then returned. The woman who saw him leave was wearing a poke bonnet. She has small eyes and a long jaw and she was sitting at the back of the church, to the left of the aisle. She saw him leave and watched to see if he would return.'

Detective Jim Leslie, acting on Gier's instructions, drove back to Mannville with the description. He had no difficulty in finding the woman. Her name was Erma Higgins, and she was a spinster who took a delight in observing what went on around her. Yes, she had seen Vernon sneak from the church and sneak back in towards the end of the service. She had thought he was going off to meet a girlfriend.

Chief Gier sat Miss Higgins and Dr Langsner in the centre of his office, facing the door. On either side of them were Detective Leslie and Inspector Longacre. When all was set, Gier marched Vernon into the office and brought him face to face with Miss Higgins. The spinster relished the drama. 'Vernon,' she told him. 'I saw you leave the church the day that Charlie's rifle was stolen.' 'I know you did,' he said. Then he began to sob. 'Let me confess. I killed them all.'

Well-respected

His statement tallied exactly with Langsner's account. The reason was rage against his mother, for throwing his girlfriend out of the house. Mrs Booher, though a kindly and well-respected woman, had thought that the daughter of a farm laborer was beneath her son's dignity. Vernon was in love with the girl, and had threatened to elope with her, but his mother had just laughed, telling him that he would not get far without money. He was tied to his father and her, whether he liked it or not. Vernon's resentment had turned to murder. On April 26, 1929, he was hanged at Edmonton for the four killings.

Dr Langsner, his task done, went back north to Alaska and to his research. The Edmonton police paid him a small fee, which he took only at the insistence of Police Chief Gier. He did not want payment, he said. He was thankful to have been able to use his extraordinary powers for the benefit of society. He never used these powers in police work again, however, for three years later he died among the Eskimos.

Blood Rushed From Face Of Young Murderer When Sentence Passed On Him

Vernon Booher, hate and resentment.

come to hate her, and he has no regret. He walked into the kitchen to kill her, and she spoke to him without turning round. In his fury he fired three shots and Fred, his brother, heard them. Vernon then realized he had to kill Fred. He did not want to, and he is sorry for it. When he ran out to hide the gun, he saw Rosyk and Cromby in the field. He was sure Rosyk had seen him and so killed the man when he had the chance. Two hours later, he decided that it was unsafe to allow Cromby to live. He felt he had to eliminate every possible witness.'

Gier thought that Dr Langsner's reconstruction of the murder sounded very plausible. But how would he prove it? The doctor again had the answer. 'Find the woman,' he suggested. 'I do not know her name. Vernon stole the gun on the Sunday that Stevenson missed his weapon. He sneaked out of church, took it

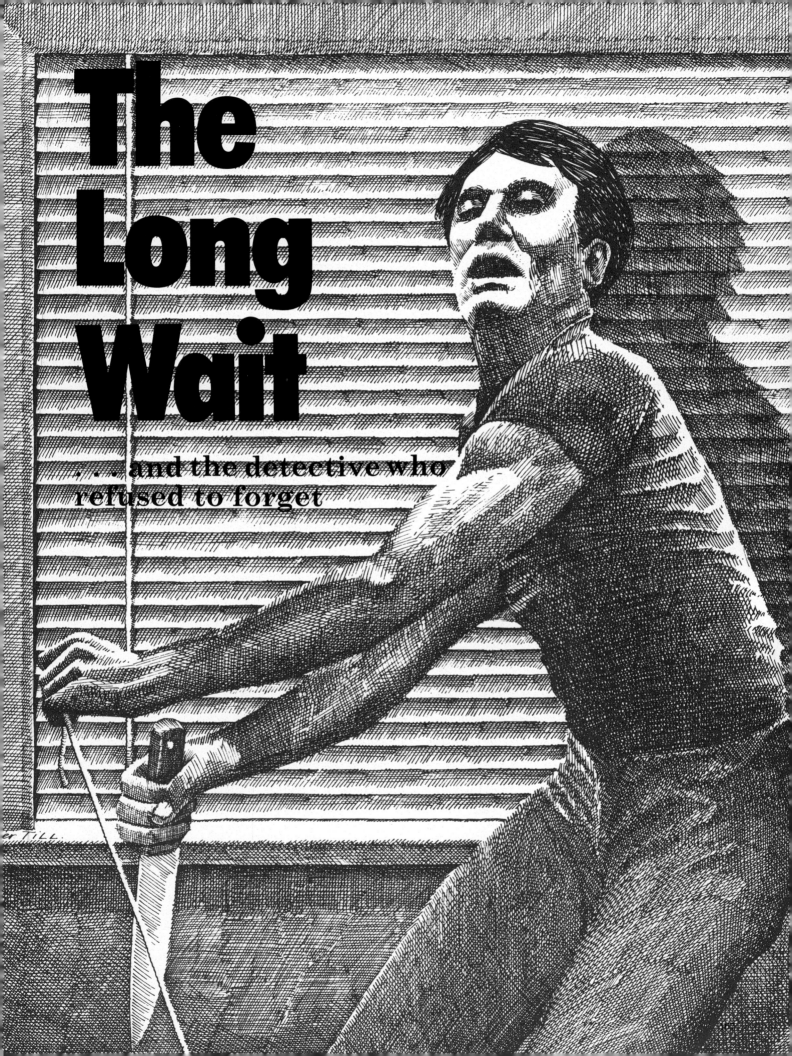

The Long Wait

. . . and the detective who refused to forget

IN THE FILES of every major police department are many records of murders and other major crimes which have never been solved, some of them dating back decades. However old, dusty and dog-eared these records may become, they are never 'closed' until a final solution is reached. The vital information the investigating officers gather at the scene of a crime remains in its folder for the benefit of successive investigators. A murderer can never relax, believing that the police have forgotten his act. The police never forget. Sometimes, the stored information produces answers to questions posed years after the original crimes are committed.

Mike Gonzalez was an Argentinian-American policeman with the Miami Homicide Department. His tenacity in hunting one killer over 14 years at first made him something of a joke, but his eventual triumph brought him a place in criminological history. In 1959, Gonzalez handed in his patrolman's uniform in order to take up his new post as detective, third grade. He felt he could make a good detective, and it was with an almost boyish eagerness that he answered a call to go to N W 31st Street, a middle-class area of Miami, on the afternoon of December 15, where a murder was reported to have been committed. The eagerness turned to nausea when he reached the white-washed, one-story cottage with his colleagues and saw the scene in the bedroom. Spreadeagled on the bed, her wrists and ankles apparently tied to the bedposts with cord, was the naked body of an elderly woman. A thinner piece of string was tied tightly around her neck, and her face was bruised and battered. Horrifically, her chest and abdomen had been stabbed repeatedly, and her left breast had been hacked off.

Disturbed

Gonzalez interviewed the woman's landlord, Mr A.E. Banks, who lived in a larger house near the murder cottage. The victim was Miss Ethel Ione Little, aged 55, a spinster who lived alone. Banks had heard her walk up the gravel path to her house the previous evening at about 8.30 pm. This was her usual time for getting home from the attorney's office in downtown Miami where she worked as a legal secretary. At

12.25 pm, Banks had received a call from Miss Little's boss, Attorney Sidney Aronovitz, asking him to call on her. Miss Little, normally a very punctual and efficient secretary, had not turned up for work, and her cottage had no telephone. Banks had found the front door locked, with the milk and the *Miami Herald* still lying on the doorstep. Using his pass key he had entered after repeatedly knocking and shouting, and had discovered the body on the bed.

Mike Gonzalez began taking notes on the state of the house. The living room was neat and tidy, as was the bathroom. On the kitchen floor were some spilled coffee grounds, but nothing else out of the ordinary. Only the bedroom had been disturbed. Besides the brutalized body, Detective Gonzalez found a bloody knife on the dressing table, and, on the floor, a flashlight, with a blood-stained, bullet-shaped end.

Irrational

The doors and windows of the cottage showed no sign of forced entry, though the back door, leading into the kitchen, was unlocked, with the key on the inside. Perhaps the murderer was someone Miss Little knew?

Investigation showed that the cord used to bind Miss Little's wrists and ankles to the bed had been cut from the Venetian blinds at her bedroom window. The person who cut them must have been extremely tall, for the remaining ends hung 6 ft 6 ins from the floor, and there were no stools or chairs in the room to stand on. Oddly, the cords binding her had been slashed through after she died, which was shown by the rigor of the still-stretched limbs. According to Dr Raymond DiJusti, the police medical examiner, it was the sort of irrational gesture that a mad slayer might well make, after his lust for blood had been slaked and contrition was beginning to seep over him. Dr DiJusti discovered another unpleasant fact. The killer had not had sexual intercourse with Miss Little, but chemical tests showed that he had sexually molested her with the flashlight. It was the act of a perverted man with a sovereign contempt for women.

Meanwhile, the fingerprint experts had come up with a promising clue. On the flashlight was a clear, double-looped print in blood, so perfect that

they were able to photograph it instead of dusting it as was normal. They also found a man's palm print on the window sill, which may or may not have been made by the intruder. Detective Gonzalez discovered another salient fact. The ligature which had strangled the woman, before the atrocities were committed on her body, had been the pull-switch string from a light in her closet.

Sidney Aronovitz, Miss Little's boss, was still distraught when Mike Gonzalez talked to him. Everyone had liked the white-haired secretary. She had taken a keen part in social and civic affairs and had taught a class in the Sunday School at the Central Baptist Church. The previous day, Monday 14, she had come into Aronovitz's office in the late afternoon and had sheepishly asked for a little time off to go Christmas shopping with her sister-in-law. Aronovitz had cheerfully given his permission, and she had told him that she would get in particularly early the following day to finish her work. She had not, of course, shown up.

The sister-in-law, Mrs Jefferson Little, told Gonzalez that she had not been able to go on the shopping jaunt after all, but apparently Ethel had gone, because partly-wrapped Christmas presents were found in her living room. Could she have gone out with a man friend, perhaps? asked Gonzalez, hinting delicately. Mrs Little did not think so. William Little, Ethel's elder brother, put it more bluntly. Managing a wan smile, he said, 'Ethel was an old maid. I don't think she ever had a date in her life.'

Unprecedented

Everything pointed to a sexual psychopath, and, like all lawmen faced with such criminals, Mike Gonzalez and his colleagues were faced with the great fear that he would strike again. Every member of the Miami Homicide Department was put onto the case, and off-duty officers came into the department to help. They all knew the importance of instant action. Over 60 known sexual offenders in the Miami area were brought in and interrogated exhaustively, but each one of them had a satisfactory alibi. Gonzalez even probed into a case which had happened a month previously, when a woman had been bound, beaten

The twenty-year vigil

For 20 years, Detective Superintendent Alec Spooner visited the scene of an unsolved murder. Spooner explained his reasons for these visits, and for his refusal to close the file on the case: 'If the murderer is about, he wants the crime forgotten. My annual return shows him that it has not been forgotten, and this may wear him down.' The detective retired from his post with the Warwickshire police force, in England, in 1964, ended his annual vigil . . . and the case remains unsolved.

The same case defeated the famous Detective Superintendent Fabian, of Scotland Yard, though he spent rather less than 20 years on his investigation.

It was a bizarre case. The murder victim was 74-year-old Charles Walton. He was found dead in a farm field, pinned to the ground by a hayfork, the prongs of which pierced either side of his neck. His shirt had been ripped open and there were two gaping wounds, in the form of a cross, hacked into his chest.

Walton had been, in the words of his niece, 'a queer old cuss'. He had never been more than a few miles from his cottage, in Lower Quinton, Warwickshire. Although he frequently visited the village pub, the 'Gay Dog', he used to take his drink home with him, often trundling away several gallons of potent rough cider in a wheelbarrow. He shunned the company of humans in preference to that of birds and animals, and his hobby was to breed toads. Some of his toads were huge grey creatures 'the size of stones', according to one of the locals. There were even people who said that he had trained a team of toads to pull a miniature plough.

Although the murder took place in the 1940s, the English countryside was at that time still alive with superstition.

One evening, when Fabian was out walking, he was startled by a large black dog which ran across his path. A moment later, a young boy walked by. 'Looking for your dog, son,' asked Fabian. 'What dog, mister,' the boy gaped. 'A big black one,' said Fabian. The boy turned on his heel and ran off like the wind.

The local policeman told Fabian that the black dog was considered locally to be a phantom, and to be an omen of death. It seemed that its first 'victim', many years earlier, may have been Charlie Walton's sister. One theory had it that Charlie Walton was a witch, and that he was ritually murdered by someone whom he had tried to put under a spell.

Years later, Walton's niece said in a television program that she believed police had a suspect throughout, but were never able to build up a case against him.

'A queer old cuss' . . . Charlie Walton was found lying dead in a farm field, pinned to the ground by a hayfork.

and raped on West Palm Beach, but he found no link with the Little killing.

By now the case was considered urgent enough for an action to be taken which was unprecedented in the history of crime in the United States. Volunteers were asked to give their fingerprints in an elimination exercise. Neighbors, friends, workmates, and tradesmen, altogether 2,500 people who had known Miss Little or had the slightest contact with her, came forward willingly, despite protests from liberal groups about the 'violation of civil liberties'. All the results were negative.

Gradually the panic died down. To the surprise of the police department no other violent sex killings were reported in the next few weeks. As months went by, detectives were taken off the case and put to other tasks, but the Ethel Ione Little case was not closed. For one man it became almost an obsession. Detective Mike Gonzalez had every detail of the killing imprinted on his memory, for it had been one of his first murder investigations, and one of the most horrific he was ever to encounter. Somewhere the maniac was still at large, and Gonzalez was determined to run him down.

Over the next few years, Gonzalez was instrumental in solving other homicides, but he always kept a careful eye on the sex crime lists. Whenever a child molester, rapist, or even a person accused of indecent exposure was brought in for questioning in the Miami area, Gonzalez was there to quiz him about his background and his whereabouts in December 1959. There were also dozens of people willing to 'confess' to Miss Little's murder. This is a phenomenon which policemen all over the world know only too well whenever a sensational crime occurs. In the two or three years following the crime, over 60 such confessions were heard by Gonzalez, who broke them all down, simply by using a series of control questions. How was she molested? How was she mutilated? What had been used to strangle her? Since the answers to none of these questions had been released to the newspapers, only the police and the killer could know them.

After seventeen months, another savage murder took place in Miami, and again Mike Gonzalez was one of the first officers to reach the scene of the crime. On May 25, 1961, the body of a 33-year-old, German-American girl named Mrs Johanna Block was found at her apartment in N W 41st Street. She was naked, and she had been strangled manually, with such force that the bones of her thorax were crushed. There were over 20 stab wounds in her body, and the long pair of scissors which had caused them were still embedded between her ribs. As with Ethel Little, Johanna Block's face had been badly beaten and her nose was broken.

Gonzalez discovered that Mrs Block had been brought to the United States by her first husband, a GI whom she had married towards the end of the Second World War. She had divorced him, and had subsequently been twice married and divorced. In 1961, she had taken work as a barmaid to help keep her three children. She certainly had no shortage of boyfriends, as Gonzalez discovered when he interviewed her best friend, Mary Alice Bratt. Miss Bratt was the talkative daughter of Captain Fred Bratt, a retired member of the Miami Police Department, and she was only too happy to help Gonzalez with his enquiries. In the next few days she put the detective in touch with no less than 20 men who had dated Mrs Block from time to time, including three truck drivers and a policeman. These four had been regular boyfriends and for a while Gonzalez felt that one of them must be the killer, for none of them knew of the existence of the others in Johanna's tangled love life. Disappointingly, they were all ruled out.

Promoted

Then came a supreme piece of irony, one which Gonzalez was not to appreciate until over a decade later. Sometime after Mrs Block's murder, when the case still had not been solved, Mary Alice Bratt dropped by the Homicide Department to clarify a few points on some of the information she had provided. When she had finished she told Mike Gonzalez that she had to hurry, because her fiancé was waiting for her outside in the car. 'Bring him in,' said Gonzalez. 'I'd like to meet him. Did he know Johanna? Maybe he could help?' 'Well we are in a hurry,' said Miss Bratt. 'He did meet her a few times, but only when he went to the bar with me. I don't think he could help you much,' she concluded.

The years went by, and the Block case joined the Little case in the 'unsolved' files. Detective Gonzalez achieved more success with other homicide crimes, and was promoted to Detective Sergeant, but the murder of Ethel Little was still fresh in his mind. Whenever the detectives of the Homicide Department got together socially or for a 'bull session', sooner or later he would bring the case up. By the late 1960s, he was the only investigating officer left on the squad who had seen the terrible corpse in the bedroom on N W 31st Street, and his juniors jokingly referred to it as 'Mike's Case'.

Confession

On Saturday, July 22, 1972, one of the telephones on Gonzalez's desk shrilled. The caller announced himself as Lieutenant Bill McElroy of the DeKalb County Police Department in Decatur, a suburb of Atlanta, Georgia. The Lieutenant explained that they had a suspect in the office who insisted on confessing to two murders he had committed years before in Miami. 'What names does he give?' asked Gonzalez. 'Little and Block. Two women,' replied McElroy. Mike Gonzalez was gripped with excitement. It was years since the last 'confession' to Ethel Little's murder, and here was something extra. None of the would-be confessors had ever tried to admit to both unsolved crimes.

In answer to Gonzalez's questions, Lieutenant McElroy gave fuller details. The suspect was named Vernon David Edwards, jnr, a native of Atlanta. He had moved to Miami when he was 21 years old, in 1958, and had subsequently married there and moved back with his wife to Atlanta in 1964. He had dark hair, was 6 ft 6 ins tall, and weighed 285 lbs. He worked as a housepainter. Immediately, Gonzalez's mental file on Ethel Little's murder brought the image of the cords cut from the Venetian blinds to the front of his mind. They had been hacked off at just about this man's eye level.

Remaining as calm as possible, Gonzalez dictated a string of his much used 'control questions.' McElroy thanked him and promised to ring back. Half an hour went by, and at the end of it, when the telephone rang, Gonzalez snatched it from its cradle. 'McElroy?' he snapped. 'Yeah,' came the reply. 'This guy scores very, very high on your questions.'

The following morning, Detective Sergeant Gonzalez left Miama on the first available flight to Atlanta. In his briefcase were the two fat files on the Little and Block murders. At Decatur Police Headquarters, he was met by Captain James T. Stanley who was carrying with him a much more slender folder containing what was known so far about their suspect. Edwards had graduated from High School, Atlanta, in 1955. He had enlisted in the Army for three years, but his record was not too good. He had been court-martialled three times for being off-limits. By the time he came out of the army his mother had moved to Miami, and he followed her there to work as a mate on a fishing boat. He married a Miami girl in 1962, and two years later brought her back to Atlanta, where he took up his present job as a house painter.

Captain Stanley took Sergeant Gonzalez into the interrogation room.

Inexorably, Gonzalez asked his vital questions and, quite steadily, Edwards answered them. Once, when he faltered on a point, the big man yelled, 'Man, you've been working on this case for years, trying to remember everything about it. All I've done is try to forget it. So I forgot a lot about it and you remember a hell of a lot about it.' There was only one thing remaining to be done at the end of the day. Gonzalez sent off a sample of Edwards' fingerprints to be checked against the killer's. They matched perfectly.

Edwards told him details about both murders which only the police and the killer could know. Then one question elicited an astonishing answer. 'What was your wife's name before you married?' asked Gonzalez. 'Mary Alice Bratt,' replied Edwards. It was the same woman who had been so helpful about Mrs Block's boyfriends. Ironically, the murderer had been sitting outside the Miami Homicide Department while Gonzalez questioned her.

Judge Paul Baker, of the Dade County Court, Miami, accepted Vernon Edwards' plea of guilty after a brief hearing. He was sentenced to life imprisonment in Florida State Penitentiary.

The original 'Pig'

His technique . . . to be a stubborn bully

SCRIPTWRITERS HAVE often been keen to portray detectives as laconic tough-guys, with a highly personal moral code, but even the most brutish of their creations fades in comparison with Marie-Francois Goron, better known as 'The Pig'.

Goron even looked similar to that unfortunate animal. He was short, fat and pale, with little eyes that glinted from behind steel-rimmed spectacles. With a small, waxed moustache bristling from under his snout-like nose, Goron was far from an attractive human being.

Born in Rennes, France in 1847, Goron entered the Paris police in 1881, after leaving the army. He rose quickly through the ranks and within four years he was Commissioner of Police in the Partin district. After just one year as Commissioner, he was made Deputy Chief of the Sûreté. In 1887, he achieved his ultimate ambition, and became Chief of the Sûreté. During his years in that position, the Sûreté became the envy of the world's law enforcement agencies.

However, there were those within Goron's force who questioned his methods, though they hesitated to do so openly. Like many little men with power, he was a bully. He was hard on his underlings, and with criminals he could be brutal. His favorite method of interrogation was to deprive a suspect of food and drink, and then question him while platters of savory stew and mugs of cool beer were placed just out of reach.

Goron had a knack of irritating the chiefs of other investigative forces to the point of fury by his needling persistence in pressing a point with which they disagreed. He was pig-headed to the point of paranoia about following his own 'hunches' to absurd lengths to prove he had been right. Goron's behavior would have undermined his chances of holding high rank in any modern police force, but his unorthodox methods made him one of the most successful detectives the world has known, and nothing illustrates this better than his triumph with the Gouffé case. Goron crossed national boundaries in order to follow up clues on this case. Information found in London, England led to the identification of the most important piece of evidence. Descriptive details circulated worldwide in the manner

Gouffé, the womanizing bailiff. Was he the victim in the sack? The Pig had a hunch that he was, and set off on one of his most spectacular hunts. Vital clues came from London and the culprits from across the Atlantic.

of Interpol led to the eventual return of the culprits to France from across the Atlantic.

On July 27, 1889, a Paris court bailiff named Gouffé was reported missing by his brother-in-law. Gouffé was described as being of slender build, 5 ft 9 in tall, always well dressed, with thick chestnut-colored hair, and a beard which was trimmed into a spade shape. He was 49 years old, a widower, and, admitted the brother-in-law, 'a womanizer'. On July 30, Goron happened to see the report on the missing man. Run-of-the-mill 'missing persons' were normally far beneath his dignity, but he pompously announced that he had a 'hunch' that Gouffé was in trouble. Junior officers sighed with resignation. There was every likelihood that Gouffé was off on some amorous jaunt. In any case, the files were filled with hundreds of missing persons. Why pick this one? Goron was adamant that he himself would launch a full investigation.

Goron's first move was to visit the bailiff's office. Everything seemed in order, except that on the floor near the safe were 18 burned matches. The female caretaker at the office block told the detective that on the night of Gouffé's disappearance she had heard a man go up the stairs and open the door of the office. He had stayed for a while, and she had assumed that it was Gouffé, but

when the man left she saw that he was a stranger.

The detective then checked into Gouffé's personal affairs. He had no money troubles and, despite his many and complex love affairs, no apparent problems with women either. Many of his girlfriends were interviewed on Goron's instructions over the next few days, but no clues to his disappearance could be found. Finally, Goron issued a description of the missing man to every police force in France.

Meanwhile, in the village of Millery, near Lyons, residents had noticed an unpleasant smell which seemed to seep up from the banks of the river Rhône. The local public works commissioner was ordered to investigate the problem, and on August 13, by the side of the river, he came across a sack, tied at the neck, from which the stench emanated. Slashing open the sack, he was horrified to find the decomposing body of a black-haired man, which tumbled out at his feet. The local police took the body to the Lyons morgue, an evil-smelling, converted barge, and the following day a police surgeon named Dr Paul Bernard performed an autopsy. Taking the putrefaction of the body as evidence, he calculated that death had taken place twelve months previously, in 1888. The body was that of a dark-haired man, aged between 35 and 45, who had stood 5 ft 7 in tall. From damage to the larynx, Dr Bernard deduced that the man had been strangled. The body had been wrapped in oil-cloth, tied with yards of string, and thrust into the bag.

The Lyons police launched a hunt for clues along the riverbank, and came across the splintered remnants of a wooden trunk. It reeked of death, and the officers presumed that the body had, at one time, been contained within the trunk. A railway dispatch ticket was stuck to the broken woodwork. It read, 'From Paris, 1231 – Paris 7/27/188–. Express train number 3. To Lyons-Perrache I.' So the trunk had been sent from Paris, on train number 3, on July 27, 188–. The last figure of the date had been obliterated.

The Millery discovery was reported in the Lyons newspapers which, like all local journals covering crime, were sent as a matter of course to the Sûreté headquarters in Paris. On

August 17, the Lyons papers were placed on Goron's desk, but the story on the body found at Millery contained no details of the label found on the trunk. Immediately on reading the report, Goron leaped to his feet and announced to his assistants that this was Gouffé's body. He dashed from the office and telegraphed Lyons police headquarters to the effect that he could solve their mystery, and offered to come down immediately to take charge of the investigation. Not unnaturally, the Lyons police chief was piqued. He had heard of Goron and his ways, and in a terse telegram in reply he told the Sûreté chief that his help was not needed. In any case, the Millery corpse did not fit Gouffé's description. The dead man at Lyons was black haired, two inches shorter, and at least four years younger. This kind of response

was exactly the sort of thing which most inflamed the ego of the podgy Paris detective. Again, he rattled off cables, this time to the Lyons newspapers themselves, asking for a full description of the body's discovery and telling them that he thought he knew who it was. They played up the story well, the Paris papers picked it up, and soon all France was eagerly attending to the latest Goron drama.

Despite the Lyons police rebuff, on August 21 Goron sent a detective and Gouffé's brother-in-law to view the body. The scene in the hot, low-decked barge-morgue was horrific. The brother-in-law almost fainted as, with handkerchief to his nose, he glanced at the rotting corpse, shook his head, and fled for the open air. Even Goron's detective stayed just long enough to make sure that the

hair and beard on the moldering head were black rather than chestnut. Before taking the train back to Paris, he cabled Goron to say that the body he had seen was definitely not that of the missing bailiff.

As if to vindicate their decision, the Lyons police felt that they had solved the mystery a couple of days later, when they had a visit from a horse-cab driver named Laforge. He told them that on July 8 he had picked up three passengers and a huge trunk at Lyons railway station. He had been told to drive to an area of Millery, unload the trunk, and wait. The three men took the trunk and a few minutes later returned, empty handed. He had then driven them back to Lyons. Shown the photographic 'rogues gallery', Laforge had picked out the three travellers without difficulty, and the police soon discovered that on July 9, three days after their taxi journey, the men had been picked up and charged with a previous robbery and murder. The crime 'solved', the Lyons police made arrangements for the burial of the body found in the trunk at the cemetery of La Guillotière.

Even Goron could find no pretext on which to continue his insistence that the Lyons body was that of Gouffé, but because of his precipitate action over the matter he now had a *cause célèbre* on his hands. The Press had sunk their teeth into the case, and would not let go. Whether he liked it or not, the Sûreté Chief was saddled with finding the bailiff, or suffering a severely damaged reputation.

No results

During the following weeks, only one further lead was forthcoming. On July 27, a couple named Michel Eyraud and Gabrielle Bompard had vanished from Paris, and they had been seen two days before with Gouffé. It was a slender clue, but by this time Goron was clutching at straws. He added Eyraud and Bompard to his wanted list.

Time went by with no results at all. In November, Goron was desperate. He wrote to the Lyons police force to find out how the trunk case was getting on. The police chief wrote back to say that the three suspects had persistently denied having anything to do with the trunk corpse, but the taxi driver, Laforge, had also been arrested as an accessory, and

Michel Eyraud went missing from Paris along with Gabrielle Bompard (inset). What attracted Goron's interest was the fact that the couple had been seen with Gouffé two days before they disappeared. By this time, Goron was desperate for a lead and he added the couple to his list.

it was assumed that questioning would eventually break down his story. However, as a sop to Goron's pride, the Lyons police chief asked him to make enquiries about the trunk at the railroad office. Presumably the victim had been killed for the contents of his trunk, and to help Goron with the enquiry, the label from the trunk was enclosed with the letter. Goron had not known about the label until then. The date, 'July 27', seemed to leap out at him. It was the exact date of the disappearance of both Gouffé and the Eyraud-Bompard couple. In a state of excitement, Goron raced around to the railroad dispatch office, and asked for the records. The Lyons police had assumed that the last figure of the date on the label was an '8', but there was no trace of a shipment on July 27, 1888. The records for July 27 of the current year, however, had Goron in a lather of triumph. 'July 27, 1889, Train number 3, 11.45 am, No 1231. Destination: Lyons-Perrache.1. One trunk, weight 105 Kilograms.' The coincidence was too much, Goron crowed to his assistants. Despite the testimonies from a doctor, police, and even Gouffé's brother-in-law, he had been right all along.

On November 11, Goron arrived at Lyons, and demanded to see the cab driver, who was still under arrest. How, Goron asked, could he have carried the trunk on July 8, when it hadn't left Paris until July 27? Laforge admitted that he had made up the entire story in an attempt to ingratiate himself with the police. Goron dismissed him and promptly made out an order for the corpse to be exhumed. By the following morning the body was on a slab in the pathology department of the University of Lyons, presided over by Dr Alexandre Lacassagne, one of France's leading exponents of criminal medicine.

Flying start

Goron and Lacassagne now faced their greatest hurdle. They had to show that, despite the apparent discrepancies in height and hair coloring, the body was that of Gouffé. But they got off to a flying start. Using simple calculations, Lacassagne showed that the dead man had been 5 ft 8 in. Gouffé's family, however, claimed that the bailiff had been 5 ft 9 in. Goron telegraphed the

Paris military authorities, who checked through Gouffé's army file. Their records showed that he had been 5 ft 8 in. For absolute confirmation, Goron also cabled Gouffé's tailor. Sure enough, his records showed 5 ft 8 in as well.

Meanwhile, Lacassagne came up with an even better lead. Examination showed that the dead man had suffered tuberculosis of the right ankle, resulting in water on the knee. He must have had a slight limp. Sûreté men in Paris checked the matter out and Gouffé's father remembered that his son had had a fall as a child and had been stiff-legged for months afterwards, and a doctor testified to having treated him for water on the knee. On November 21, the one remaining question of the hair was quickly solved. Using ordinary soap and water, Lacassagne rinsed the head of the corpse and the hair turned from oily black to burnished chestnut. Goron and the doctor beamed at each other in triumph. Tapping the remains with his scalpel, Lacassagne exclaimed, 'Voila. I present to you Monsieur Gouffé.'

With the problem of the body solved, Goron now turned his attention to the trunk. Where had it come from? Who had owned it? Using the shattered remains of the original as a guide, a carpenter made a replica, and Goron had it put on public display at the Sûreté headquarters in Paris. By now the newspapers were hysterical over the mystery, and in three days over 25,000 people came to look at the trunk. On November 26, Goron received a call from a baggage manufacturer who said that in his expert opinion the trunk had been made in England. Pictures of the replica appeared in the London newspapers, and a Frenchman living in the city recognized it. He wrote to Goron with the information that on June 4, 1889, a Frenchwoman named Madame Vespres, who also lived in London, had sent a couple to him for lodgings. They had apparently been father and daughter. On arrival they had bought a large trunk, identical to the Paris one, from the baggage firm of Zwanziger, in the Euston Road. The couple had left in mid-July, taking the trunk with them.

The energetic Goron went to London. A salesman at Zwanzigers recognized photographs of the trunk and recalled selling one like it to a

short, balding Frenchman of about 50 years of age, who had large hands. His companion had been a pretty, young woman. From his records, the sale had taken place on June 11. The Frenchman who had written the original letter to Goron also recognized the trunk, as did Madam Vespres. Madam Vespres had one vital fact to add. She had suspected all along that the couple were not father and daughter, because their names were different. They were a Michel Eyraud and Gabrielle Bompard.

'Dear friend'

On his return to Paris, Goron looked into the police files which had amassed since he first suspected that the couple were implicated. Eyraud, it appeared, was a professional swindler, an ugly man who nevertheless 'had a way with women'. Gabrielle Bompard was the pretty daughter of a middle-class family who had run away from home and turned to prostitution. Goron was jubilant when his men uncovered a photograph of Eyraud.

Now the Sûreté chief cast his dragnet world-wide, sending copies of the photograph, along with descriptions of the missing couple, to every newspaper and French embassy and consulate throughout the world. But even Goron was unprepared for the response he received. In mid-January, 1890, he received three letters from New York, written in the handwriting of and signed in the name of Michel Eyraud. The hunted man explained that he was very upset that he was wanted for the killing of his 'dear friend' Gouffé. He had fled Paris only to avoid financial difficulties which had been caused by the wicked Gabrielle Bompard. She was a greedy woman who might easily have arranged the slaying to get at Gouffé's money, he added.

Two days after the arrival of the final letter, the detective had another shock. On January 22, two people walked into his office, an American named George Garanger, and Gabrielle Bompard. Goron sat, fascinated, as Garanger told his tale.

It appeared that, while on a

An impression of how the murder took place. 1, Eyraud attempts to strangle Gouffé. 2, The body is put into a sack, and 3, dumped on the bank. 4, Bompard accuses Eyraud.

1

2

3

4

Gabrielle Bonipétard

Complainte
Créée par **SULBAC** à l'Eldorado

business trip to Vancouver, Canada, Garanger had met a French businessman named Vanaert and his lovely daughter Berthe. Garanger had fallen wildly in love with Berthe, and had even given money to Vanaerd for a proposed deal in order to stay with her. When the Frenchman asked him to escort Berthe back to Paris, he had leaped at the chance. In Europe, Garanger had seen the papers and had recognized Vanaerd as none other than the fugitive Eyraud. 'Berthe' had tearfully confessed to him that she was Gabrielle Bompard, and had told him her story. According to Gabrielle she had come completely under the fatal charm of Eyraud, and had blindly carried out his every whim, even to making love to Gouffé, whom Eyraud hoped to swindle. On July 26, 1889, she had invited Gouffé to her apartment on the Rue Tronson-Ducoudray, at Eyraud's instructions, and had left him there alone. When she returned, Eyraud was there with a red-haired stranger, and the large, London trunk. Gouffé, Eyraud had told her, had gone home. The following morning, she had unsuspectingly set out with Eyraud on a railroad trip to Lyons, taking the trunk with them. On arrival, Eyraud had rented a self-drive carriage, and had driven her and the trunk to Millery. There, the red-haired stranger had appeared again and had taken the trunk. Eyraud had driven back to Lyons, and suggested a trip to America. That was all Gabrielle knew, said Garanger. She had had no part at all in any murder.

Inquisition

The fat little detective smiled at the American when he had finished. 'What a sad story,' he said. Then, nodding to a uniformed gendarme, he snapped, 'Lock her up.'

The next day, Goron took the manacled Gabrielle to see her former landlady at the Rue Tronson-Ducoudray. The landlady remembered that she had come home on the evening of July 26, 1889, with a gentleman with chestnut-colored hair, and no one else had called during the evening. Gabrielle stuck to her own story.

Gabrielle Bompard, or Bompétard, escaped the guillotine because she claimed to have been hypnotized as a child, and was consequently easily lead by powerful men.

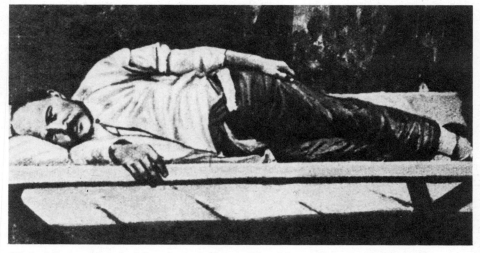

Michel Eyraud lies in his prison cell, awaiting his walk to the guillotine.

It was at this point that Goron put into practice his feared inquisition techniques which had never been known to fail. For a fortnight he had Gabrielle marched up and down her cell for long periods, allowing her only 'cat naps' here and there. He starved her and then gave her only dry biscuits to eat, without any water. For a few days he put her on a diet of water only, and kept the cell light burning. Every time she began to nod off to sleep, he shook her awake and questioned her. Strong men had cracked under the treatment, and Gabrielle was not strong. In February, 1890, she told her story again – a different one this time, and one which Goron was more inclined to believe. She had agreed to lure Gouffé to her apartment, where, behind the couch, was a curtained-off alcove in which Eyraud had waited. In his hand he had held a rope, which had been looped over the ceiling beam. Gouffé arrived and the voluptuous Gabrielle had welcomed him in her dressing gown. Settling him upon the couch, she had playfully wrapped the dressing gown sash around his neck.

While the lusty Gouffé fondled Gabrielle, Eyraud had stealthily tied one end of the rope to the sash, and had then hauled on the other, in an attempt to hang the bailiff from the ceiling beam. The plan had not worked. Gouffé had kicked and struggled, and Eyraud was forced to strangle him by hand. The next day, after vainly trying to open Gouffé's office safe by the light of matches, they had loaded his body into the trunk and taken it to Lyons. There they had disposed of both pieces of evidence in the river near Millery.

Goron took the broken Gabrielle with him to the murder apartment where she showed him the beam where the rope had been hidden. She also went with him to Millery, and pointed out the exact place where the body had been found. As she and Goron embarked on the train at Lyons for Paris, a squadron of cavalry had to hold back the excited crowd. The vain Goron revelled in the publicity.

On May 19, 1890, Eyraud was recognized by a Frenchman in Havana, Cuba, and was arrested. When his ship docked at St Nazaire on June 30, the crowds were as thick as they had been for his mistress at Lyons. On December 16, 1890, the trial of Bompard and Eyraud opened and lasted for four days. Because of a testimony that Gabrielle had been hypnotized as a child, and had ever since been a 'toy' in the hands of more forceful personalities, she received a sentence of 20 years in jail. Eyraud, inevitably, went to the guillotine.

The case had been a triumph for Marie-François Goron, but a curious one. It was his absurd vanity which had led him to investigate the case in the first place, and his belligerent stubbornness which had kept him kicking at the stone wall of the Lyons evidence, with not a single rational clue to go on. He had broken Gabrielle with methods which would be condemned today. If he had failed in the task he had so arbitrarily set himself, scorn, instead of laurels, would have been his reward. When he died at the age of 86 in 1933, Goron had scored dozens of successes with a similar lack of scruples or conscience, but none had been so dramatic as the Lyons case.

A detective's doubts

Was an innocent man condemned to die?

'IS IT NOT BETTER that twelve innocent people go to the stake, rather than have one guilty person escape?' was the cry of the Spanish Inquisition. Exactly the reverse of the question was put, more recently, as an argument by reformers against capital punishment. It was the possibility that Sacco and Vanzetti in the United States, and Timothy Evans and James Hanratty in Britain, might have been wrongfully executed which eventually helped to bring about the abolition of the death sentence. Long before that, conscientious homicide officers had often pondered the question uneasily, for theirs was a fearsome responsibility. Once a man was dead, no amount of posthumous free pardons could bring him back to life if his innocence were to be proved. Sometimes, amid a welter of damning evidence, there remained an awful nagging doubt.

Textbook

On April 28, 1955, two 14-year-old girls named Stephanie Bryan and Mary Ann Stewart left the Willard School in Alameda, near Oakland, California, at about 3.00 in the afternoon. They stopped at the public library, where the bespectacled Stephanie took out some books, and then went on to the local pet shop, where Stephanie bought a pamphlet on the care of parakeets. Reaching the Claremont Hotel, Stephanie told Mary Ann that she was going to take a short cut through the hotel gardens to her parents' home on the Canyon Road. The girls parted company, and Stephanie was never seen alive again. For several weeks the Alameda and Contra Costa County police, under the guidance of Inspector Charles O'Meara of the Oakland force, combed the surrounding area, without much success. The one positive clue they had was that on May 2, a man in Contra Costa County had found a French textbook by the roadside, and had given it to his son. The book was wet, and the son tore off the soaked jacket and laid it to one side. A week later, throwing out rubbish, the boy's mother found the soggy jacket and noticed Stephanie's name on it. Since then there had been nothing. On the evening of June 15, Inspector O'Meara received a telephone call from a Mrs Georgia Abbott of Alameda. She said that she had found a red leather wallet which, judging by a snap-shot and other items inside it, she took to have been owned by the missing girl. Inspector O'Meara climbed into his police sedan and drove over to the Abbott house, a white building near the sea shore. There he found Burton K. Abbott, a 28-year-old accountancy student at the University of California.

With him were Georgia, his pretty red-haired wife, and a friend, Otto Dezman. Dezman was introduced to the inspector as the owner of a beauty parlor in which Georgia Abbott worked.

O'Meara examined the wallet, and nodded in confirmation. The snap was of Stephanie all right, and when he withdrew the few papers he found a card which bore her name. 'How and where did you find this?' he asked Mrs Abbott. The redhead explained that the three of them had been discussing a fancy-dress party to which they had been invited. She wanted to go as a Gibson girl, and had gone down to the basement to see if she could find an old-fashioned hat which had belonged to her aunt. She and her husband rarely used the basement except to store junk, she explained. While down there she found the wallet lying under the stairs.

O'Meara noticed that Burton Abbott was only half-attending to the conversation. He was idly glancing at a crossword in the *San Francisco Chronicle*. O'Meara followed Mrs Abbot through the kitchen door and down the steps which led to the basement. It was large and concreted, with a back door which opened onto the street at the back of the house. Was the back door usually unlocked, asked the Inspector, opening it? Mrs Abbott replied that it was. They usually only locked the door leading to the kitchen as there was nothing of value in the basement. In any case, it was sometimes rented to the local town council, and it had been used as a polling station a couple of weeks back, during a municipal election.

Persistence

The basement was dark by this time, and the Inspector followed Mrs Abbott back up the stairs. He had one question to ask Abbott, now totally immersed in his crossword. 'Could you tell me where you where on April 28?' Abbott looked up and thought for a while. Then he smiled.

'Sure,' he said. 'It was the opening day of the fishing season. I left at 11.00 in the morning to go to the family cabin in Trinity County up by the California and Oregon border. Mrs Frakes, our housekeeper, put up food for me and saw me off.'

O'Meara said that he would be back and wished the couple goodnight. Before his return the following day, however, he did some checking on the Abbotts. They were a happily married couple with a four-year-old son Chris, he discovered, and 'Bud', as Burton was known to his friends, was much liked and admired for his persistence in taking a degree.

Four years earlier, he had undergone serious surgery at the Livermore Veterans' Hospital after being injured during his army service. The operation had left him with only one lung and six ribs missing.

Back at the Abbott's house, the inspector and two colleagues went down to the basement. The area under the stairs where the wallet was found had not been concreted over, and O'Meara began to prod the sandy soil.

A few inches beneath the surface he came across a pair of horn-rimmed spectacles, then a white brassiere, a pamphlet on parakeets, and a small red purse. The purse contained a comb, a few pennies, and Stephanie Bryan's identification card. Rather unnecessarily, he turned to Mrs Abbott and aked, 'Are these yours?' She was very pale and replied, 'No, I've never seen them before. I cannot imagine how they came to be buried here.'

Distraught

When they got upstairs and O'Meara laid the things on the table before Abbott, he looked astonished and confused for the first time. He, too, had no idea where the objects came from, or what they were doing buried in his basement. 'Unless,' he added, 'someone's playing a dreadful trick, or is trying to frame me in some way.'

The inspector then asked Abbott to accompany him to headquarters to make a statement. Georgia Abbott became distraught. Surely, she asked the inspector, he didn't think her husband had anything to do with these things, or the girl's disappearance? 'Of course not, honey,' said Abbott, squeezing her hand. 'You don't think that if I knew anything

I would be dumb enough to hide her brassiere and gear in my own basement?' Inspector O'Meara had been thinking along much the same lines. If there had been any connection between the student and the missing girl, he had had plenty of time to dispose of the evidence. Even after O'Meara's visit the previous night, he could have got rid of the brassiere and purse. But he had not done so. Did this mean that he was innocent, or did it mean that he had some giant idea of the power of his own intelligence, that he could bluff his way out of the situation into which he had fallen?

Fruitless

Abbott's statement was taken down by an official stenographer. He claimed that until his wife had found the wallet, he had no idea that it had lain in his basement. In fact, until his wife and Otto Dezman had told him about the case that evening, he had no idea that the girl was missing. He had, he pointed out, been away on a fishing trip the day Stephanie disappeared.

'Anyone see you on the trip who can substantiate your story?' asked the inspector. Abbott replied that 'lots of people' could. He had left home about 11.00 am, and had first driven to Sacramento to try and find the Bureau of Land Management, as his brother Mark wanted to buy some land adjoining his. Unfortunately, the one-way street system of Sacramento baffled him, and after spending a fruitless 40 minutes

roaming around it, he gave up the task and set out for Trinity County. He reached the township of Dunnigan at about 2.30 pm and stopped at a restaurant for a sandwich. At 5.30 pm he had filled up with gas at Corning, and shortly afterwards stopped for another sandwich at Red Bluff.

'I made it fast on the last 45 miles to Wildwood,' he said, 'and at around 8.30 pm I got up into the mountains. I stopped for a drink at Delbert Cox's bar, and then went to the cabin.'

The following day he spent most of the morning clearing thick snow, which had fallen a few days before, from around the cabin, then had a short spell of fishing until it began to rain. He then drove into Wildwood, telephoned his brother Mark, and spent the rest of the day and evening in Cox's bar. Mark and his wife Mary came up the following day, and the day afterwards, May 1, they all drove home together in the rain. Inspector O'Meara made a brief note. Stephanie's text book had been found on May 2 on the Contra Costa road, one of the roads Abbott might have taken on his way back from the mountains.

While Abbott was being interviewed, Detective Dean had been examining his car, a grey-green Chevrolet, and had returned with specimens of lint, threads, and dirt, which were taken to the Criminology Department of the University of California to be examined by the Department Head, Dr Paul Kirk.

The following morning, Inspector O'Meara arranged to follow the

Burton Abbott and his counsel Stanley Whitney endured a three-month trial.

An element of doubt... James Hanratty

The doubts about the Murder on Deadman's Hill remain a recurrent issue nearly two decades after the event. One evening in August, 1961, Michael Gregsten, a married man, had gone out in his car with his girlfriend, Valerie Storie. They were parked on the edge of a cornfield not far from London when an intruder held them at gunpoint, subsequently killing Gregsten and raping Storie. He then shot her seven times and left her for dead, though she eventually recovered.

A matter of days later, the widow of the murdered man had an 'overpowering hunch' that she had seen the killer in a shop, a dry cleaner's. A relative then traced this person by way of his cleaning ticket, since the police were hesitant to pursue someone whom they had no reason to suspect. The police's understandable reluctance to investigate at this stage is just one of the remarkable features of this case. In due course they did check on the man, James Hanratty, and several facts emerged which made him a possible suspect. As other possibilities were discounted, Hanratty damaged his own position by changing alibis.

He was finally implicated when the victim Miss Storie shifted her own evidence on identification. Nonetheless, many observers remained convinced of her innocence even when a jury decided otherwise after the longest murder trial in British history. While Hanratty awaited his ultimate fate at the gallows, one of the prosecution witnesses committed suicide, and there have since emerged further strands of evidence which increase doubts about Hanratty's guilt. Within a few years of his execution, the death penalty for murder was replaced by life imprisonment. Soon afterwards, an earlier suspect – who had been 'cleared' in an identification parade – made a series of 'confessions.' Although these statements were subsequently withdrawn, they were a bizarre postscript to a disturbing case.

Hanratty as viewed by the tabloid Press.

The murder car (above) after its journey from Deadman's Hill.

route Abbott said he had taken. Abbott had been released, but told to wait at home. O'Meara set out at 11.00 accompanied by two detectives and Dave Broderick, a police reporter who was an old friend of the inspector, and a former sheriff of Marin County, California.

They reached the Abbott's three-roomed cabin, and dusted it for fingerprints. It yielded none except those of Burton Abbott. Then, with the aid of local police and tracker dogs, they began quartering the ground for yards around the little building. About one hundred yards up the steep hillside at the rear of the cabin, the dogs stopped and began howling. After carefully digging for five minutes, they found first a brown and white saddle shoe, and then the dishevelled, pitiful body of a young girl.

The girl's brassiere was missing, and her panties had been wound around her neck. Dr and Mrs Bryan, Stephanie's parents, identified the body as that of their daughter when it reached Alameda, and their identification was confirmed by fingerprints and dental charts.

Inspector Charles O'Meara drove once more to the Abbott house by the shore, and arrested its owner for the capital murder of Stephanie Bryan. The student was fairly composed. He willingly handed over the clothes he had been wearing for the fishing trip, which were a pair of jeans and a scuffed leather jacket.

Confirmed

Inspector O'Meara was now faced with the task of filling out the case against his suspect. Although he intended to charge his prisoner under the State of California's Lindberg kidnapping law, as well as for the murder, he had yet to produce a weapon, eye witness, and motive.

Delbert Cox, the owner of the bar Abbott said that he had used on the day of Stephanie's disappearance, was not much help to either O'Meara or Abbott's possible defense. He couldn't swear to having seen Abbott on April 28, because he had been watching his favorite TV show at the time Abbott was supposed to have had a drink. He confirmed that Abbott had spent much of the following day, April 29, there. Tom Daly, a lumber-mill worker, confirmed this. He had had a nine-hour drinking session with Abbott at Cox's on

An element of doubt . . . Timothy Evans

At least seven women and a baby girl were murdered at number ten Rillington Place, in west London, during the late 1940s and early 1950s, but who was the killer? Terrible doubts on this score will always haunt the people who were involved in the initial investigation at Rillington Place. The first victims to be found at the house were the wife and small child of Timothy Evans, who lived there. Evans, who was mentally subnormal, broke down under police questioning and made a confession. He was subsequently found guilty and hanged, despite having blamed his neighbor John Christie during the trial for the killings. Christie testified against him, and was complimented by the judge on the clarity of his evidence. It now seems that Evans, worried at his wife's pregnancy, had agreed to let Christie perform an abortion. Christie had, instead, raped and murdered the wife. Some years later, more bodies were found at Rillington Place. Christie was arrested, revealed as a multiple murderer and probably a necrophiliac, and hanged. In the light of this, the doubts about Evans' guilt

Christie and his wife Ethel in the back yard of 10 Rillington Place. He was already a murderer and she was soon to become one of his victims.

were greatly magnified. A long-running and successful campaign for his pardon was mounted by several investigative journalists and public figures.

Police at work behind the house, while crowds throng the street. The case against Christie was hardening, but it was too late for Evans (right).

April 29. He also said that Abbott appeared quite normal.

At Corning, where Abbott claimed that he had stopped for gas at 5.30 pm on April 28, the garage owner James A. Craig was a little more helpful. Although he couldn't positively identify Abbott, he remembered servicing a Chevrolet with an unusual red fanbelt at about that time. Abbott's car had such a belt. Corning was about 200 miles away from the Claremont Hotel, outside which Stephanie was last seen alive, about two hours before Abbott's garage stop.

The waitress and owner of the Chuck Wagon Diner at Red Bluff were more positive. They both said that Abbott had eaten there at 7.30 pm on the evening of April 28. The waitress remembered the date because she had left her job at the Chuck Wagon the following day.

All this helped to fix times. Inspector O'Meara knew that it had taken him nine and a half hours to drive out to Abbott's cabin, and five-and-a-half back, so that the suspect's estimate that it had taken him eight hours to drive from Alameda to Wildwood was perfectly possible.

Now O'Meara turned to the forensic evidence. Dr George S. Loquvan, the Oakland pathologist who had carried out an autopsy on the body, could say little beyond the fact that the girl had been strangled. The wet, sandy soil in which she had lain buried until June 20 had attacked the body tissues in such a way that it was impossible to tell how long had elapsed between the time of her death and the burial, or even if she had been sexually assaulted. Dr Paul Kirk was more positive. Traces of hair and blood had been found in the ridges of the floor mat in Abbott's Chevrolet, but it was impossible to say whether or not they were Stephanie's. There were no traces of the girl's fingerprints in either the car or Abbott's cabin. On the other hand, 18 fibres and two human hairs had been found in the car, and the hairs were indistinguishable from Stephanie's hair. One fibre matched her turquoise skirt and several matched her sweater. Precipitation tests carried out by Dr Kirk proved that soil found on the accused's mountain boots were identical with the soil found in Stephanie's shallow grave. Furthermore, fresh sand from the basement of Abbott's home matched deposits from a pair of his shoes, although he said that he 'never' went down to the basement.

One further point had been nagging at the back of O'Meara's mind. Stephanie Bryan had weighed 105 pounds, and she had been found buried on a steep hillside 100 yards from Abbott's cabin. Was it possible that a man with one lung could have hauled such a weight that distance? The inspector went to see Dr Elmer J. Shabart, Abbott's surgeon, at the Livermore Veterans' Hospital.

Routine

Shabart's reply puzzled O'Meara. His patient, said Dr Shabart, had made a good recovery from the operation, as far as was possible. He did a lot of fishing and walking in the mountains. In fact, he had called at the hospital on May 2 complaining of chest pain and had asked for further surgery to cure it. 'He seemed almost over-anxious,' said the doctor. 'We told him that another operation was unnecessary, that he was quite fit. On May 13 he called again, and again we turned him away.'

To the inspector, the coincidence was curious. Abbott's original operation had been four years ago, and apart from routine checks he had not visited the hospital since then. Why should he suddenly turn up at Livermore five days after the Bryan girl's disappearance, and more or less demand surgery? To establish an alibi? To show that he was too weak to commit such a crime? All the evidence collected so far was circumstantial. But if Burton Abbott had not killed Stephanie Bryan, who had? Why should anyone want to rig evidence against Abbott. No one seemed to have a grudge against the handsome, pleasant-natured student. Nor could a motive be established since sexual assault had not been evident.

Influence

It was O'Meara's friend, Dave Broderick, the ex-sheriff, who came up with a possible answer. He was old enough to recall the Leopold and Loeb case which was similarly without motive. 'Dickie' Loeb was the wealthy son of a vice-president of Sears Roebuck. With Leopold, he had kidnapped and killed a 14-year-old boy named Robert Franks. Loeb had been under the influence of the

An element of doubt . . . Sacco and Vanzetti

No case has generated such long-standing doubts as that which started with an armed payroll robbery and double murder in South Braintree, Massachusetts, in 1920. This crime was linked by police with an armed holdup in the state the previous year, at which the attackers were said to have been 'Italian-looking.' The police arrested Nicola Sacco and Bartolomeo Vanzetti, who were initially accused of being illegally in possession of guns. When they were brought to trial on murder charges, the case against them was ostensibly based on their lack of wholly convincing alibis, and on questionable evidence of identification. They were found guilty, and sentenced to death, though it was six years before they were finally executed. A reprieve was refused even when a known killer who was already in jail confessed to the double murder. Today, it is argued that Sacco and Vanzetti's only crime was to be known radical activists at a time when the revolution in Russia had precipitated the United States into an anti-'Red' panic. The chief prosecutor in the case had openly declared his determination to 'crucify these damned, God-hating radicals.'

Sacco and Vanzetti. The jail was ringed by guns on execution day, to control the volatile crowds of sightseers who surrounded the walls. A few days later the crowds were out again, lining the route to pay tribute as the anarchists were driven slowly to their burial.

Judge Webster Thayer, who pronounced the death sentence on the two men. He boasted to his friends, 'Did you see what I did with those anarchist bastards the other day?'

rather strange young man Nathan Leopold, who was known as 'the Crazy Genius' because of his very powerful intellect. That crime had been committed 21 years earlier in Chicago, and had been widely reported at the time, and commented upon ever since. Leopold and Loeb had had an arrogant belief in their own ability to flout the law, and literally to get away with murder!

In the sense that they escaped execution, they succeeded, but only through the inspired pleading of the famous lawyer, Clarence Darrow. Could it be that Abbott, a young man whose determined intellect had helpovercome the steepest physical odds, had consciously or unconsciously imitated the Leopold and Loeb crime, just to prove his own superiority? This would certainly explain the fact that he had left damning evidence in his own basement. He could be trying a monstrous double bluff, not only on the police but on society in general.

At his trial, which started on November 7, 1955, before Superior Court Judge Charles Wade Shook, Burton Abbott denied any such suggestion and stuck rigidly to his story. He knew nothing about Stephanie Bryan, had never seen her, and had not even heard of her disappearance until his wife had found the wallet in the basement. He could only suggest that he had been framed. But even he could suggest no culprit.

Red-faced

The defense did come up with one suggestion. Otto Dezman, who had been in his house on the night of the discovery, and who employed Georgia Burton, might have had a motive. Could Dezman have been having an affair with Georgia, and rigged the evidence against her husband? The red-faced Dezman shouted his denial from the dock.

Certainly the evidence could have been planted by anyone determined enough. But then the prosecution came up with two very damaging witnesses, a Mrs Bessie Wells, who had been a customer at Dezman's beauty parlor on April 28, and Mrs Leona Dezman, manager of the parlor. Mrs Wells claimed that she had seen Abbott come into the shop that afternoon at between 2.15 pm and 2.30 pm and speak to his wife. Mrs Dezman made the same claim,

adding that he had also been in the shop at 10.00 that morning.

The defense made an attempt to show that Mrs Dezman had acted out of malice in giving her statement, that she was jealous of Mrs Abbott and her husband. Like Otto Dezman, Leona roundly denied the charge.

In February, after the trial had dragged on for over three months, Burton Abbott was sentenced to the gas chamber for capital murder. He stuck steadfastly to his story until the verdict. Then he instructed his lawyers to lodge an appeal.

Nagging

Two top lawyers who had become interested in the case volunteered to defend him, Leo Sullivan and George T. Davis. In May 1956, while they were preparing their brief, an event of possible significance occurred. Their offices were burgled and a bundle of documents relating to the case 'twice the size of a telephone book' were stolen. Sullivan claimed that they had been taken by someone who 'had it in' for Abbott in a big way. Despite the theft, the appeal court upheld the ruling of Judge Shook. Burton Abbott would die in the gas chamber at St Quentin on March 23, 1957.

It was with very mixed feelings that Inspector O'Meara and police reporter Dave Broderick drove up to the prison on that bitter and blustery morning. O'Meara had gone over the case thoroughly, not once but several times. All his painstakingly collected evidence pointed to the young man who was now sitting out his few final moments on Death Row. And yet there remained an awful nagging element of doubt. Fate was brutally cruel that day, especially to Abbott, but also to the police inspector.

At 11.18 am precisely, the executioner pulled the lever which released 16 small pellets of cyanide into a bucket of sulphuric acid under the condemned man's glassed-off chair. Abbott strained at his bonds and died almost instantly.

At 11.20 am, a telephone rang. It was a temporary stay of execution from California Governor Goodwin Knight. It had been relayed from an airplane out over the Pacific, on which the Governor was travelling. For Abbott, and for O'Meara's conscience, it came exactly two minutes too late.

Tomorrow's detectives

ANYONE WITH a flair for detection – and a clean record – can become a successful private eye in the United States. In order to acquire a license, it is necessary to be vetted by the local police chief, and in most states by the District Attorney's office. Applicants are usually required to take an oral and written examination to prove that they are familiar with the laws of trespass and intrusion and other legislation which may affect their work.

Since this license can be revoked, without any right of appeal in most states, the private eye is careful to maintain goodwill with the police department. Private investigators usually understand this well enough, as many of them are former police detectives.

Depending upon the force in which he works, a police officer may have to spend between two and four years as a uniformed patrolman on the beat before he can apply to be considered for the position of detective, third grade.

A career-minded detective may be keen to work his way up the ladder – second and first grades, sergeant, lieutenant, Bureau of Inspectors – but not all officers think this way. Those who enjoy practical detective work often feel that, beyond the rank of sergeant or lieutenant, they may become tangled in administrative paperwork.

One alternative route is private practice. Another prospect, for the really enthusiastic and talented detective, is to look beyond the confines of his own city or county and apply to join the Federal Bureau of Investigation.

The F.B.I. National Academy in Washington, D.C., opened its doors

The traditional British Bobby, the rank from which every career in London's Metropolitan Police force must start.

in July, 1935, with a twelve-week course for 23 officers. Each of the candidates had been selected by their local police departments for their high sense of responsibility and dedication. Since then, the Academy has released a steady stream of graduates, some of whom go on to complete the intensive F.B.I. 'special agent' course.

Increasingly, F.B.I. trainees are men of high qualifications; detectives with university degrees in law, accountancy, and the sciences are given priority. Their training involves a broad curriculum which ranges from weaponry to a general study of the many Federal statutes with whose violation the F.B.I. is concerned. Among these are the White Slave Act, the Anti-Trust Act, and since the Lindbergh kidnapping of 1932, the laws making abduction across a State line a Federal offense. In recent years the violation of Civil Rights has concerned the Bureau more than any other law agency.

Recruits are given exhaustive training in the use of firearms ranging from small caliber pistols to the Thompson sub-machine gun – the 'Tommy gun' – which was the staple tool of both F.B.I. men and gangsters during the days of Prohibition. If his on-target rate is less than 60 per cent, the recruit is considered unsuitable as a special agent, however well he does in other fields.

As a final part of their training, recruits are given snap oral and written tests of alertness and observation, and are assigned to an actual investigation before their closing examination.

Progressive

There is nothing quite like the F.B.I. anywhere else in the world, although Scotland Yard comes closest. Scotland Yard is not a national organization, but merely the headquarters of the London Metropolitan Police Force. The skill of detectives and forensic scientists there is such, however, that they are frequently called out to aid not only provincial British forces, but to investigate crimes throughout the British Commonwealth and other friendly countries.

Unlike the United States, where some progressive police departments take on particularly promising college graduates for immediate detective training, Britain still expects all its detectives to rise through the ranks. Every aspiring detective, therefore, patrols a beat in uniform for a minimum of two years.

After that, he can apply to join the Criminal Investigation Department – the C.I.D. – as a detective. If he is successful, he goes through a further two years' probation with the rank of Temporary Detective Constable, though he is always referred to as 'Aid' by his senior colleagues.

Interrogation

An 'Aid' carries out fairly humdrum tasks of observation and usually spends most of his time patrolling the streets watching for petty criminals such as shoplifters and pickpockets. If he manages to serve his two years without being the subject of a complaint by a member of the public, he is then made Detective Constable – an odd

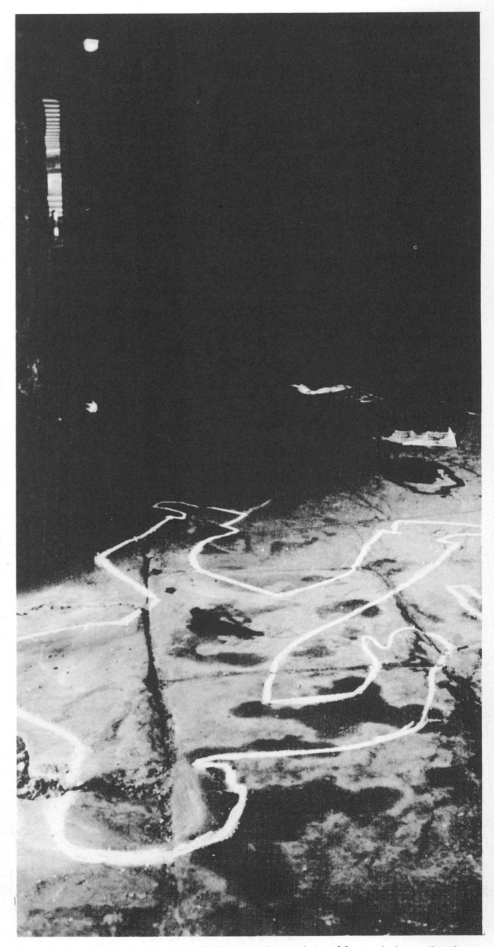

The chalk outline of a murder victim, starting points of forensic investigation.

A Scotland Yard fingerprint expert works on the door of a stolen car.

The 'voiceprint' machine is typical of modern forensic sophistication.

qualification to American police department eyes – and goes to Detective Training School.

For 13 weeks during his course at the school in Victoria, London, the recruit studies English Criminal Law, and has to achieve a very high mark in order to continue in the C.I.D. He is also given lectures on weaponry, explosives, pathology, and interrogation. Curiously nothing is taught about detection as such. Rightly or wrongly, the C.I.D. believes that this can only be learned by practical experience.

Once his examinations are passed, the Detective Constable is assigned to a division – the British equivalent of a precinct. Later he may be transferred to one of the dozen specialist branches within the C.I.D., each of which is headed by a Detective Commander. If he joins Special Branch – the British equivalent of the American Secret Service – he will carry a pistol as a matter of course. Or he may opt for the Flying Squad, an elite and hard-bitten body of men who fight organized crime.

Diehards

The Flying Squad is nicknamed the 'Sweeney' and is genuinely feared by villains and looked on with awe even by detectives in other branches. No one quite knows how the nickname came about. The popular assumption is that it is London rhyming slang (Sweeney Todd – Flying Squad), but the department's first head was a saturnine Irishman named John Sweeney. In his day, the squad was known as 'Sweeney's Mob'.

Other branches include the Obscene Publication Branch (popularly known as the 'Porn Squad'), the Fraud Squad, the Drugs Squad, and the Forgeries Squad. Since the troubles in Northern Ireland escalated, a Bomb Squad has also been formed. Officers from all branches are called upon to make up the Murder Squad when necessary.

To a certain extent, such specialization is creeping into the average American police department, too. Despite the diehards on both sides of the Atlantic, it seems that the day is fast approaching when at least 50 per cent of any detective force will have to be composed of specialists brought in from outside. The era of the detective as crime buffs know it will then be over.

INDEX

PICTURE CREDITS

Reading from left to right across the page and from top to bottom. Front cover, Michael Busselle; frontispiece, Kobal Collection; Page 6 Kobal Collection; 8 Topham; 9 Kobal Collection, Topham; 10/11 Topham, Kobal Collection, Metropolitan Police; 14 Kobal Collection; 15 Associated Press; 16/17 Topham; 18 Keystone; 19 Associated Press; 21 Keystone; 22 Keystone; 23 Associated Press, (bottom right) Keystone; 24 Topham; 25 Keystone, Popperfoto, Popperfoto; 26 Popperfoto; 27 Topham; 28 Topham; 29 Popperfoto; 30 Topham; 31 Syndication International; 32 Radio Times Hulton Picture Library, Syndication International; 42–51 Public Archives of Canada; 45 Radio Times Hulton Picture Library; 46/47 Radio Times Hulton Picture Library; 52 Syndication International, Radio Times Hulton Picture Library; 54 Radio Times Hulton Picture Library; 55 Syndication International; 56/57 Popperfoto, Popperfoto, Syndication International, Syndication International, Radio Times Hulton Picture Library; 58 Syndication International; 59 Topham; 60 John Frost Collection; 61 Popperfoto, Syndication International; 62 Syndication International; 63 Syndication International; 64/65 Radio Times Hulton Picture Library, Mary Evans Picture Library; 66/67 Radio Times Hulton Picture Library; 68 Mary Evans Picture Library; 69 Mary Evans Picture Library; 70 Trevor Goring; 72/73 Newsday; 75 Topham; 76/77 René Dazy; 78 Radio Times Hulton Picture Library; 79 Radio Times Hulton Picture Library; 81 Radio Times Hulton Picture Library; 82 Topham; 84 Syndication International; 85 Radio Times Hulton Picture Library, John Frost Collection; 87 Popperfoto; 88 Syndication International, Popperfoto; 89 Topham, Radio Times Hulton Picture Library; 90 Syndication International; 91 Topham; 92 Syndication International; 93 Syndication International, Popperfoto, Topham; 94/95 Syndication International; 97 Syndication International; 98 Sun, London; 99 Popperfoto, Syndication International; 100 Topham; 101 Syndication International; 102 Syndication International; 103 Popperfoto; 104/105 Popperfoto; 106 Topham, Popperfoto; 107 Keystone; 108/109 Topham; 110 Associated Press; 111 Radio Times Hulton Picture Library, Association Press; 112/113 Associated Press, Topham; 114 Topham; 115 John Frost Collection; 116 John Frost Collection, Jon Wyand; 117 Radio Times Hulton Picture Library; 119 Radio Times Hulton Picture Library; 121 Jon Wyand; 122 Kyodo News Enterprise; 123 Topham; 124–127 Kyodo News Enterprise; 128–135 Topham; 136/137 John Frost Collection; 138/139 Associated Press; 140 John Frost Collection; 142/143 Topham; 144/145 Syndication International; 146 Associated Press; 147 Topham; 148 Popperfoto; 149 Popperfoto; 150 Topham, Popperfoto; 151 Topham; 152 Topham; 153 Zoological Society of London; 154 Topham; 155 Radio Times Hulton Picture Library; 156 Topham; 157 Zoological Society of London; 158 Jon Wyand; 163–166 Edmonton Journal; 165 Psychic News; 167 Peter Till; 171–177 René Dazy; 178 Syndication International; 180 Associated Press; 181 Syndication International, Topham; 182 Syndication International; 183 Syndication International, Popperfoto; 184 Syndication International; 185 Popperfoto; 186 F.B.I.; 187 Metropolitan Police; 188 Quarto; 189 Syndication International, Topham. Color realization by Bill Payne.